THE NEW AVENGERS

POWERLOSS

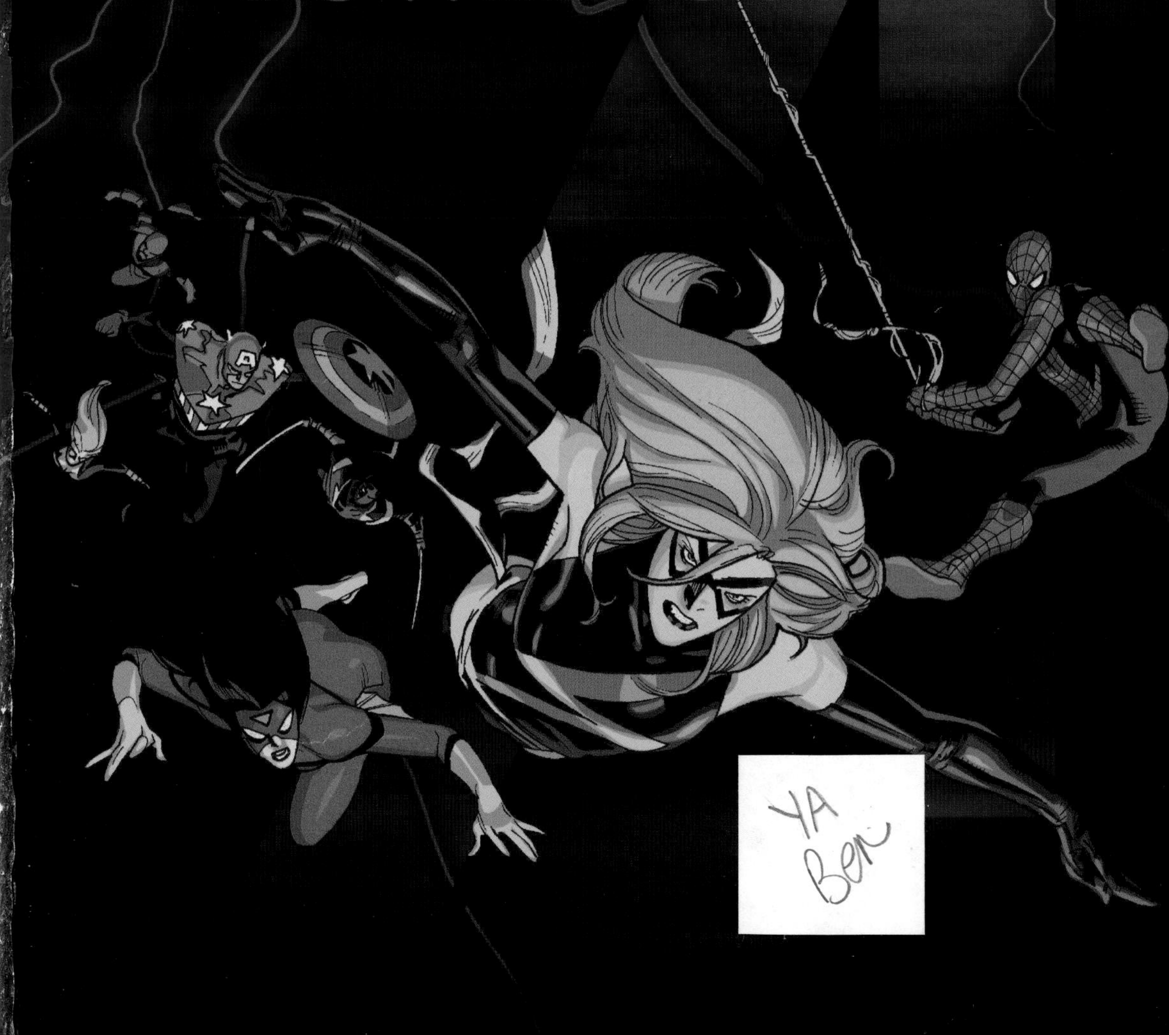

NEW AVENGERS VOL. 12: POWERLOSS. Contains material originally published in magazine form as NEW AVENGERS #55-60. First printing 2010. Hardcover ISBN# 978-0-7851-4575-2. Softcover ISBN# 978-0-7851-4576-9. Published by MARVEL PUBLISHING, INC., a subsidiary of MARVEL ENTERTAINMENT, INC. OFFICE OF PUBLICATION: 417 5th Avenue, New York, NY 10016. Copyright © 2009 and 2010 Marvel Characters, Inc. All rights reserved. Hardcover: $19.99 per copy in the U.S. (GST #R127032852). Softcover: $14.99 per copy in the U.S. (GST #R127032852). Canadian Agreement #40668537. All characters featured in this issue and the distinctive names and likenesses thereof, and all related indicia are trademarks of Marvel Characters, Inc. No similarity between any of the names, characters, persons, and/or institutions in this magazine with those of any living or dead person or institution is intended, and any such similarity which may exist is purely coincidental. **Printed in the U.S.A.** ALAN FINE, EVP - Office Of The Chief Executive Marvel Entertainment, Inc. & CMO Marvel Characters B.V.; DAN BUCKLEY, Chief Executive Officer and Publisher - Print, Animation & Digital Media; JIM SOKOLOWSKI, Chief Operating Officer; DAVID GABRIEL, SVP of Publishing Sales & Circulation; DAVID BOGART, SVP of Business Affairs & Talent Management; MICHAEL PASCIULLO, VP Merchandising & Communications; JIM O'KEEFE, VP of Operations & Logistics; DAN CARR, Executive Director of Publishing Technology; JUSTIN F. GABRIE, Director of Publishing & Editorial Operations; SUSAN CRESPI, Editorial Operations Manager; ALEX MORALES, Publishing Operations Manager; STAN LEE, Chairman Emeritus. For information regarding advertising in Marvel Comics or on Marvel.com, please contact Ron Stern, VP of Business Development, at rstern@marvel.com. For Marvel subscription inquiries, please call 800-217-9158. **Manufactured between** [illegible]

THE NEW AVENGERS

POWERLOSS

Writer: **Brian Michael Bendis**
Penciler: **Stuart Immonen**
Inker: **Wade von Grawbadger**
Colorist: **Dave McCaig**
Letterer: **RS & Comicraft's Albert Deschesne**
Associate Editors: **Lauren Sankovitch & Jeanine Schaefer**
Editor: **Tom Brevoort**

Collection Editor: **Jennifer Grünwald**
Assistant Editors: **Alex Starbuck & John Denning**
Editor, Special Projects: **Mark D. Beazley**
Senior Editor, Special Projects: **Jeff Youngquist**
Senior Vice President of Sales: **David Gabriel**

Editor in Chief: **Joe Quesada**
Publisher: **Dan Buckley**
Executive Producer: **Alan Fine**

PREVIOUSLY: The Avengers are on the run! Until they can be sure who's on their side, Spider-Man, Captain America, Luke Cage, Ronin, Mockingbird, Spider-Woman and Ms. Marvel are using Captain America's hideout in Brooklyn as a safe house. Collectively they try to keep the values of the Avengers name alive even though they're living on the wrong side of the law.

Norman Osborn is the new political and media darling, and is now running H.A.M.M.E.R., the national peacekeeping task force, which includes his own team of Avengers.

After Norman had the Hood's crime syndicate stage a surprise attack on the New Avengers, Clint Barton, aka Ronin, finally took matters into his own hands and went on national television to out Osborn as the former villain called the Green Goblin.

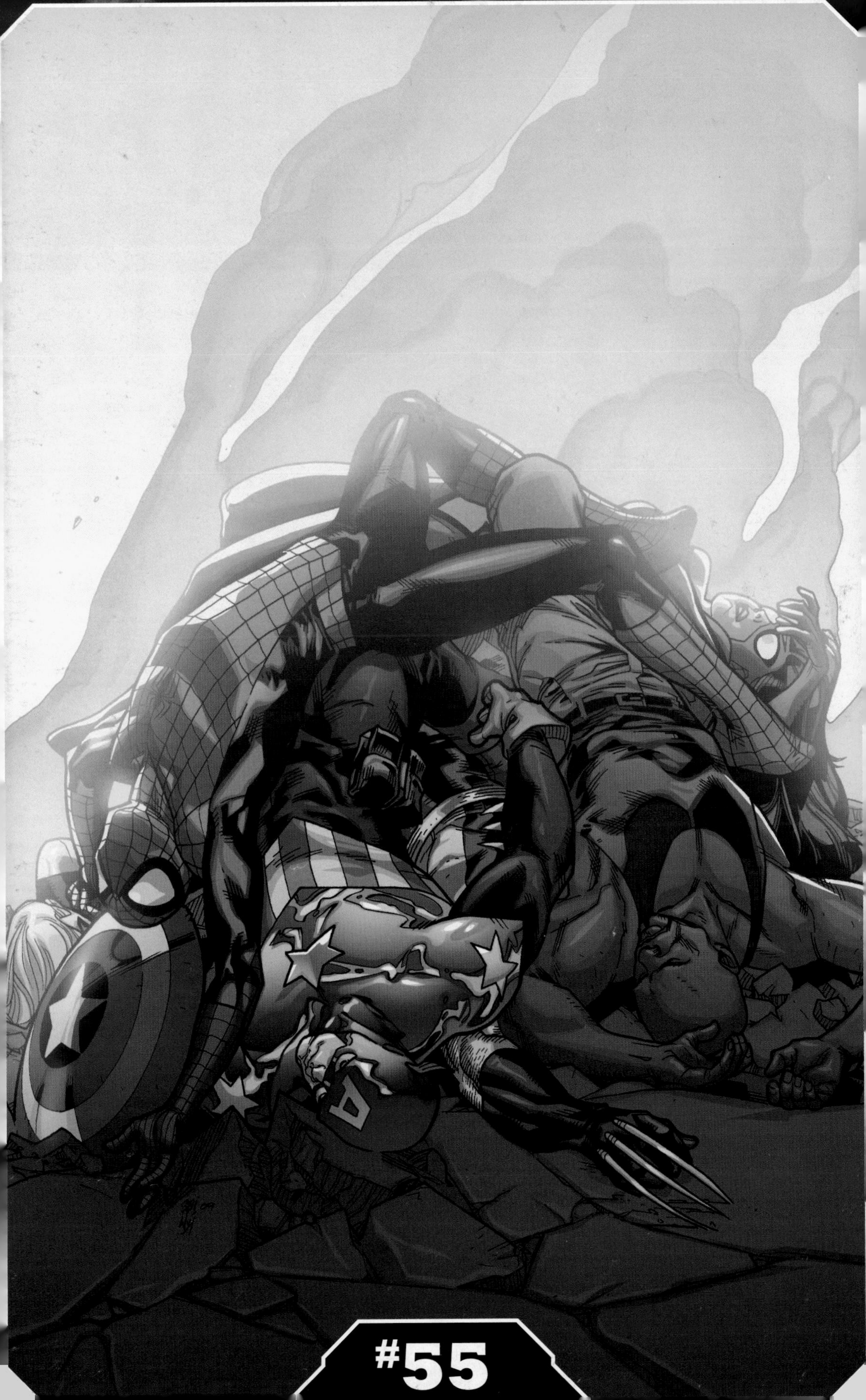
#55

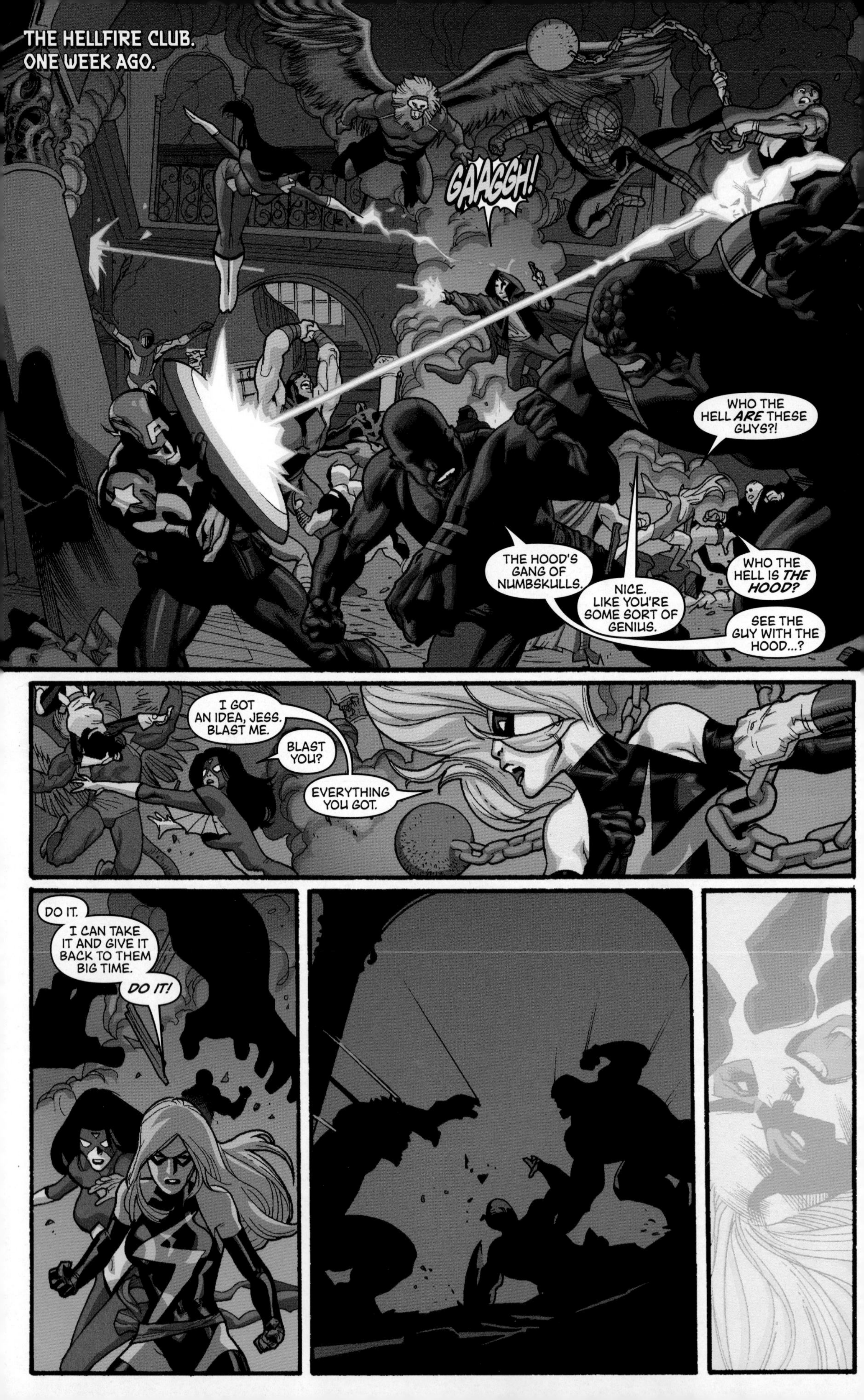
THE HELLFIRE CLUB.
ONE WEEK AGO.
GAAAGH!
WHO THE HELL ARE THESE GUYS?!
THE HOOD'S GANG OF NUMBSKULLS.
WHO THE HELL IS THE HOOD?
SEE THE GUY WITH THE HOOD...?
NICE. LIKE YOU'RE SOME SORT OF GENIUS.
I GOT AN IDEA, JESS. BLAST ME.
BLAST YOU?
EVERYTHING YOU GOT.
DO IT.
I CAN TAKE IT AND GIVE IT BACK TO THEM BIG TIME.
DO IT!

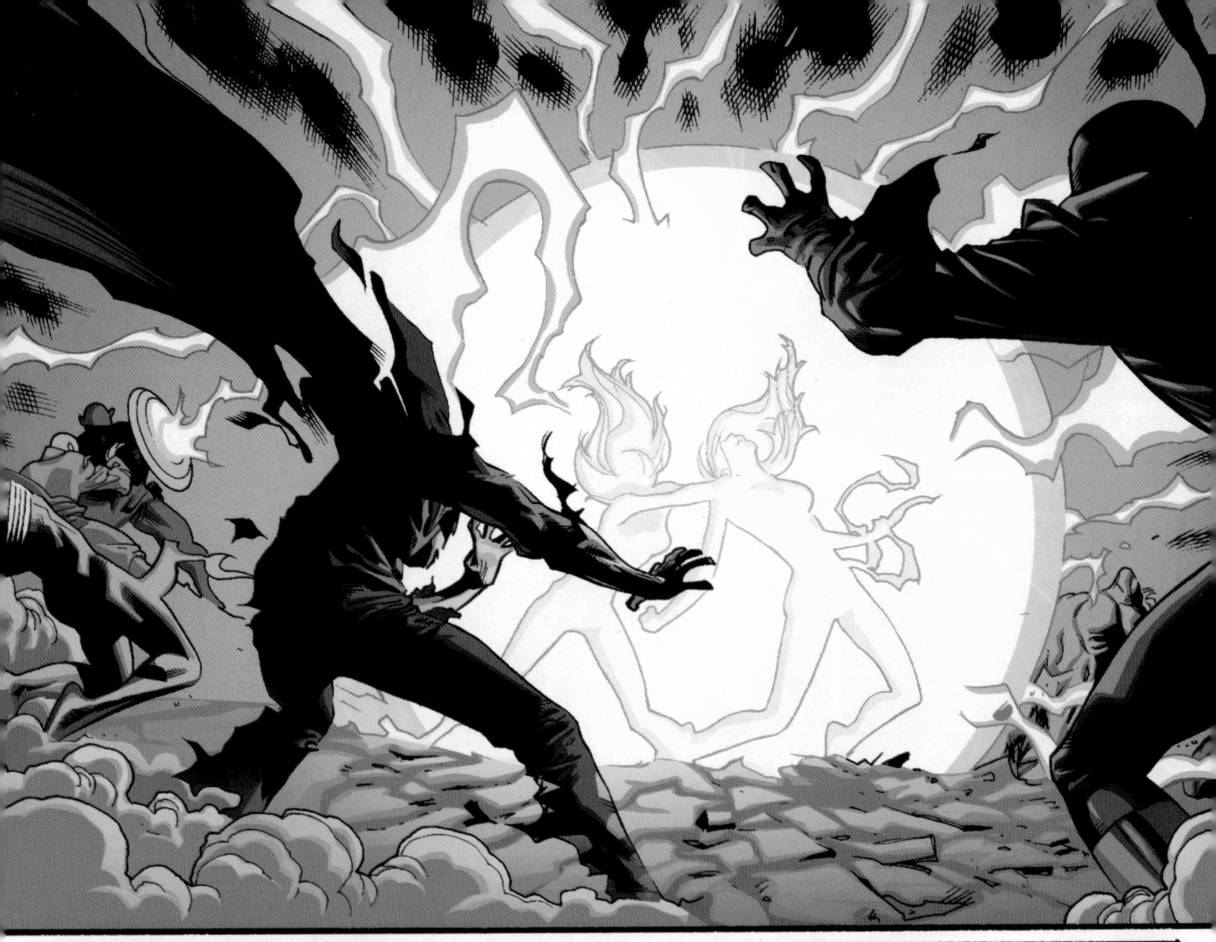

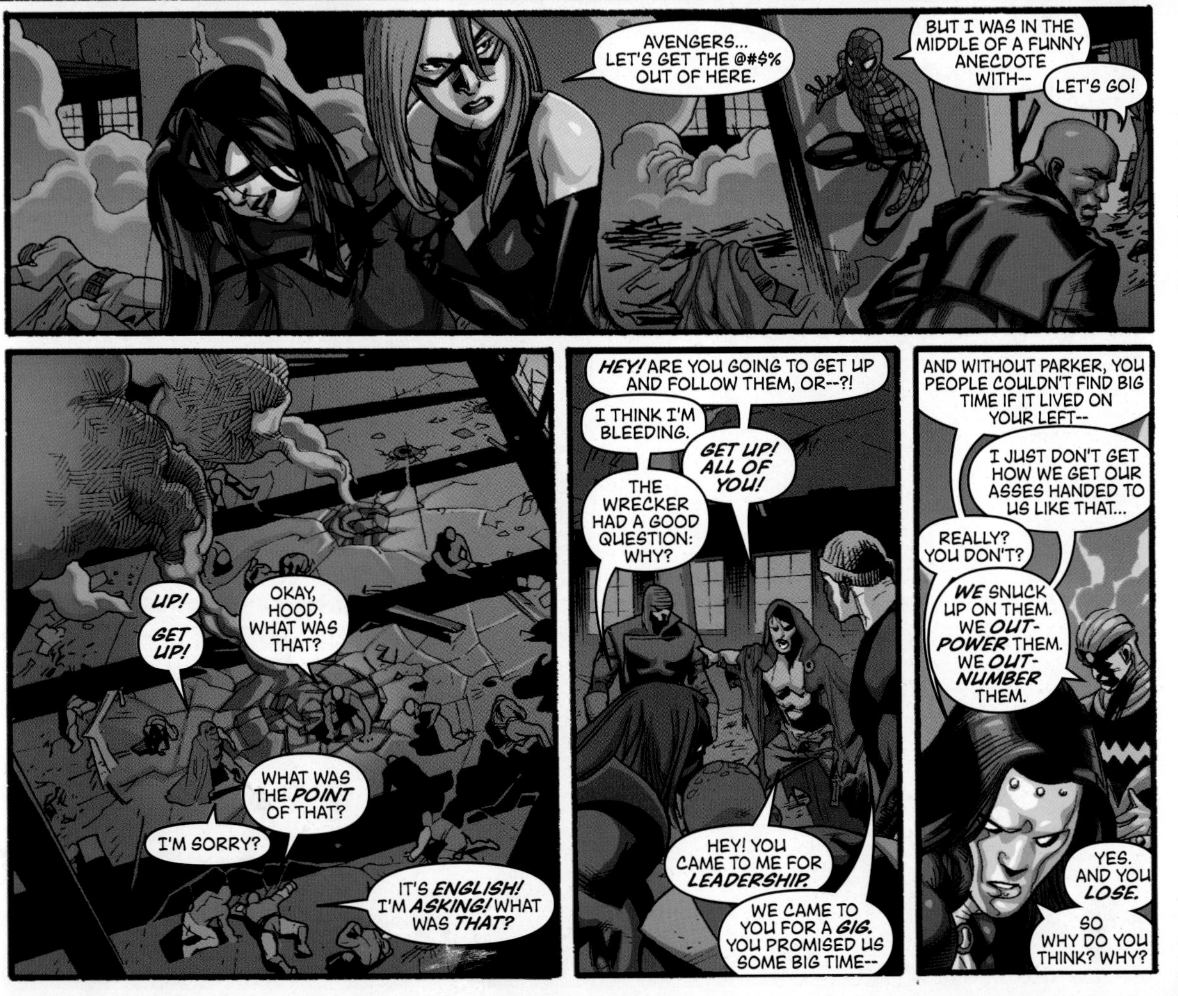

AVENGERS... LET'S GET THE @#$% OUT OF HERE.
BUT I WAS IN THE MIDDLE OF A FUNNY ANECDOTE WITH--
LET'S GO!
UP! GET UP!
OKAY, HOOD, WHAT WAS THAT?
WHAT WAS THE POINT OF THAT?
I'M SORRY?
IT'S ENGLISH! I'M ASKING! WHAT WAS THAT?
HEY! ARE YOU GOING TO GET UP AND FOLLOW THEM, OR--?!
I THINK I'M BLEEDING.
GET UP! ALL OF YOU!
THE WRECKER HAD A GOOD QUESTION: WHY?
HEY! YOU CAME TO ME FOR LEADERSHIP.
WE CAME TO YOU FOR A GIG. YOU PROMISED US SOME BIG TIME--
AND WITHOUT PARKER, YOU PEOPLE COULDN'T FIND BIG TIME IF IT LIVED ON YOUR LEFT--
I JUST DON'T GET HOW WE GET OUR ASSES HANDED TO US LIKE THAT...
REALLY? YOU DON'T?
WE SNUCK UP ON THEM. WE OUT-POWER THEM. WE OUT-NUMBER THEM.
YES. AND YOU LOSE.
SO WHY DO YOU THINK? WHY?

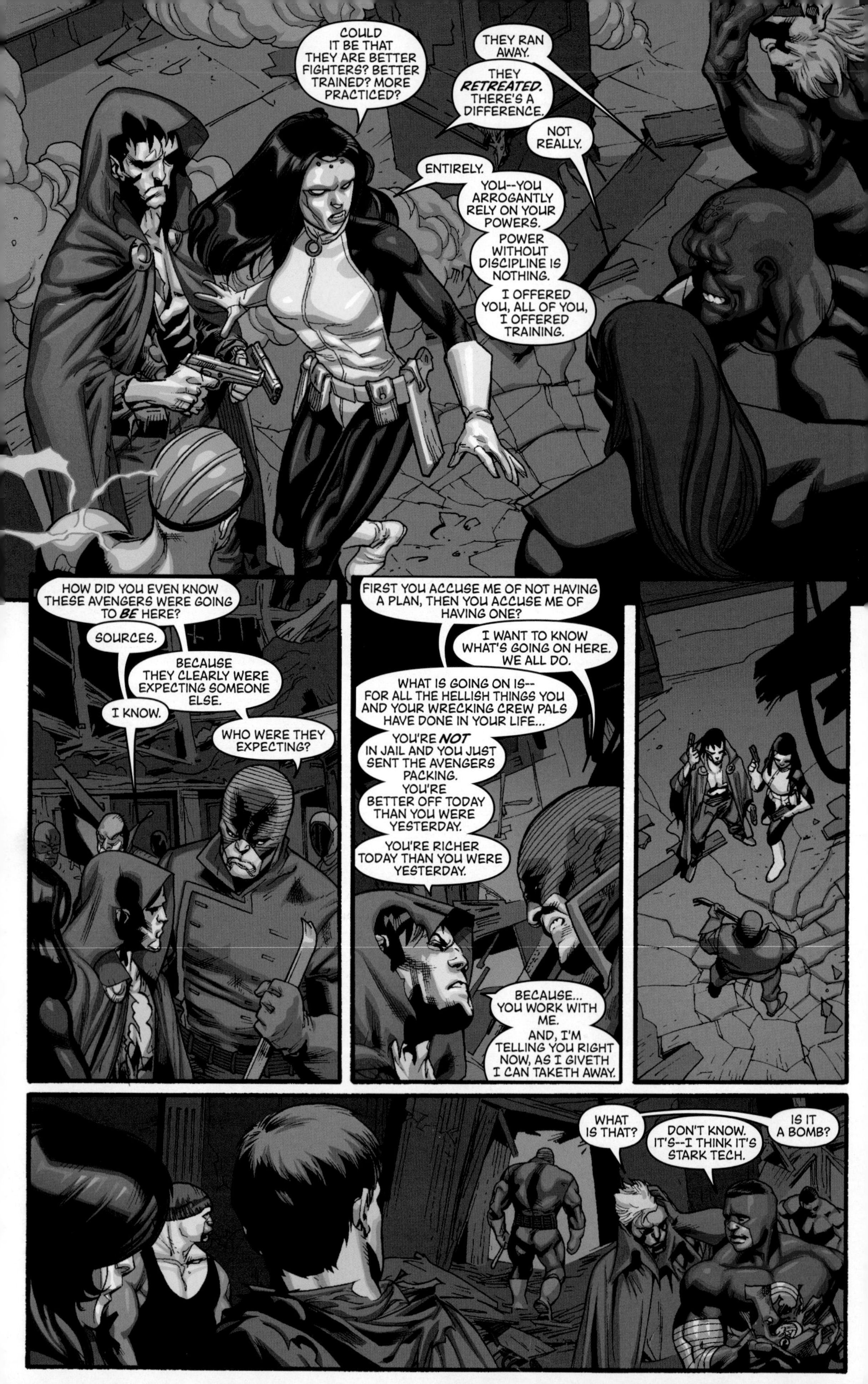
COULD IT BE THAT THEY ARE BETTER FIGHTERS? BETTER TRAINED? MORE PRACTICED?
THEY RAN AWAY.
THEY RETREATED. THERE'S A DIFFERENCE.
NOT REALLY.
ENTIRELY.
YOU--YOU ARROGANTLY RELY ON YOUR POWERS.
POWER WITHOUT DISCIPLINE IS NOTHING.
I OFFERED YOU, ALL OF YOU, I OFFERED TRAINING.
HOW DID YOU EVEN KNOW THESE AVENGERS WERE GOING TO BE HERE?
SOURCES.
BECAUSE THEY CLEARLY WERE EXPECTING SOMEONE ELSE.
I KNOW.
WHO WERE THEY EXPECTING?
FIRST YOU ACCUSE ME OF NOT HAVING A PLAN, THEN YOU ACCUSE ME OF HAVING ONE?
I WANT TO KNOW WHAT'S GOING ON HERE. WE ALL DO.
WHAT IS GOING ON IS-- FOR ALL THE HELLISH THINGS YOU AND YOUR WRECKING CREW PALS HAVE DONE IN YOUR LIFE...
YOU'RE NOT IN JAIL AND YOU JUST SENT THE AVENGERS PACKING.
YOU'RE BETTER OFF TODAY THAN YOU WERE YESTERDAY.
YOU'RE RICHER TODAY THAN YOU WERE YESTERDAY.
BECAUSE... YOU WORK WITH ME.
AND, I'M TELLING YOU RIGHT NOW, AS I GIVETH I CAN TAKETH AWAY.
WHAT IS THAT?
DON'T KNOW. IT'S--I THINK IT'S STARK TECH.
IS IT A BOMB?

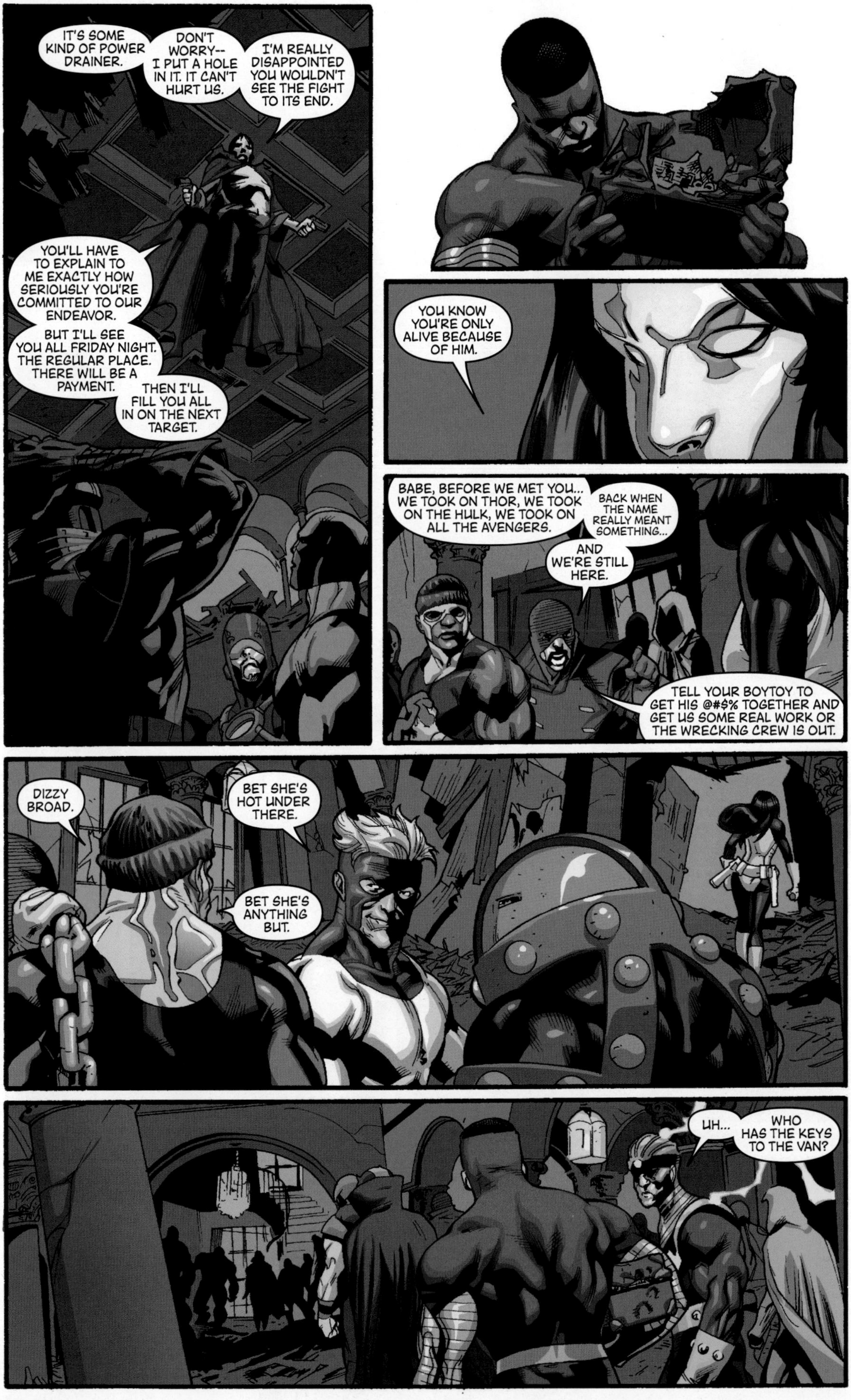
IT'S SOME KIND OF POWER DRAINER.
DON'T WORRY-- I PUT A HOLE IN IT. IT CAN'T HURT US.
I'M REALLY DISAPPOINTED YOU WOULDN'T SEE THE FIGHT TO ITS END.
YOU'LL HAVE TO EXPLAIN TO ME EXACTLY HOW SERIOUSLY YOU'RE COMMITTED TO OUR ENDEAVOR.
BUT I'LL SEE YOU ALL FRIDAY NIGHT. THE REGULAR PLACE. THERE WILL BE A PAYMENT.
THEN I'LL FILL YOU ALL IN ON THE NEXT TARGET.
YOU KNOW YOU'RE ONLY ALIVE BECAUSE OF HIM.
BABE, BEFORE WE MET YOU... WE TOOK ON THOR, WE TOOK ON THE HULK, WE TOOK ON ALL THE AVENGERS.
BACK WHEN THE NAME REALLY MEANT SOMETHING...
AND WE'RE STILL HERE.
TELL YOUR BOYTOY TO GET HIS @#$% TOGETHER AND GET US SOME REAL WORK OR THE WRECKING CREW IS OUT.
DIZZY BROAD.
BET SHE'S HOT UNDER THERE.
BET SHE'S ANYTHING BUT.
UH...
WHO HAS THE KEYS TO THE VAN?

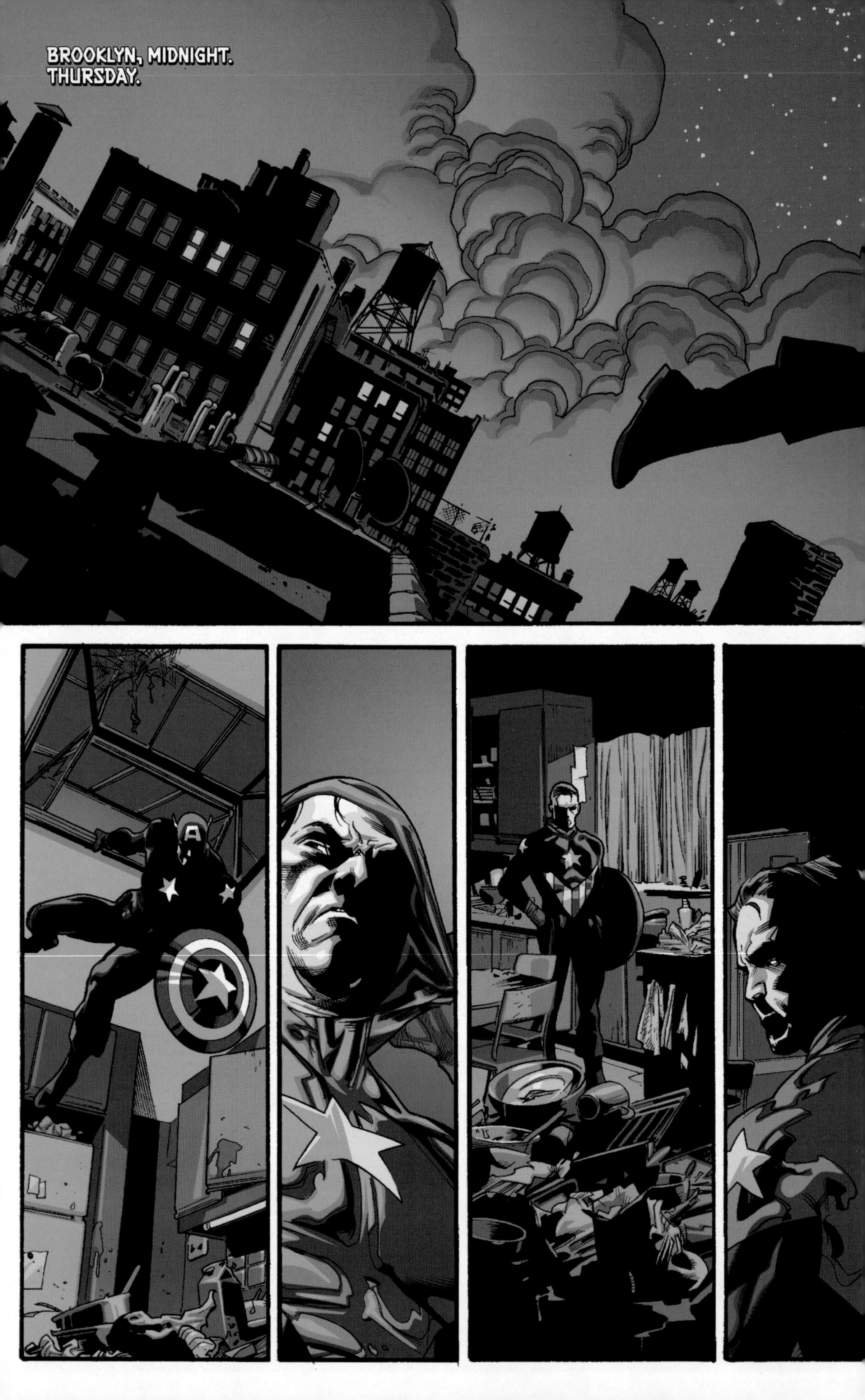
BROOKLYN, MIDNIGHT.
THURSDAY.

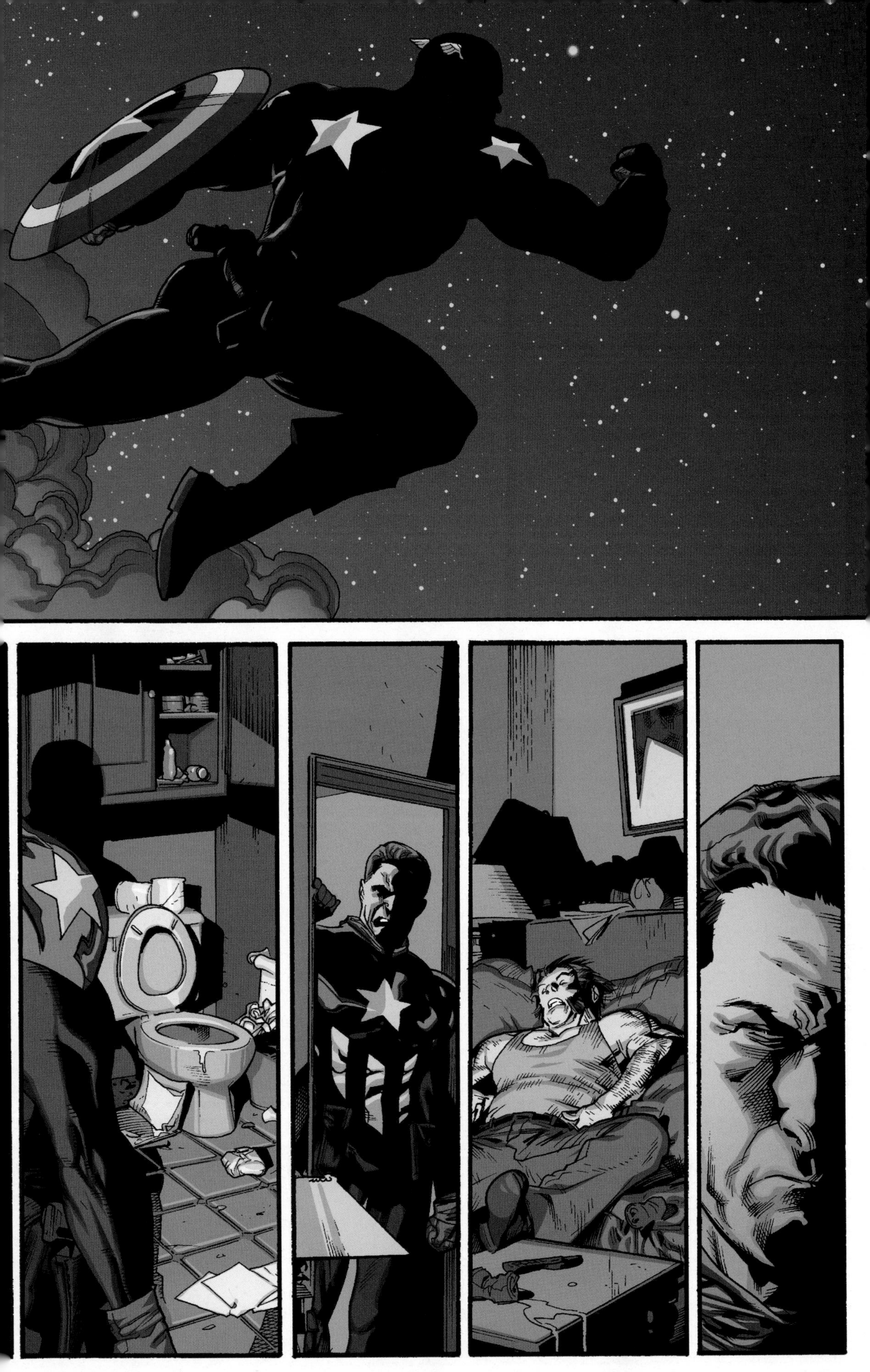

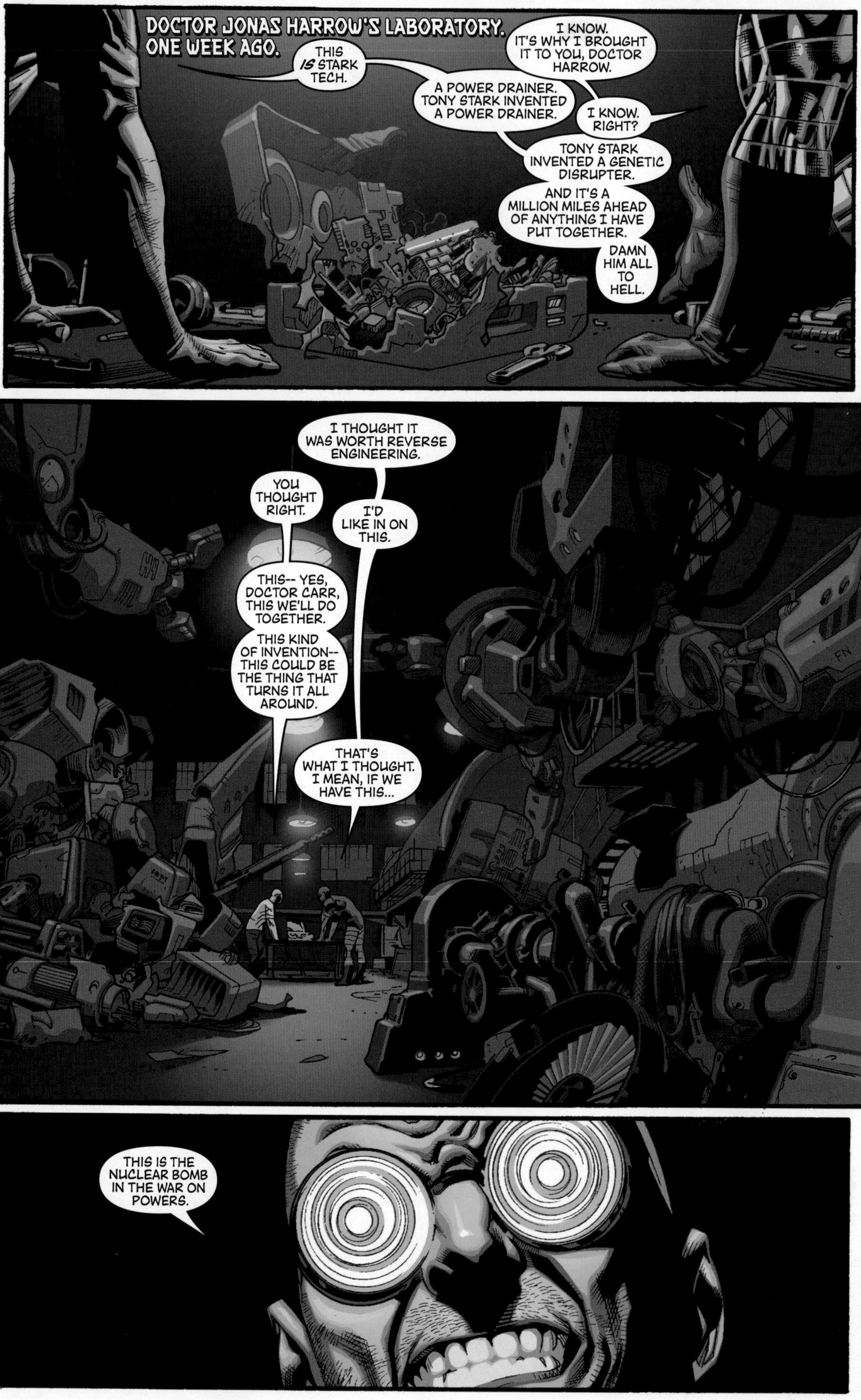
DOCTOR JONAS HARROW'S LABORATORY. ONE WEEK AGO.
THIS *IS* STARK TECH.
I KNOW. IT'S WHY I BROUGHT IT TO YOU, DOCTOR HARROW.
A POWER DRAINER. TONY STARK INVENTED A POWER DRAINER.
I KNOW. RIGHT?
TONY STARK INVENTED A GENETIC DISRUPTER.
AND IT'S A MILLION MILES AHEAD OF ANYTHING I HAVE PUT TOGETHER.
DAMN HIM ALL TO HELL.
I THOUGHT IT WAS WORTH REVERSE ENGINEERING.
YOU THOUGHT RIGHT.
I'D LIKE IN ON THIS.
THIS-- YES, DOCTOR CARR, THIS WE'LL DO TOGETHER.
THIS KIND OF INVENTION-- THIS COULD BE THE THING THAT TURNS IT ALL AROUND.
THAT'S WHAT I THOUGHT. I MEAN, IF WE HAVE THIS...
THIS IS THE NUCLEAR BOMB IN THE WAR ON POWERS.

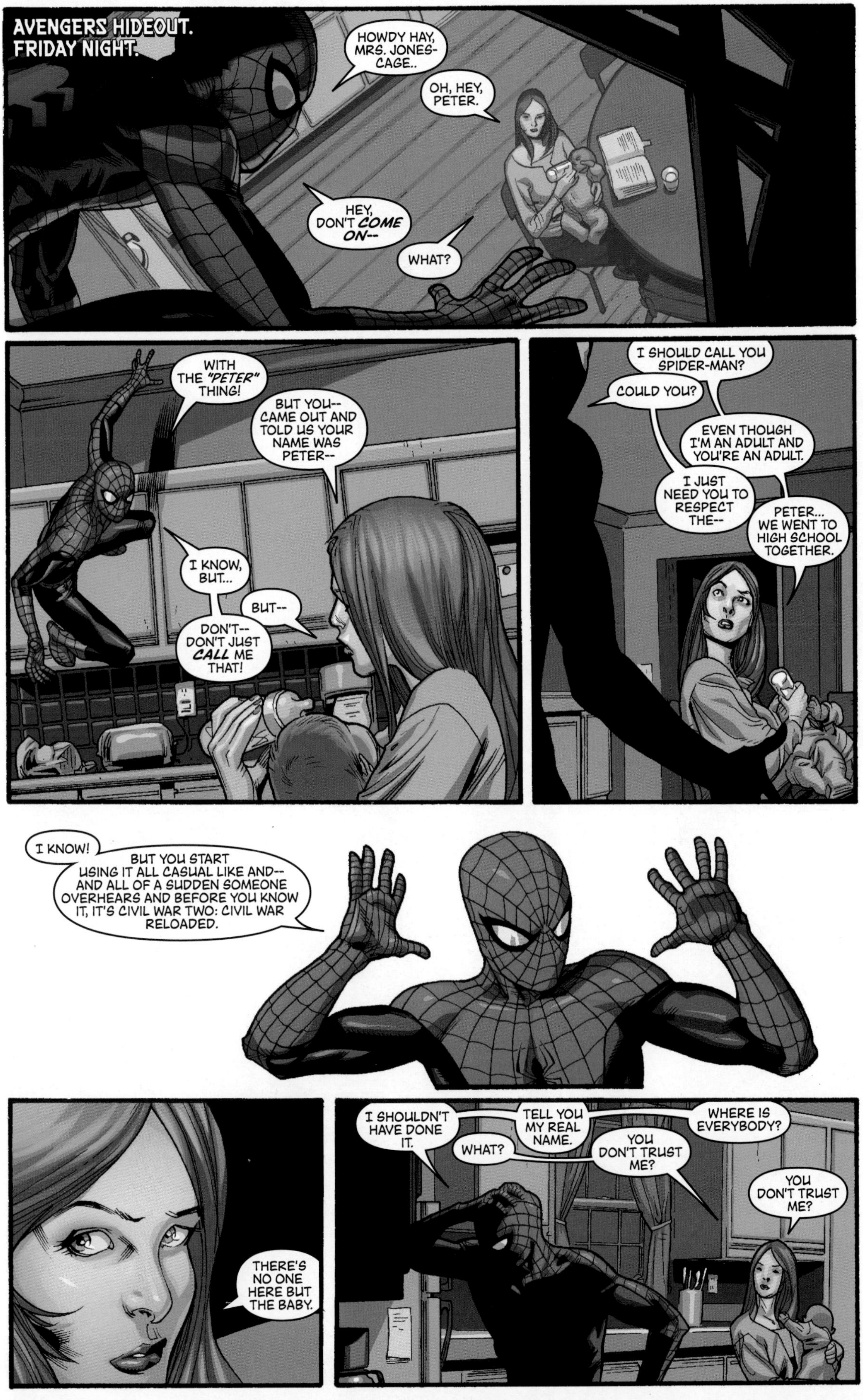
AVENGERS HIDEOUT. FRIDAY NIGHT.
HOWDY HAY, MRS. JONES-CAGE..
OH, HEY, PETER.
HEY, DON'T COME ON--
WHAT?
WITH THE "PETER" THING!
BUT YOU-- CAME OUT AND TOLD US YOUR NAME WAS PETER--
I KNOW, BUT...
BUT--
DON'T-- DON'T JUST CALL ME THAT!
I SHOULD CALL YOU SPIDER-MAN?
COULD YOU?
EVEN THOUGH I'M AN ADULT AND YOU'RE AN ADULT.
I JUST NEED YOU TO RESPECT THE--
PETER... WE WENT TO HIGH SCHOOL TOGETHER.
I KNOW!
BUT YOU START USING IT ALL CASUAL LIKE AND-- AND ALL OF A SUDDEN SOMEONE OVERHEARS AND BEFORE YOU KNOW IT, IT'S CIVIL WAR TWO: CIVIL WAR RELOADED.
THERE'S NO ONE HERE BUT THE BABY.
I SHOULDN'T HAVE DONE IT.
TELL YOU MY REAL NAME.
WHERE IS EVERYBODY?
WHAT?
YOU DON'T TRUST ME?
YOU DON'T TRUST ME?

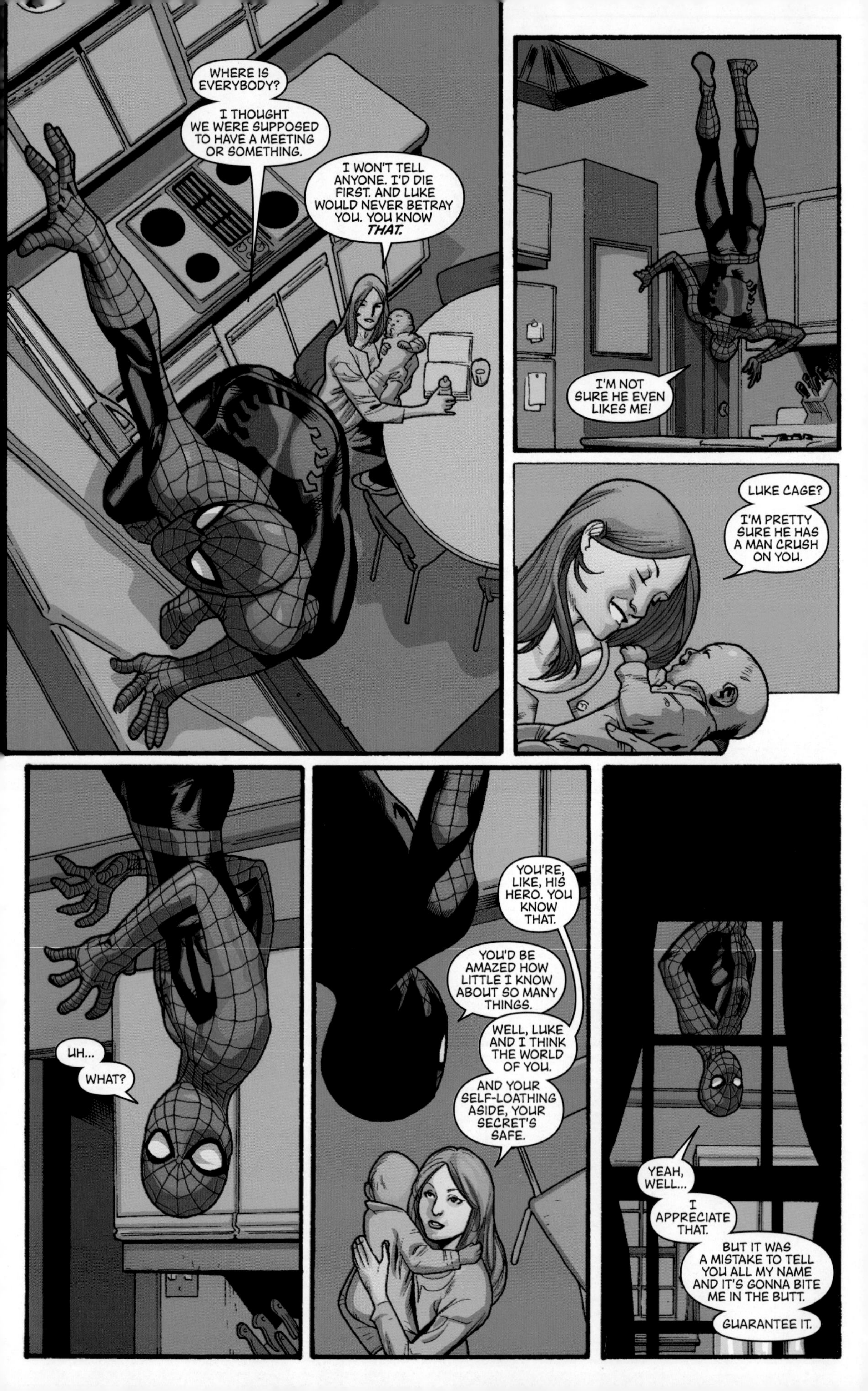
WHERE IS EVERYBODY?
I THOUGHT WE WERE SUPPOSED TO HAVE A MEETING OR SOMETHING.
I WON'T TELL ANYONE. I'D DIE FIRST. AND LUKE WOULD NEVER BETRAY YOU. YOU KNOW *THAT.*
I'M NOT SURE HE EVEN LIKES ME!
LUKE CAGE?
I'M PRETTY SURE HE HAS A MAN CRUSH ON YOU.
UH...
WHAT?
YOU'RE, LIKE, HIS HERO. YOU KNOW THAT.
YOU'D BE AMAZED HOW LITTLE I KNOW ABOUT SO MANY THINGS.
WELL, LUKE AND I THINK THE WORLD OF YOU.
AND YOUR SELF-LOATHING ASIDE, YOUR SECRET'S SAFE.
YEAH, WELL...
I APPRECIATE THAT.
BUT IT WAS A MISTAKE TO TELL YOU ALL MY NAME AND IT'S GONNA BITE ME IN THE BUTT.
GUARANTEE IT.

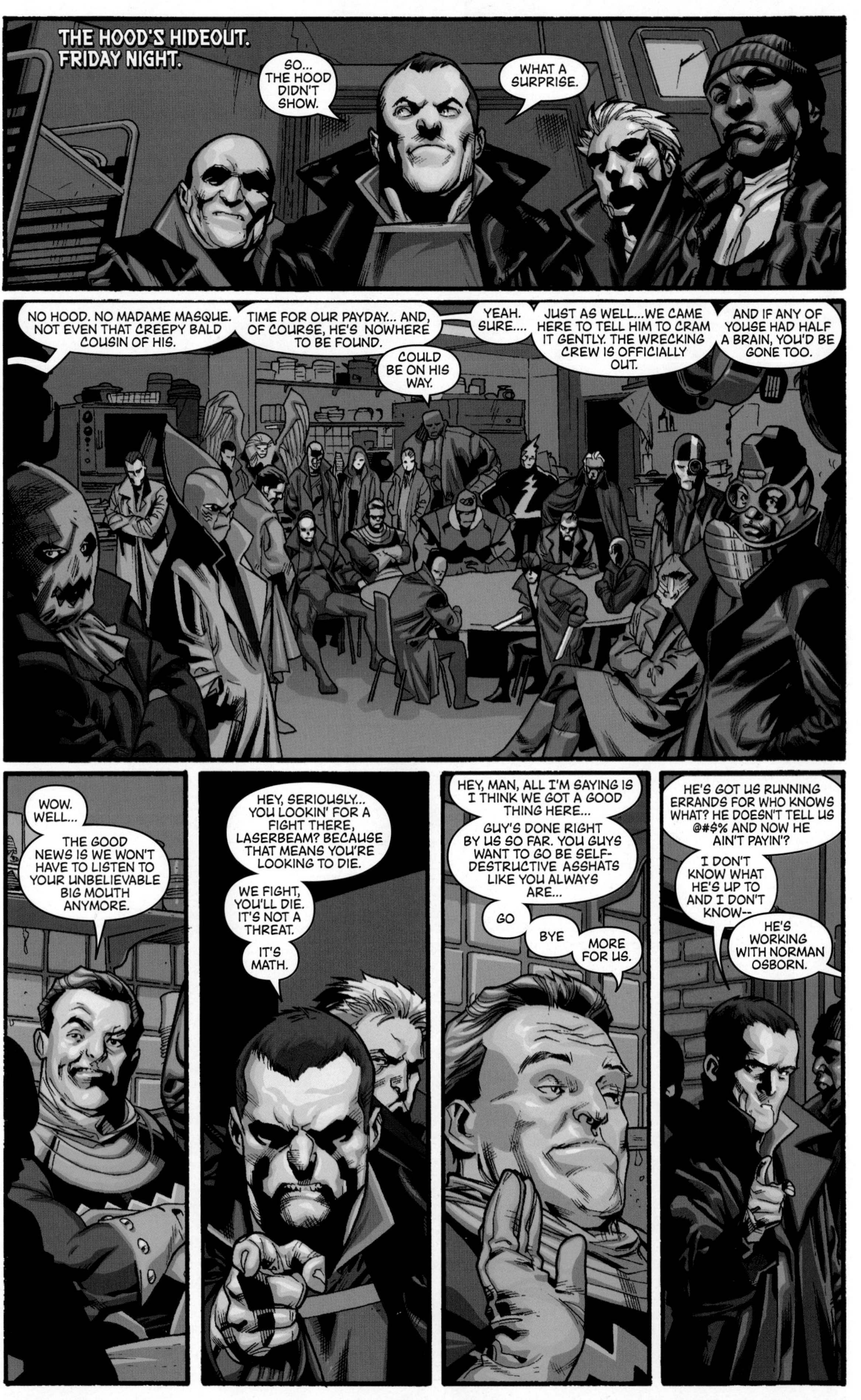
THE HOOD'S HIDEOUT. FRIDAY NIGHT.
SO... THE HOOD DIDN'T SHOW.
WHAT A SURPRISE.
NO HOOD. NO MADAME MASQUE. NOT EVEN THAT CREEPY BALD COUSIN OF HIS.
TIME FOR OUR PAYDAY... AND, OF COURSE, HE'S NOWHERE TO BE FOUND.
COULD BE ON HIS WAY.
YEAH. SURE....
JUST AS WELL...WE CAME HERE TO TELL HIM TO CRAM IT GENTLY. THE WRECKING CREW IS OFFICIALLY OUT.
AND IF ANY OF YOUSE HAD HALF A BRAIN, YOU'D BE GONE TOO.
WOW. WELL...
THE GOOD NEWS IS WE WON'T HAVE TO LISTEN TO YOUR UNBELIEVABLE BIG MOUTH ANYMORE.
HEY, SERIOUSLY... YOU LOOKIN' FOR A FIGHT THERE, LASERBEAM? BECAUSE THAT MEANS YOU'RE LOOKING TO DIE.
WE FIGHT, YOU'LL DIE. IT'S NOT A THREAT.
IT'S MATH.
HEY, MAN, ALL I'M SAYING IS I THINK WE GOT A GOOD THING HERE...
GUY'S DONE RIGHT BY US SO FAR. YOU GUYS WANT TO GO BE SELF-DESTRUCTIVE ASSHATS LIKE YOU ALWAYS ARE...
GO
BYE
MORE FOR US.
HE'S GOT US RUNNING ERRANDS FOR WHO KNOWS WHAT? HE DOESN'T TELL US @#$% AND NOW HE AIN'T PAYIN'?
I DON'T KNOW WHAT HE'S UP TO AND I DON'T KNOW--
HE'S WORKING WITH NORMAN OSBORN.

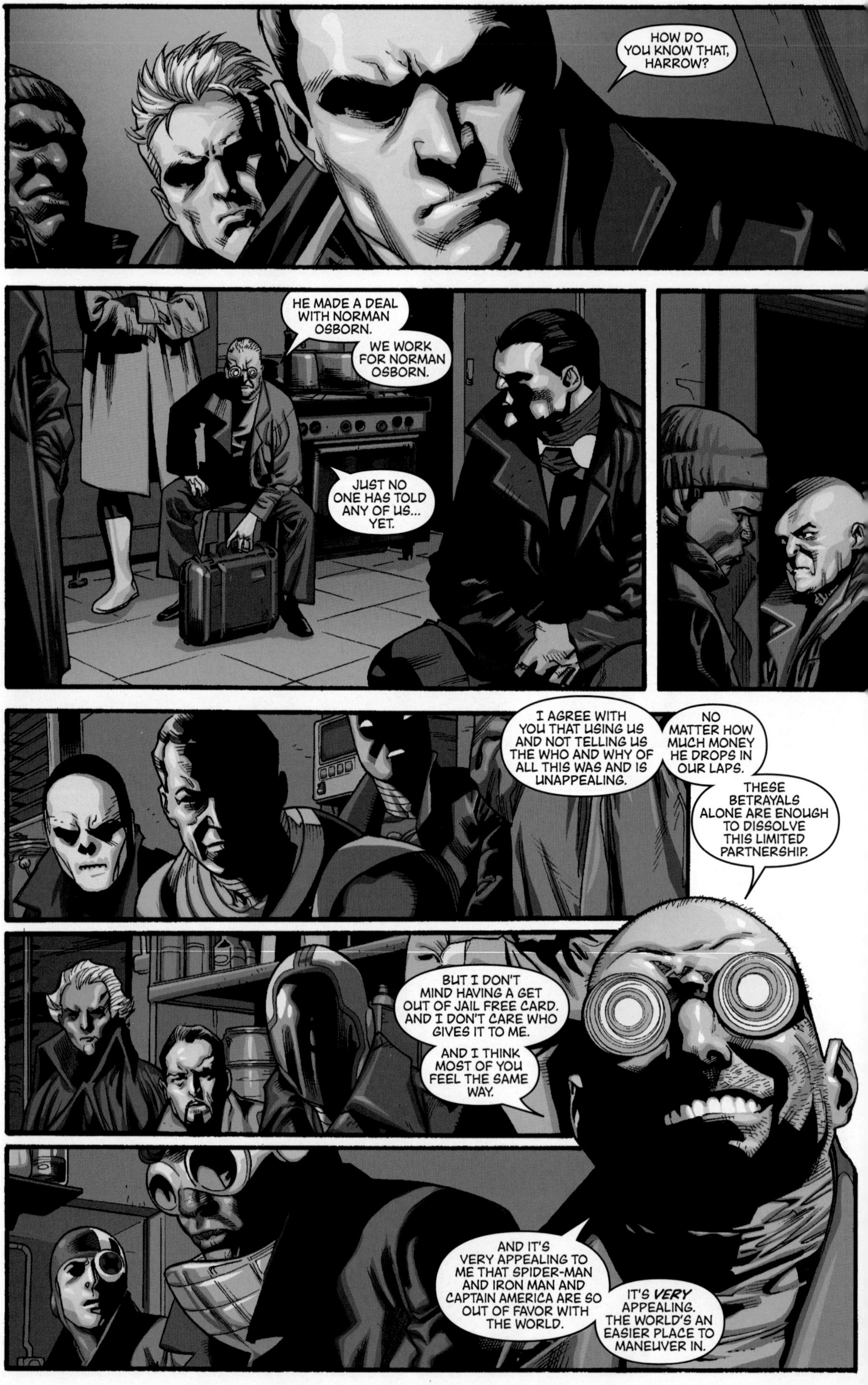
HOW DO YOU KNOW THAT, HARROW?
HE MADE A DEAL WITH NORMAN OSBORN.
WE WORK FOR NORMAN OSBORN.
JUST NO ONE HAS TOLD ANY OF US... YET.
I AGREE WITH YOU THAT USING US AND NOT TELLING US THE WHO AND WHY OF ALL THIS WAS AND IS UNAPPEALING.
NO MATTER HOW MUCH MONEY HE DROPS IN OUR LAPS.
THESE BETRAYALS ALONE ARE ENOUGH TO DISSOLVE THIS LIMITED PARTNERSHIP.
BUT I DON'T MIND HAVING A GET OUT OF JAIL FREE CARD. AND I DON'T CARE WHO GIVES IT TO ME.
AND I THINK MOST OF YOU FEEL THE SAME WAY.
AND IT'S VERY APPEALING TO ME THAT SPIDER-MAN AND IRON MAN AND CAPTAIN AMERICA ARE SO OUT OF FAVOR WITH THE WORLD.
IT'S *VERY* APPEALING. THE WORLD'S AN EASIER PLACE TO MANEUVER IN.

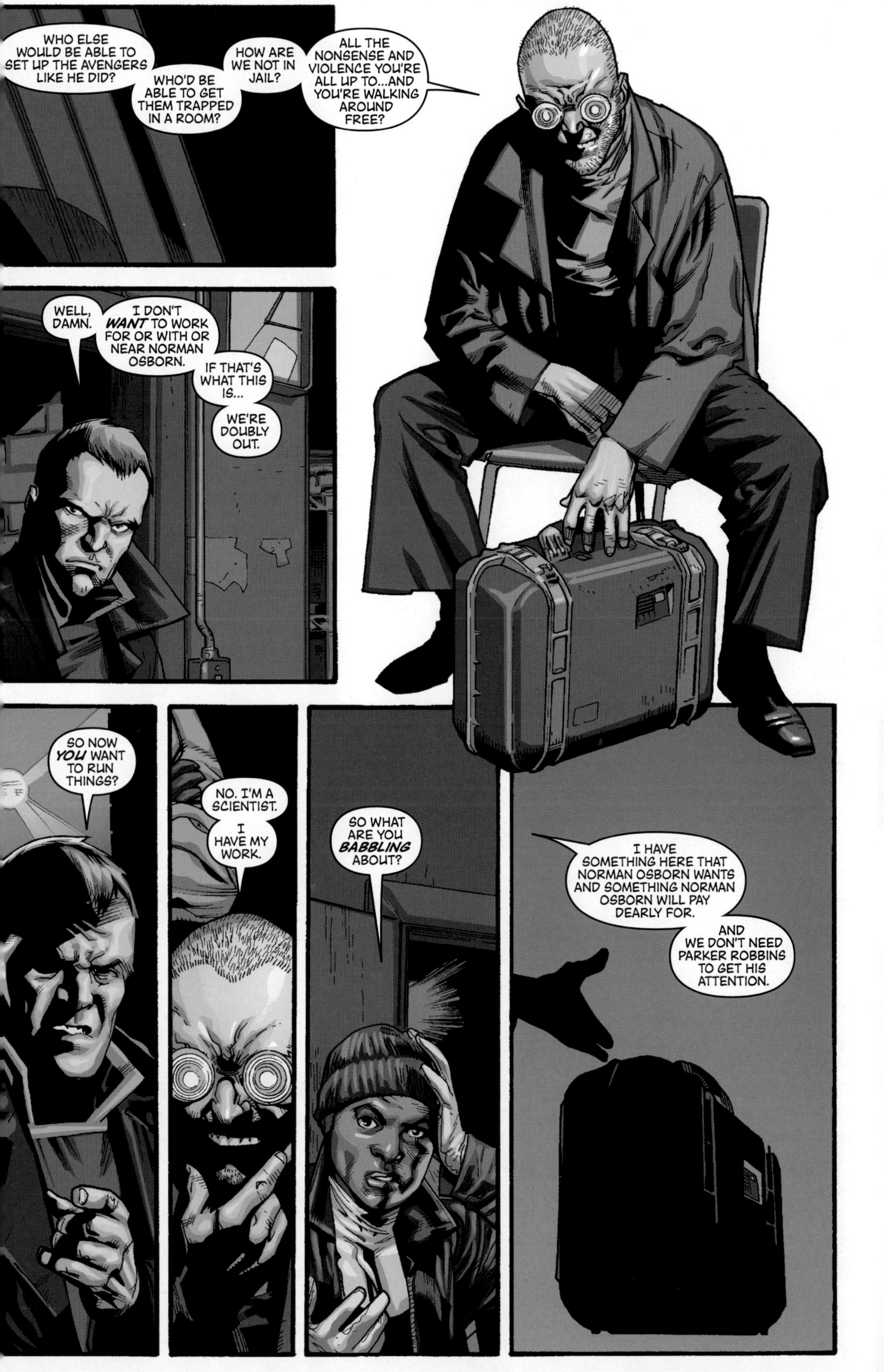
WHO ELSE WOULD BE ABLE TO SET UP THE AVENGERS LIKE HE DID?
WHO'D BE ABLE TO GET THEM TRAPPED IN A ROOM?
HOW ARE WE NOT IN JAIL?
ALL THE NONSENSE AND VIOLENCE YOU'RE ALL UP TO...AND YOU'RE WALKING AROUND FREE?
WELL, DAMN.
I DON'T *WANT* TO WORK FOR OR WITH OR NEAR NORMAN OSBORN.
IF THAT'S WHAT THIS IS...
WE'RE DOUBLY OUT.
SO NOW *YOU* WANT TO RUN THINGS?
NO. I'M A SCIENTIST.
I HAVE MY WORK.
SO WHAT ARE YOU *BABBLING* ABOUT?
I HAVE SOMETHING HERE THAT NORMAN OSBORN WANTS AND SOMETHING NORMAN OSBORN WILL PAY DEARLY FOR.
AND WE DON'T NEED PARKER ROBBINS TO GET HIS ATTENTION.

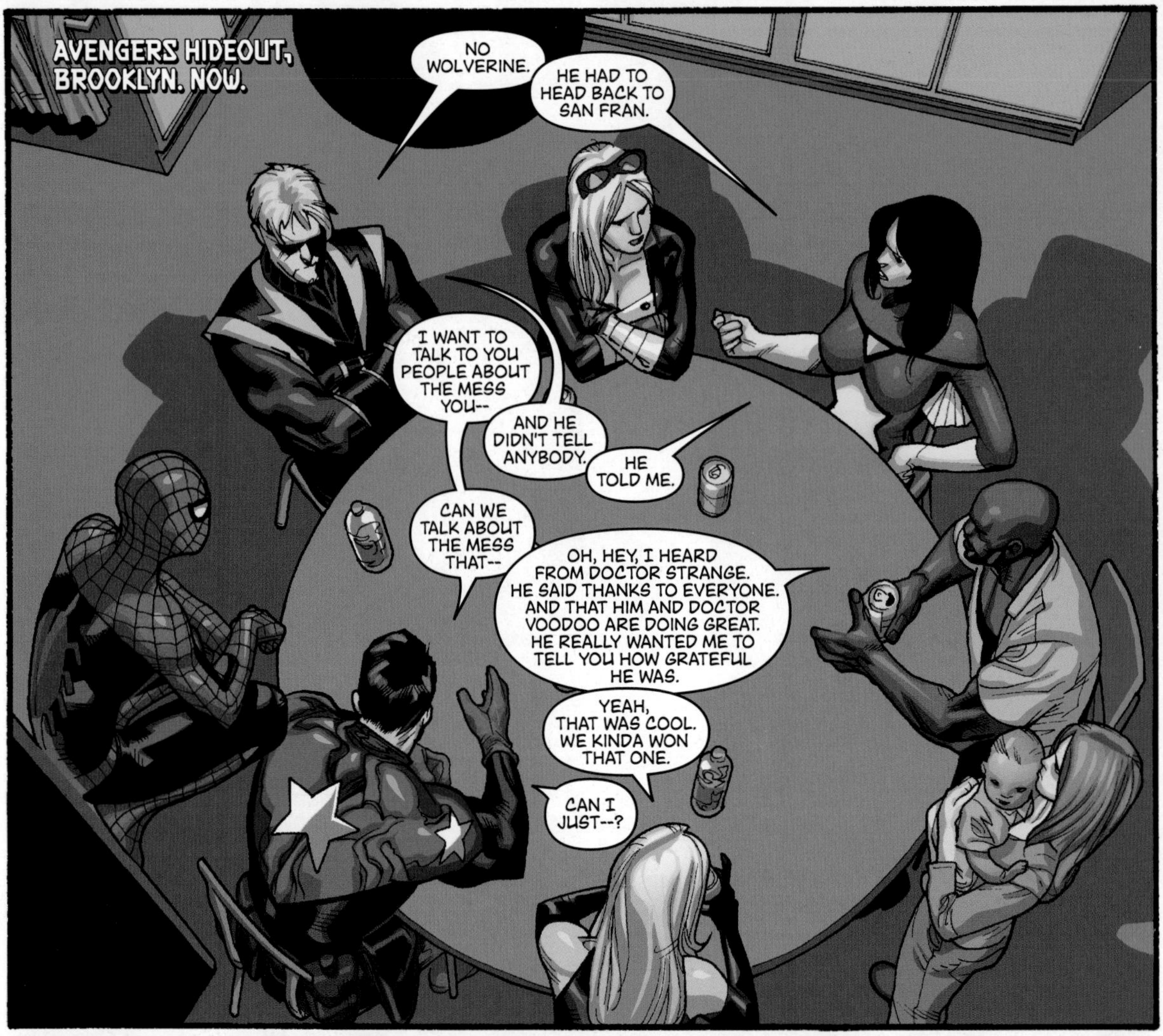
AVENGERS HIDEOUT, BROOKLYN. NOW.
NO WOLVERINE.
HE HAD TO HEAD BACK TO SAN FRAN.
I WANT TO TALK TO YOU PEOPLE ABOUT THE MESS YOU--
AND HE DIDN'T TELL ANYBODY.
HE TOLD ME.
CAN WE TALK ABOUT THE MESS THAT--
OH, HEY, I HEARD FROM DOCTOR STRANGE. HE SAID THANKS TO EVERYONE. AND THAT HIM AND DOCTOR VOODOO ARE DOING GREAT. HE REALLY WANTED ME TO TELL YOU HOW GRATEFUL HE WAS.
YEAH, THAT WAS COOL. WE KINDA WON THAT ONE.
CAN I JUST--?

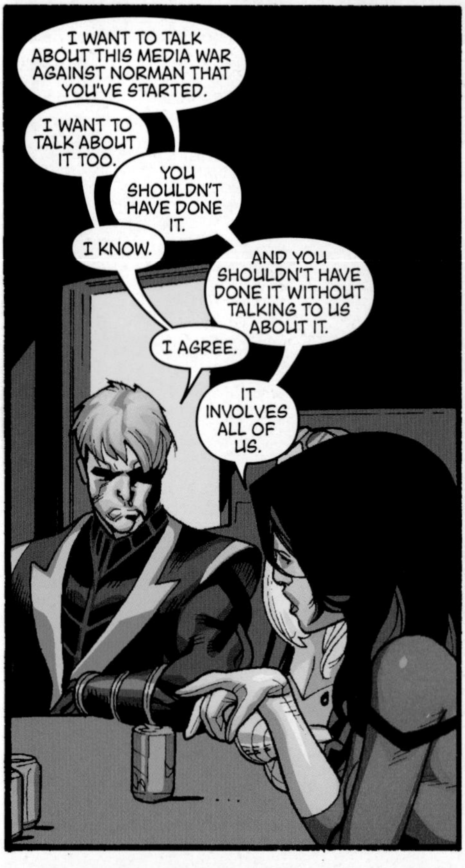
I WANT TO TALK ABOUT THIS MEDIA WAR AGAINST NORMAN THAT YOU'VE STARTED.
I WANT TO TALK ABOUT IT TOO.
YOU SHOULDN'T HAVE DONE IT.
I KNOW.
AND YOU SHOULDN'T HAVE DONE IT WITHOUT TALKING TO US ABOUT IT.
I AGREE.
IT INVOLVES ALL OF US.

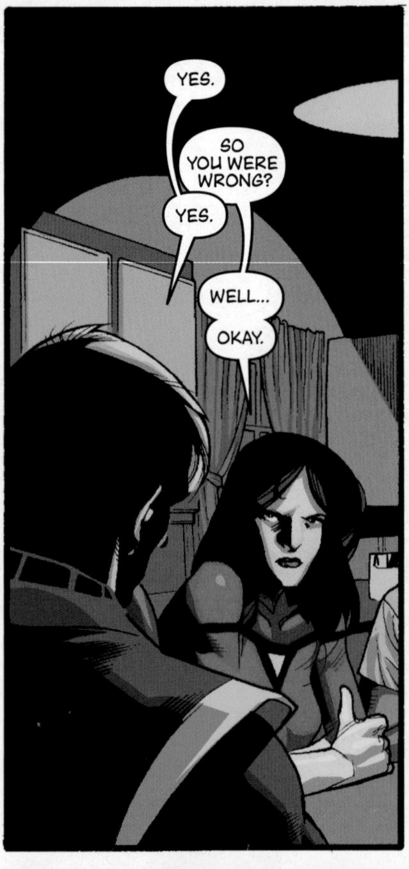
YES.
SO YOU WERE WRONG?
YES.
WELL...
OKAY.

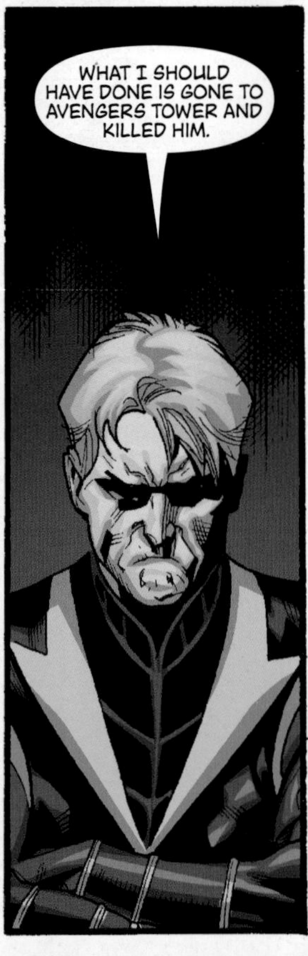
WHAT I SHOULD HAVE DONE IS GONE TO AVENGERS TOWER AND KILLED HIM.

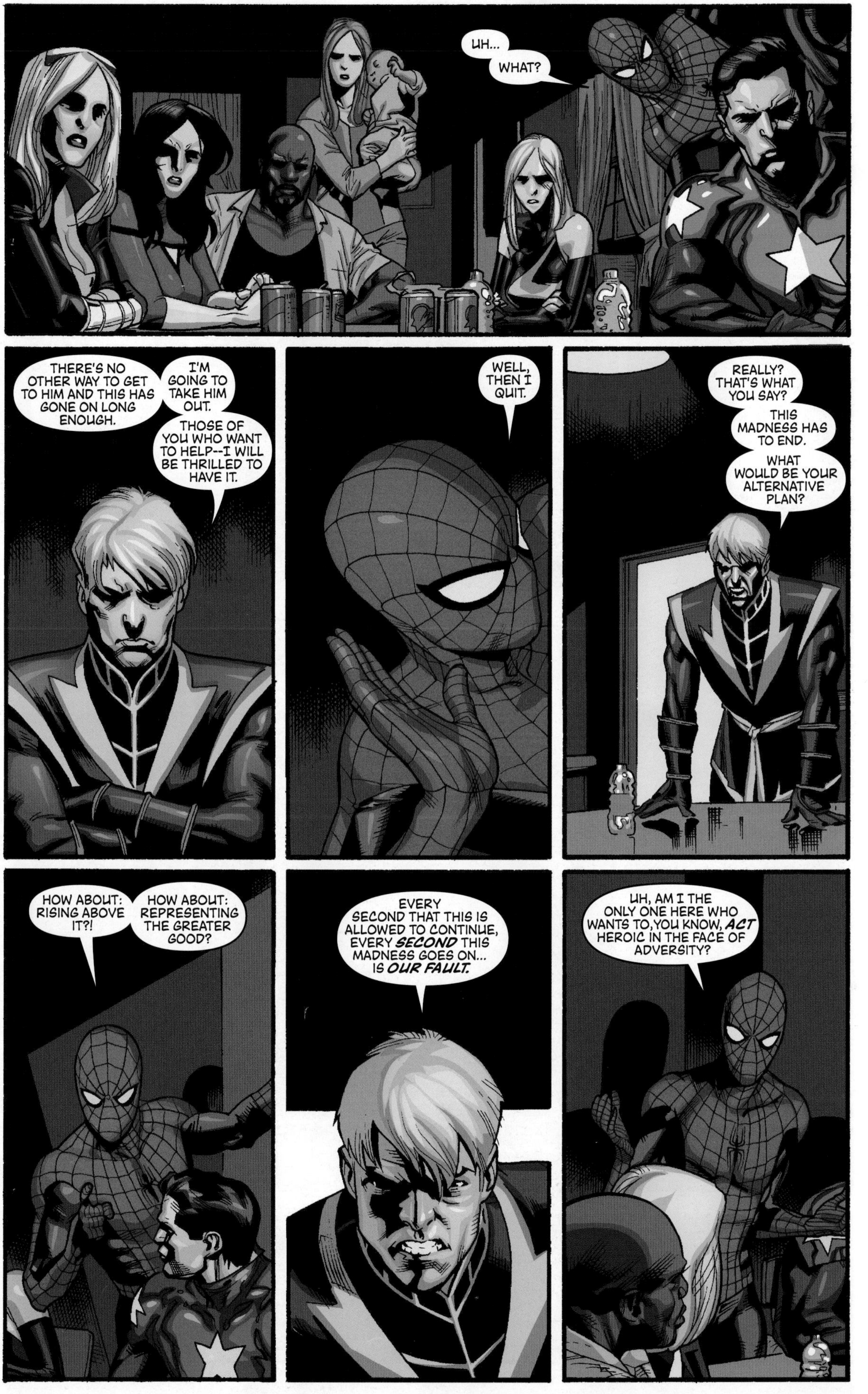
UH... WHAT?
THERE'S NO OTHER WAY TO GET TO HIM AND THIS HAS GONE ON LONG ENOUGH.
I'M GOING TO TAKE HIM OUT.
THOSE OF YOU WHO WANT TO HELP--I WILL BE THRILLED TO HAVE IT.
WELL, THEN I QUIT.
REALLY? THAT'S WHAT YOU SAY?
THIS MADNESS HAS TO END.
WHAT WOULD BE YOUR ALTERNATIVE PLAN?
HOW ABOUT: RISING ABOVE IT?!
HOW ABOUT: REPRESENTING THE GREATER GOOD?
EVERY SECOND THAT THIS IS ALLOWED TO CONTINUE, EVERY SECOND THIS MADNESS GOES ON... IS OUR FAULT.
UH, AM I THE ONLY ONE HERE WHO WANTS TO, YOU KNOW, ACT HEROIC IN THE FACE OF ADVERSITY?

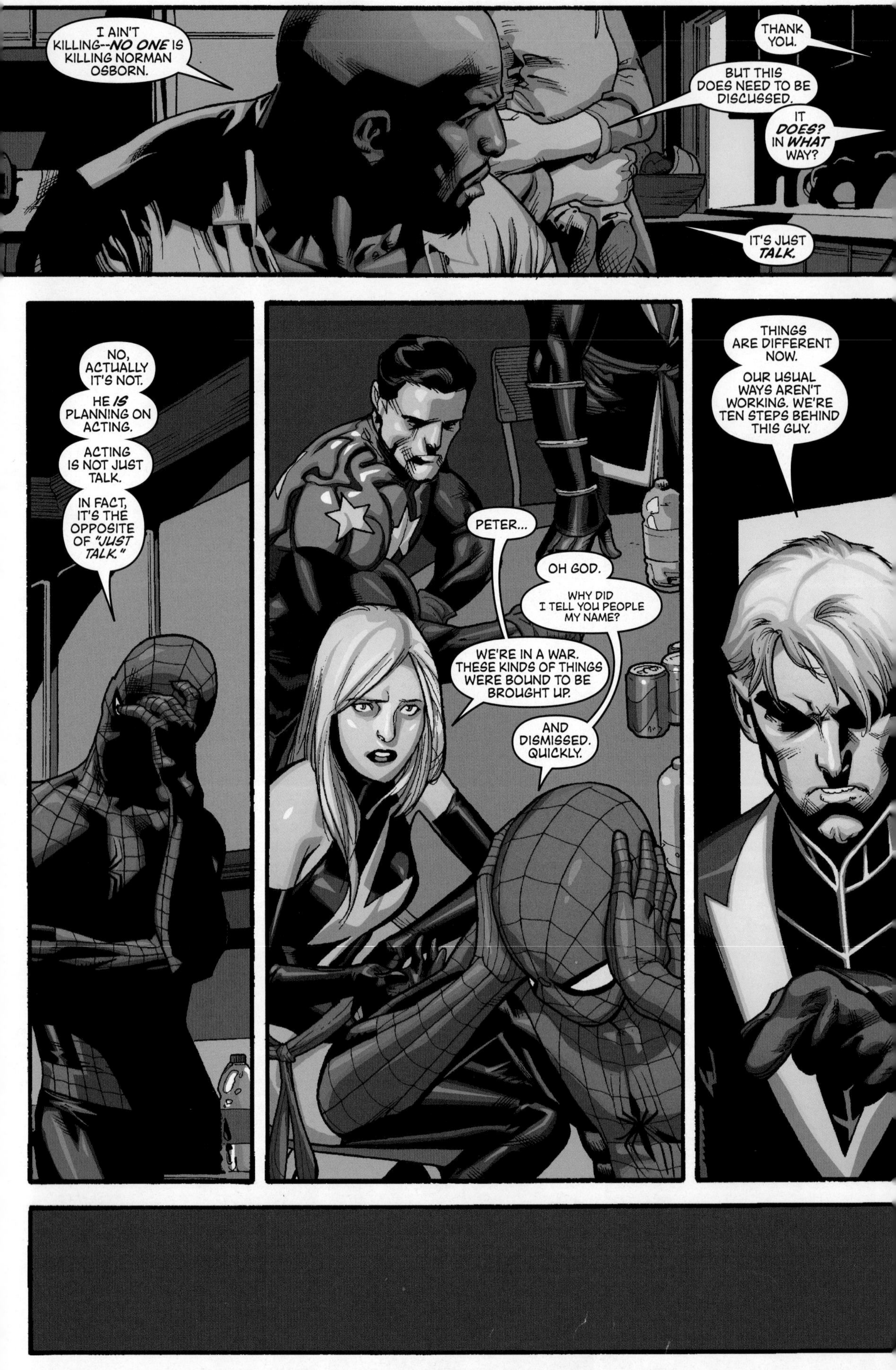
I AIN'T KILLING--*NO ONE* IS KILLING NORMAN OSBORN.
THANK YOU.
BUT THIS DOES NEED TO BE DISCUSSED.
IT *DOES?* IN *WHAT* WAY?
IT'S JUST *TALK.*
NO, ACTUALLY IT'S NOT.
HE *IS* PLANNING ON ACTING.
ACTING IS NOT JUST TALK.
IN FACT, IT'S THE OPPOSITE OF *"JUST TALK."*
PETER...
OH GOD.
WHY DID I TELL YOU PEOPLE MY NAME?
WE'RE IN A WAR. THESE KINDS OF THINGS WERE BOUND TO BE BROUGHT UP.
AND DISMISSED. QUICKLY.
THINGS ARE DIFFERENT NOW.
OUR USUAL WAYS AREN'T WORKING. WE'RE TEN STEPS BEHIND THIS GUY.

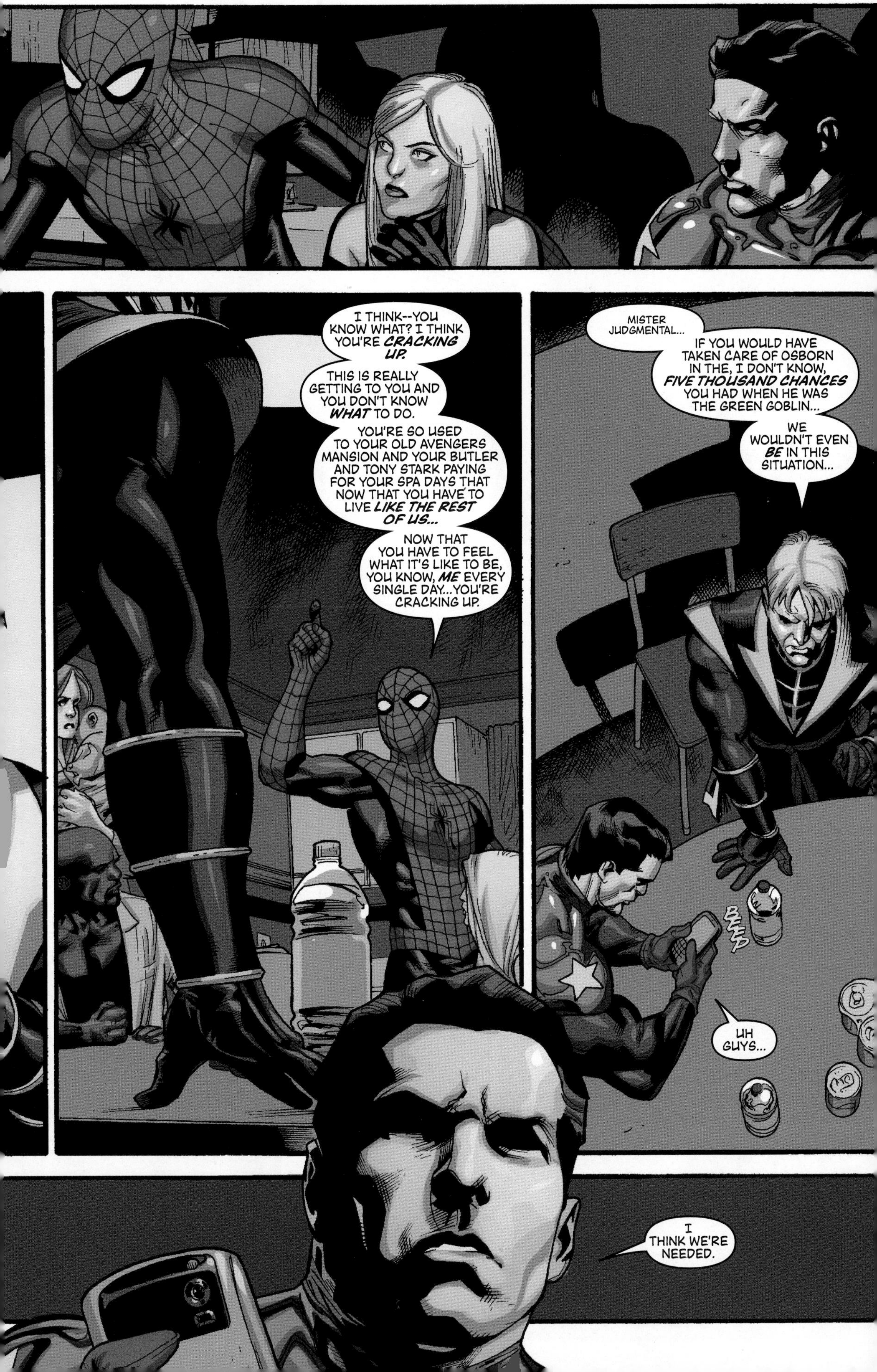
I THINK--YOU KNOW WHAT? I THINK YOU'RE CRACKING UP.
THIS IS REALLY GETTING TO YOU AND YOU DON'T KNOW WHAT TO DO.
YOU'RE SO USED TO YOUR OLD AVENGERS MANSION AND YOUR BUTLER AND TONY STARK PAYING FOR YOUR SPA DAYS THAT NOW THAT YOU HAVE TO LIVE LIKE THE REST OF US...
NOW THAT YOU HAVE TO FEEL WHAT IT'S LIKE TO BE, YOU KNOW, ME EVERY SINGLE DAY...YOU'RE CRACKING UP.
MISTER JUDGMENTAL...
IF YOU WOULD HAVE TAKEN CARE OF OSBORN IN THE, I DON'T KNOW, FIVE THOUSAND CHANCES YOU HAD WHEN HE WAS THE GREEN GOBLIN...
WE WOULDN'T EVEN BE IN THIS SITUATION...
BEEP
UH GUYS...
I THINK WE'RE NEEDED.

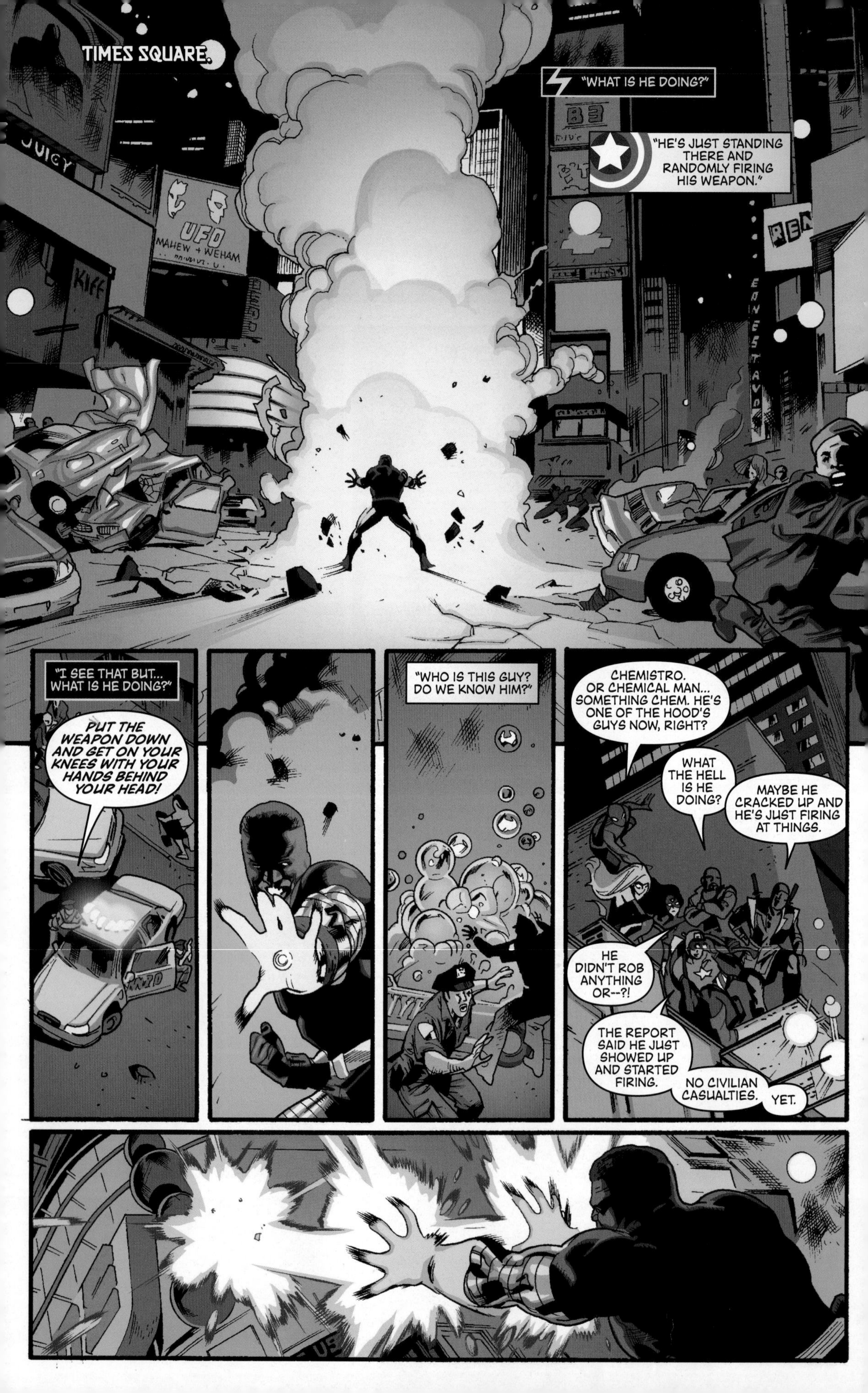
TIMES SQUARE.
"WHAT IS HE DOING?"
"HE'S JUST STANDING THERE AND RANDOMLY FIRING HIS WEAPON."
"I SEE THAT BUT... WHAT IS HE DOING?"
PUT THE WEAPON DOWN AND GET ON YOUR KNEES WITH YOUR HANDS BEHIND YOUR HEAD!
"WHO IS THIS GUY? DO WE KNOW HIM?"
CHEMISTRO. OR CHEMICAL MAN... SOMETHING CHEM. HE'S ONE OF THE HOOD'S GUYS NOW, RIGHT?
WHAT THE HELL IS HE DOING?
MAYBE HE CRACKED UP AND HE'S JUST FIRING AT THINGS.
HE DIDN'T ROB ANYTHING OR--?!
THE REPORT SAID HE JUST SHOWED UP AND STARTED FIRING.
NO CIVILIAN CASUALTIES.
YET.

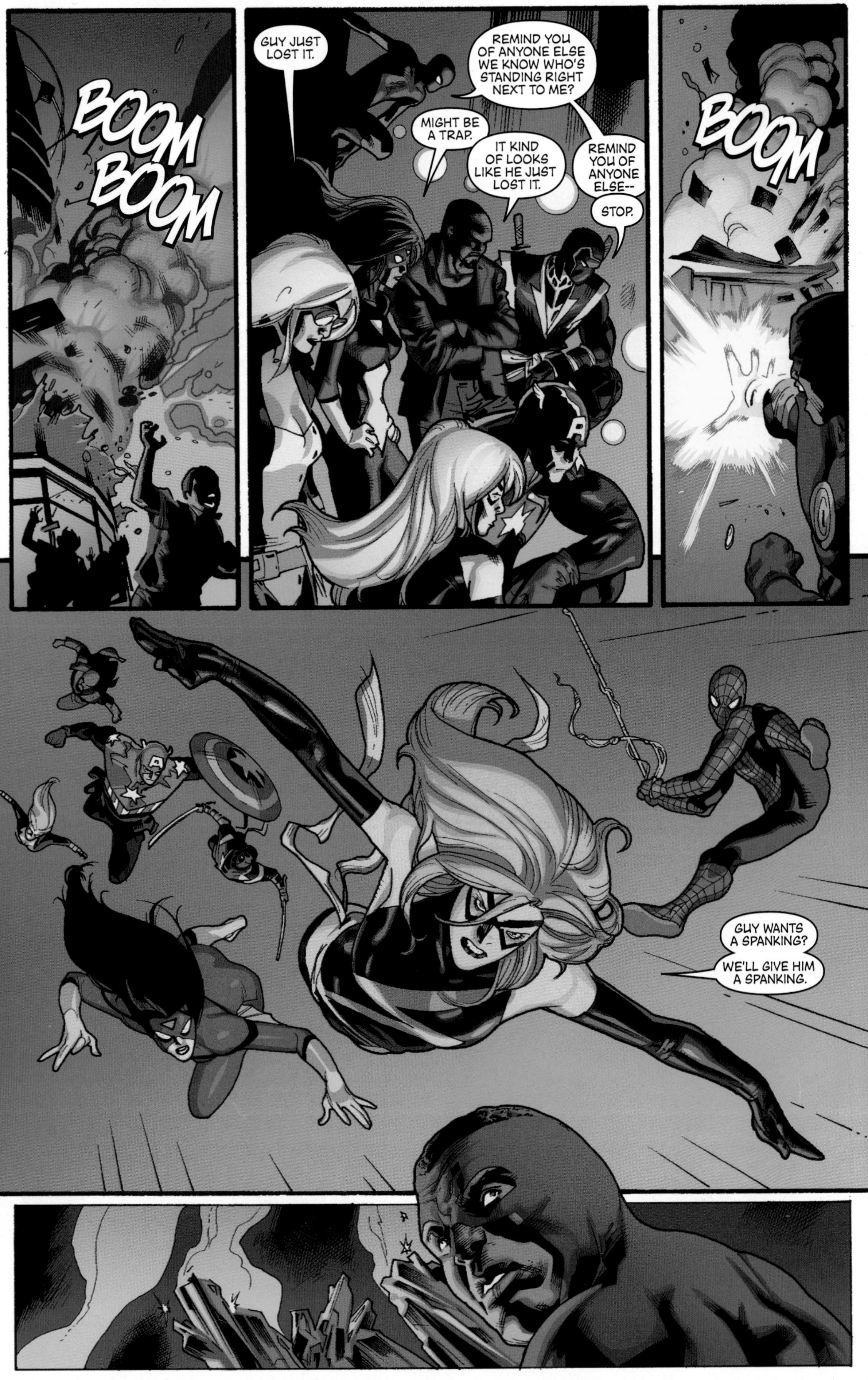
BOOM BOOM BOOM
GUY JUST LOST IT.
REMIND YOU OF ANYONE ELSE WE KNOW WHO'S STANDING RIGHT NEXT TO ME?
MIGHT BE A TRAP.
IT KIND OF LOOKS LIKE HE JUST LOST IT.
REMIND YOU OF ANYONE ELSE--
STOP.
BOOM
GUY WANTS A SPANKING?
WE'LL GIVE HIM A SPANKING.

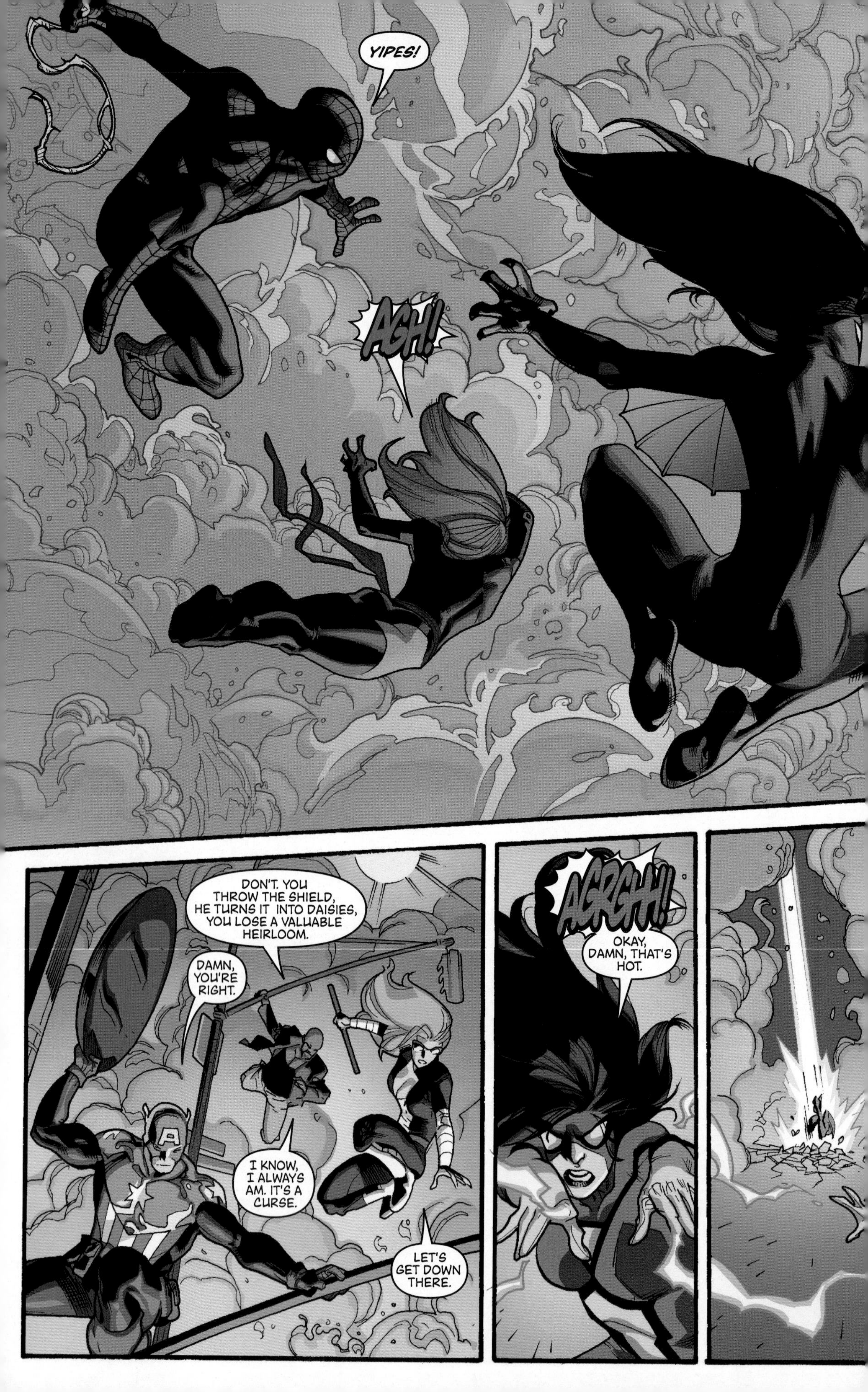
YIPES!
AGH!
DON'T. YOU THROW THE SHIELD, HE TURNS IT INTO DAISIES, YOU LOSE A VALUABLE HEIRLOOM.
DAMN, YOU'RE RIGHT.
I KNOW, I ALWAYS AM. IT'S A CURSE.
LET'S GET DOWN THERE.
AGRGHH!
OKAY, DAMN, THAT'S HOT.

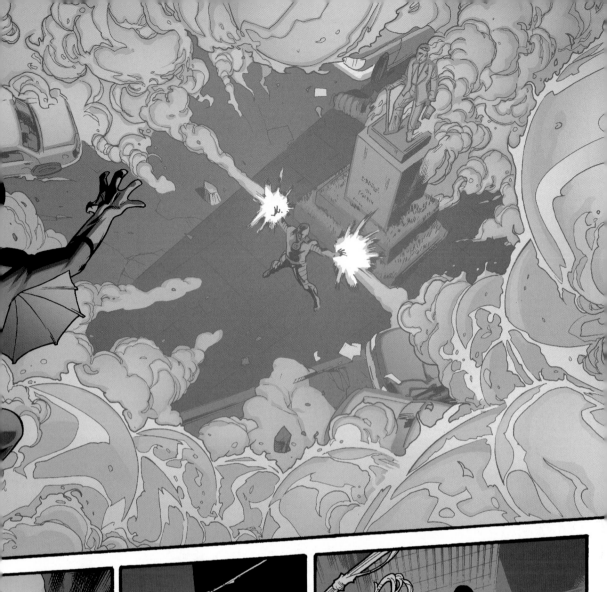

CAROL!

YOU KNOW WHAT, CHEMICAL BOY? I KIND OF APPRECIATE YOUR COMPLETELY POINTLESS RANDOM TANTRUM KIND OF...

UH...

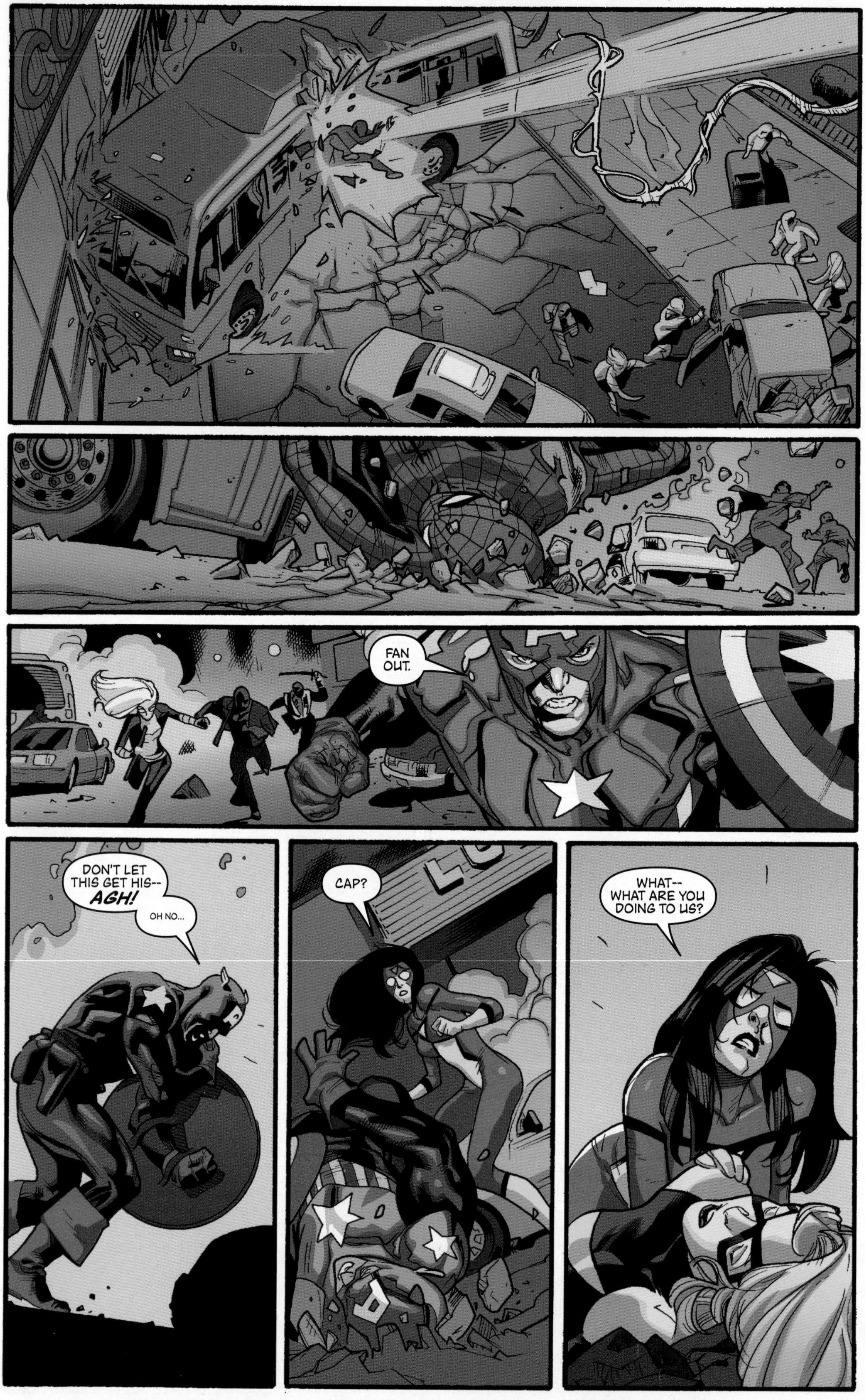
FAN OUT.
DON'T LET THIS GET HIS-- AGH!
OH NO...
CAP?
WHAT-- WHAT ARE YOU DOING TO US?

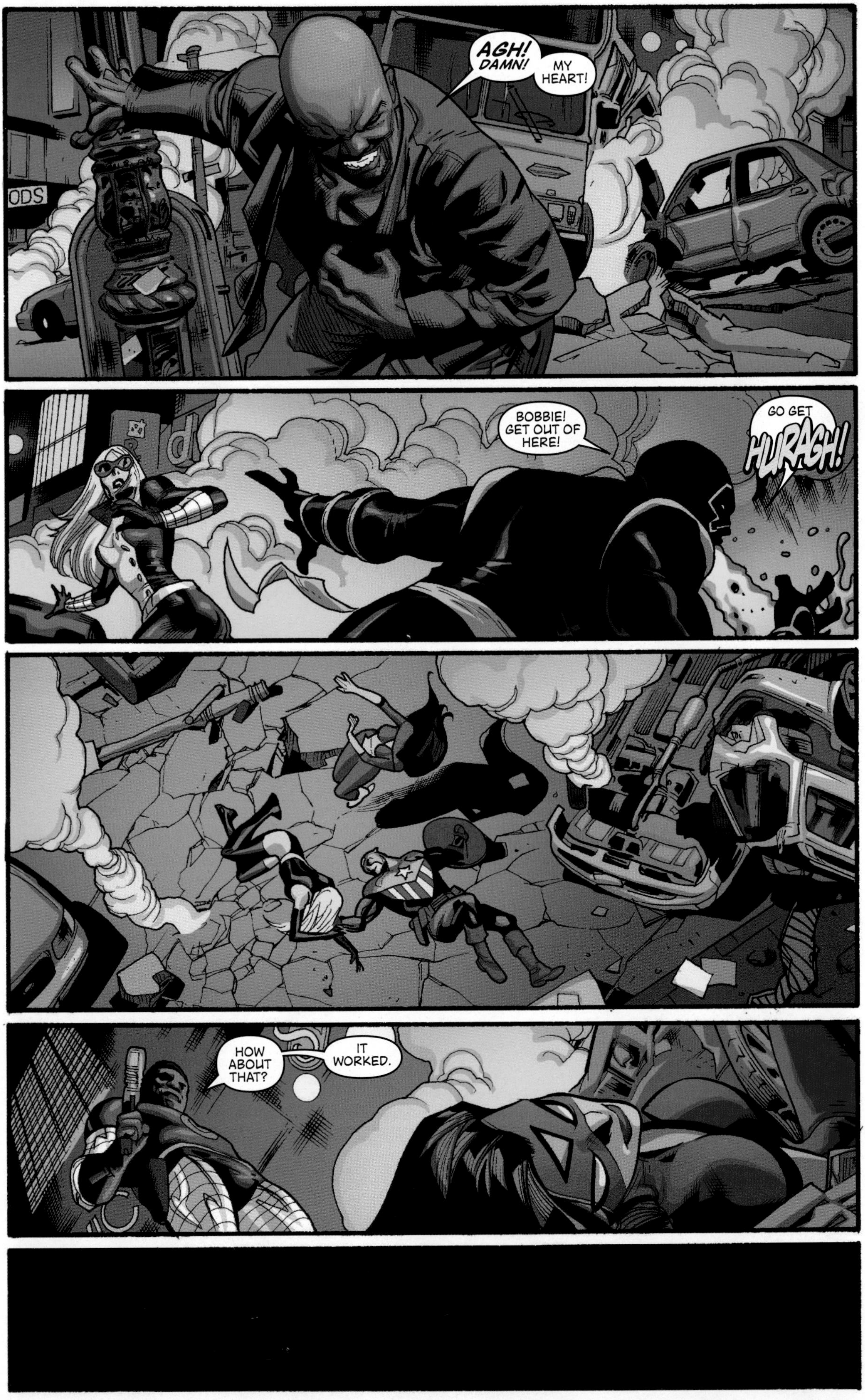
AGH! DAMN!
MY HEART!
ODS
BOBBIE! GET OUT OF HERE!
GO GET
HURAGH!
HOW ABOUT THAT?
IT WORKED.

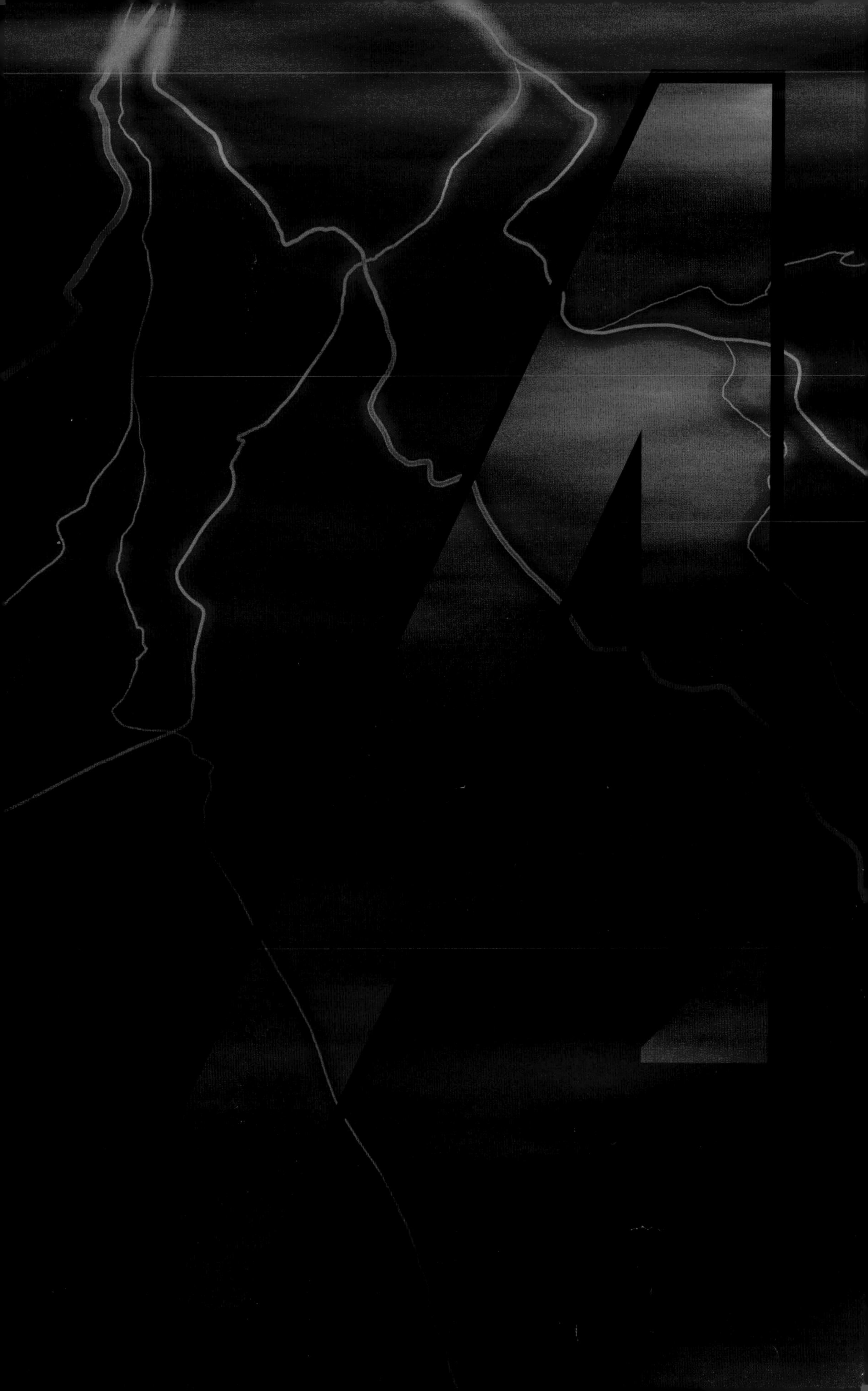

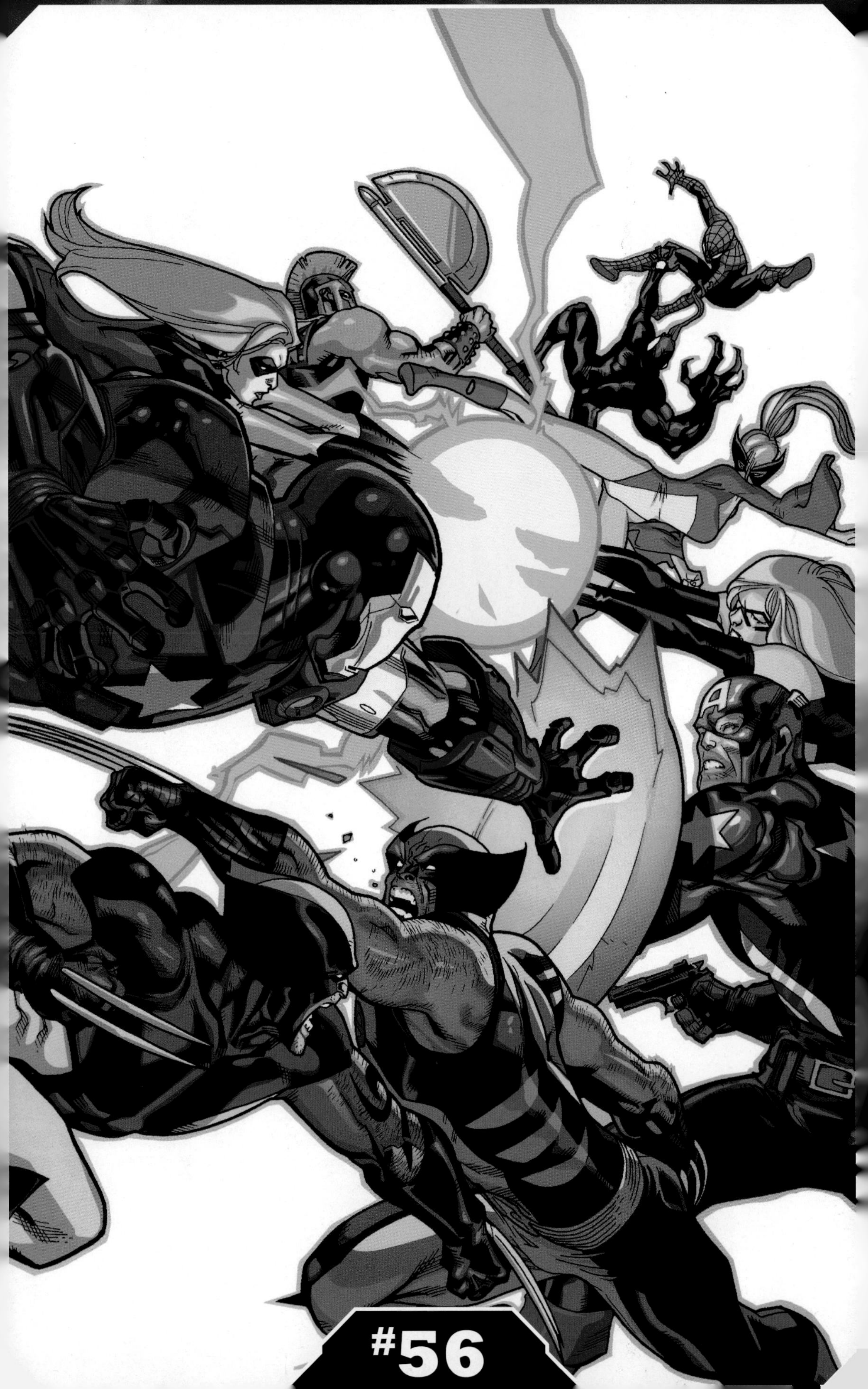
#56

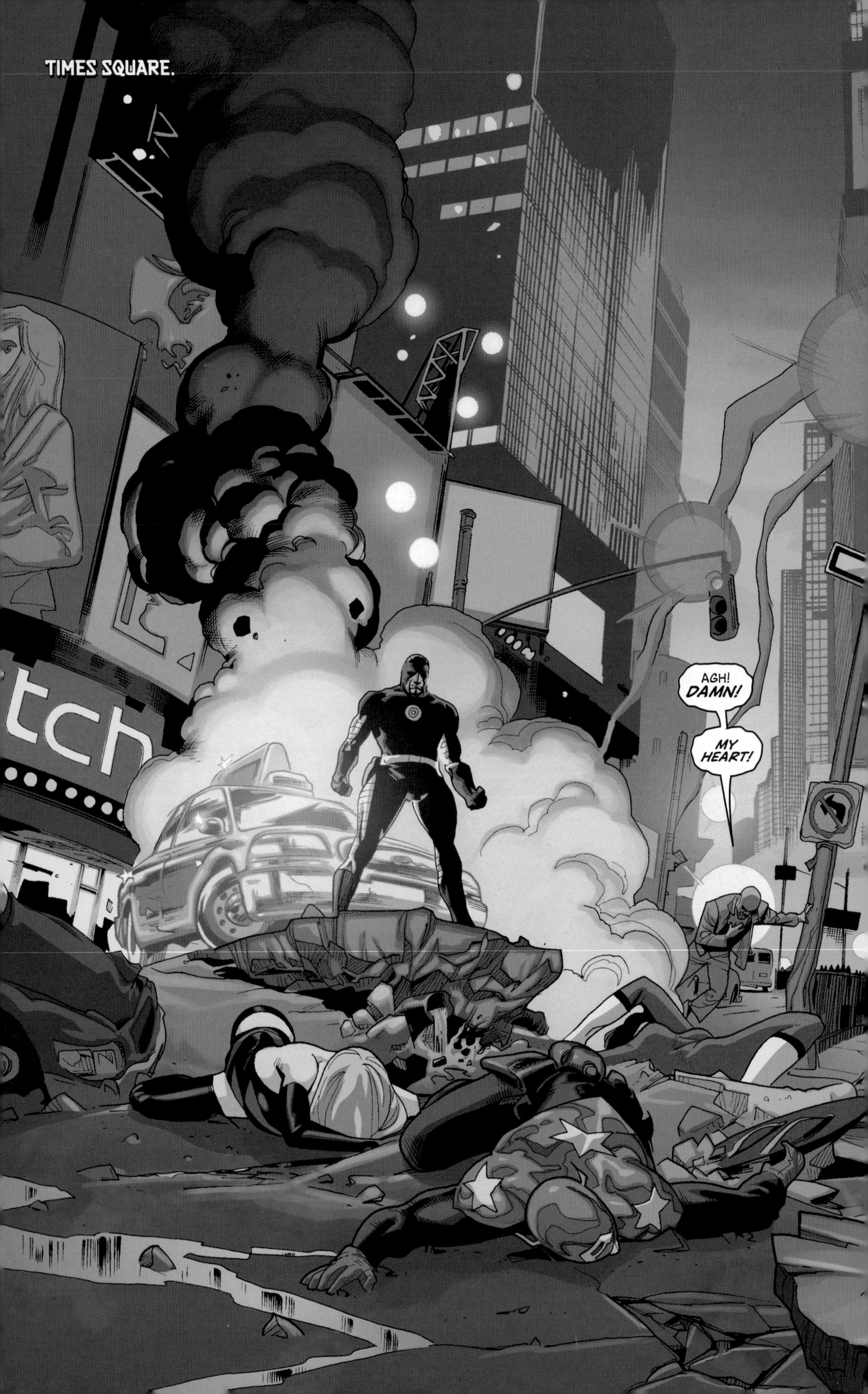
TIMES SQUARE.
AGH! DAMN!
MY HEART!

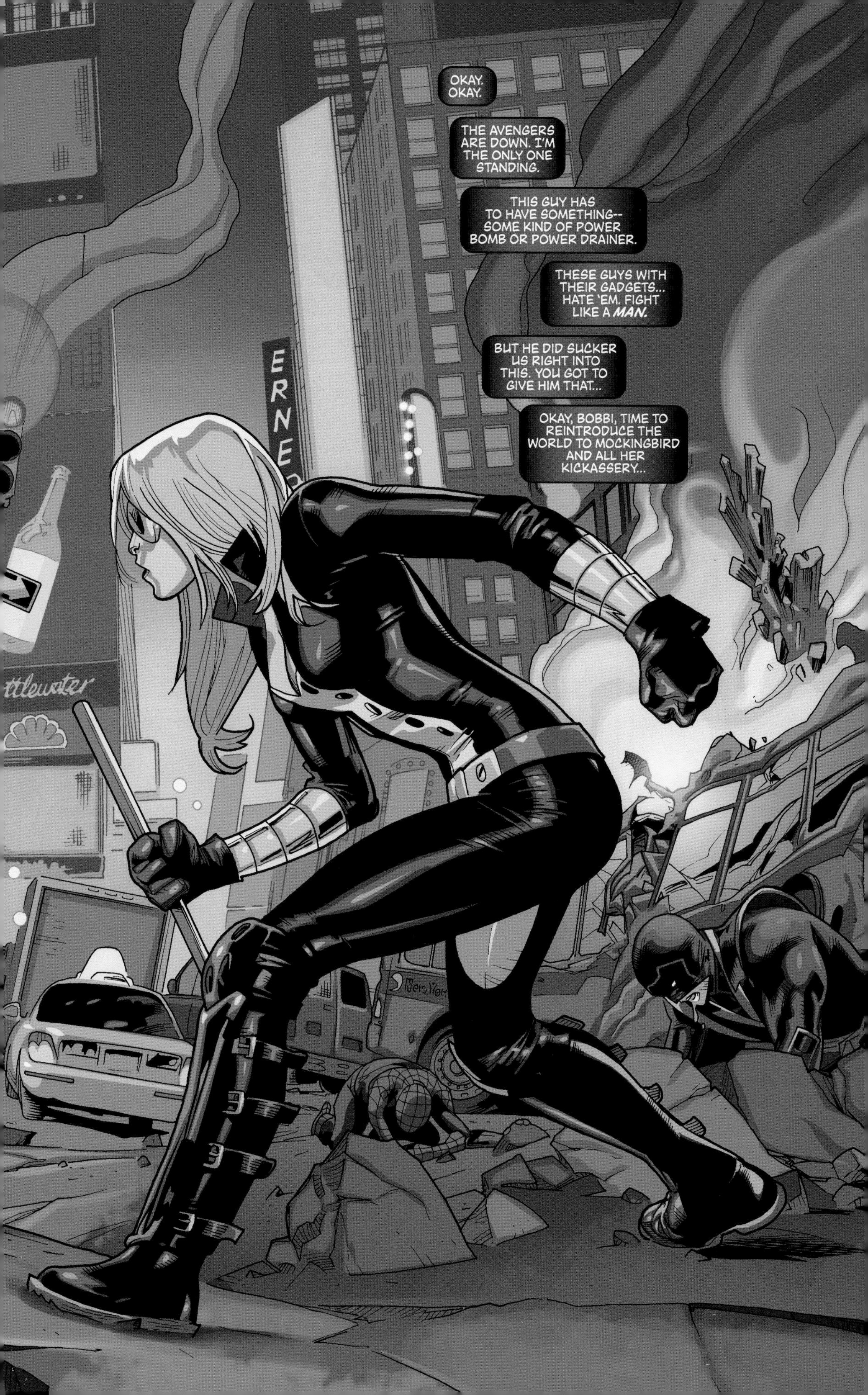
OKAY. OKAY.
THE AVENGERS ARE DOWN. I'M THE ONLY ONE STANDING.
THIS GUY HAS TO HAVE SOMETHING-- SOME KIND OF POWER BOMB OR POWER DRAINER.
THESE GUYS WITH THEIR GADGETS... HATE 'EM. FIGHT LIKE A *MAN.*
BUT HE DID SUCKER US RIGHT INTO THIS. YOU GOT TO GIVE HIM THAT...
OKAY, BOBBI, TIME TO REINTRODUCE THE WORLD TO MOCKINGBIRD AND ALL HER KICKASSERY...

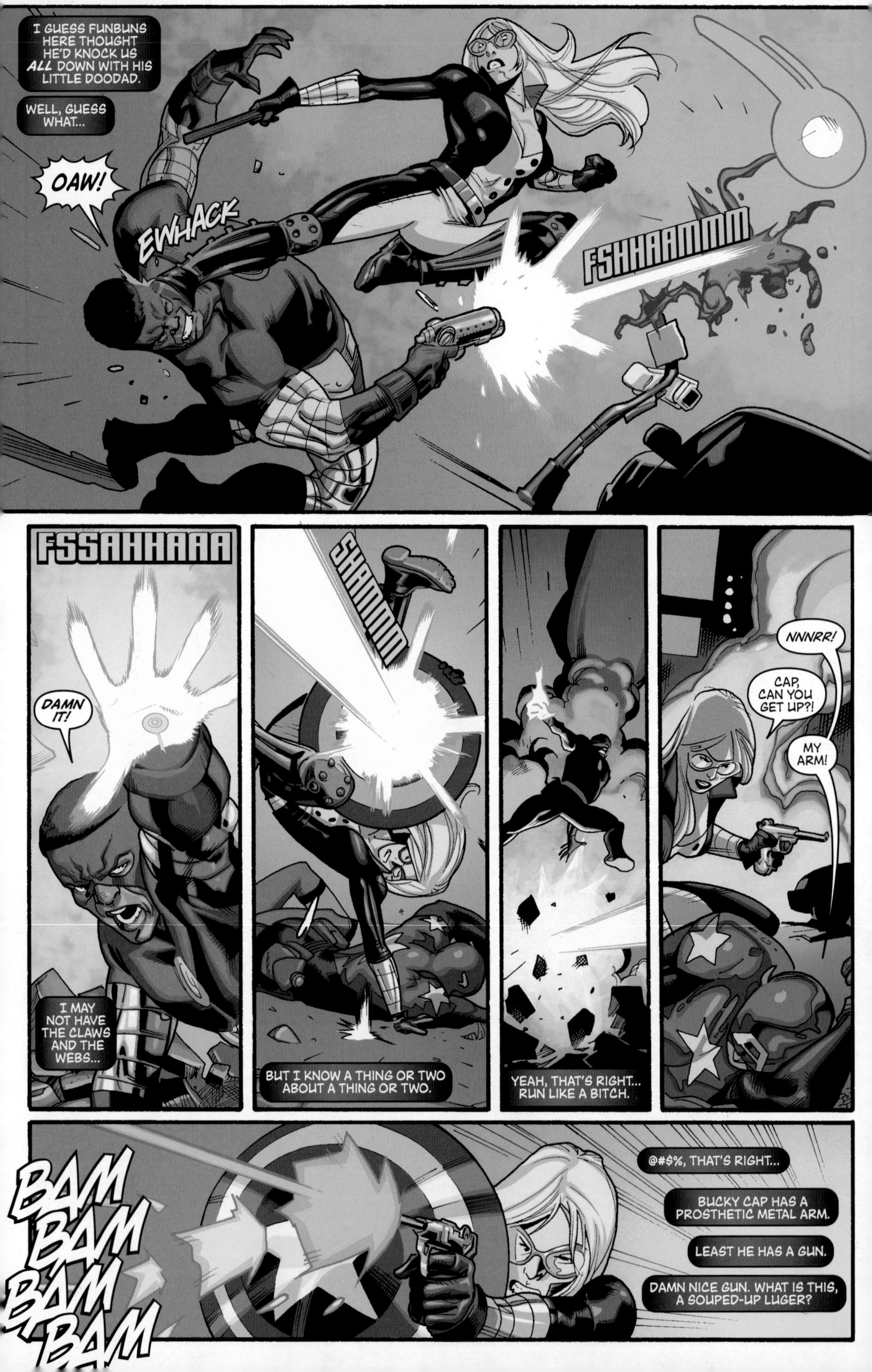
I GUESS FUNBUNS HERE THOUGHT HE'D KNOCK US ALL DOWN WITH HIS LITTLE DOODAD.
WELL, GUESS WHAT...
OAW!
EWHACK
FSHHAAMMM
FSSAHHAAA
DAMN IT!
I MAY NOT HAVE THE CLAWS AND THE WEBS...
SHAMMM
BUT I KNOW A THING OR TWO ABOUT A THING OR TWO.
YEAH, THAT'S RIGHT... RUN LIKE A BITCH.
NNNRR!
CAP, CAN YOU GET UP?!
MY ARM!
BAM BAM BAM BAM
@#$%, THAT'S RIGHT...
BUCKY CAP HAS A PROSTHETIC METAL ARM.
LEAST HE HAS A GUN.
DAMN NICE GUN. WHAT IS THIS, A SOUPED-UP LUGER?

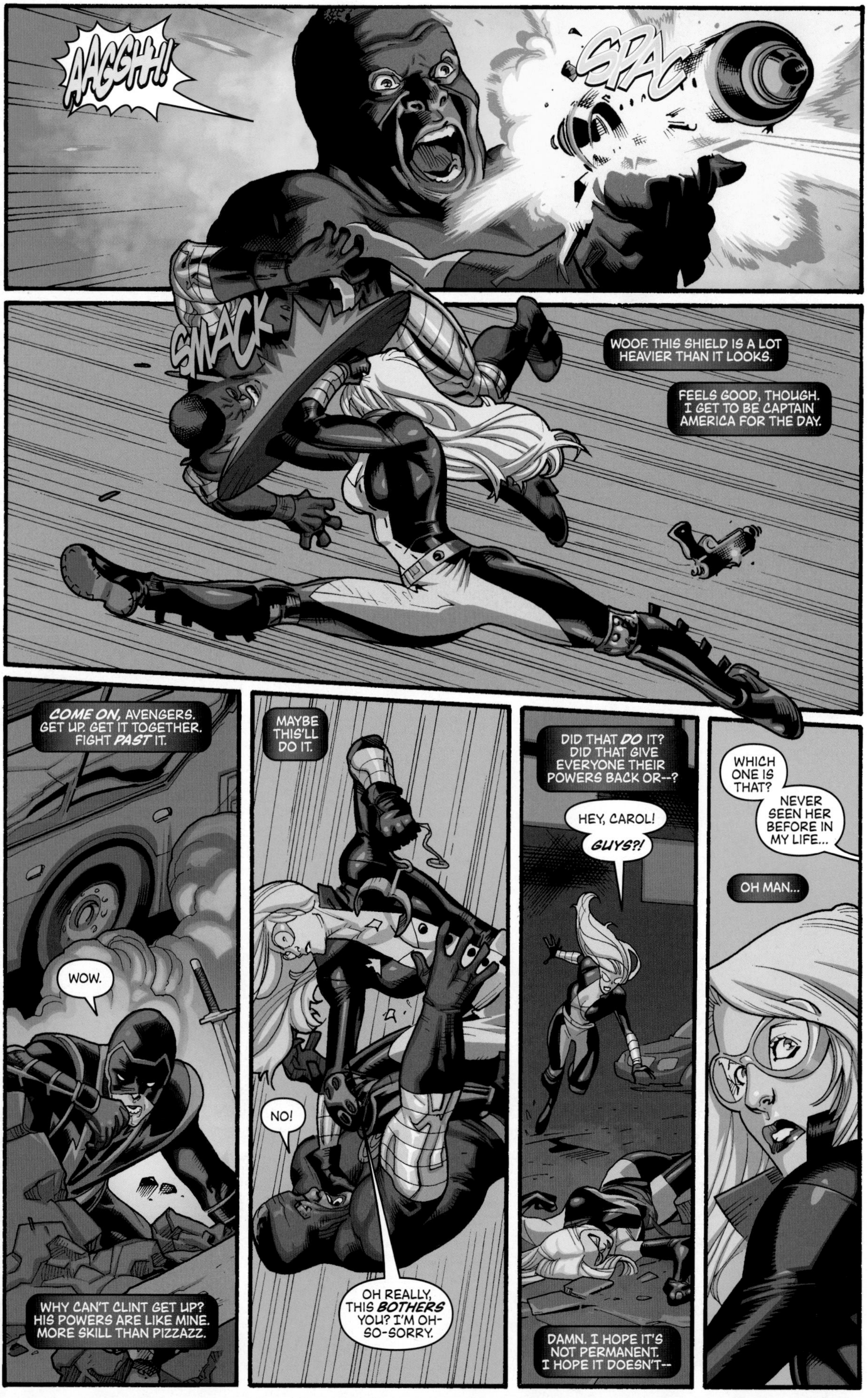
AAGGHH!
SPAC
SMACK
WOOF. THIS SHIELD IS A LOT HEAVIER THAN IT LOOKS.
FEELS GOOD, THOUGH. I GET TO BE CAPTAIN AMERICA FOR THE DAY.
COME ON, AVENGERS. GET UP. GET IT TOGETHER. FIGHT PAST IT.
WOW.
WHY CAN'T CLINT GET UP? HIS POWERS ARE LIKE MINE. MORE SKILL THAN PIZZAZZ.
MAYBE THIS'LL DO IT.
NO!
OH REALLY, THIS BOTHERS YOU? I'M OH-SO-SORRY.
DID THAT DO IT? DID THAT GIVE EVERYONE THEIR POWERS BACK OR--?
HEY, CAROL!
GUYS?!
DAMN. I HOPE IT'S NOT PERMANENT. I HOPE IT DOESN'T--
WHICH ONE IS THAT?
NEVER SEEN HER BEFORE IN MY LIFE...
OH MAN...

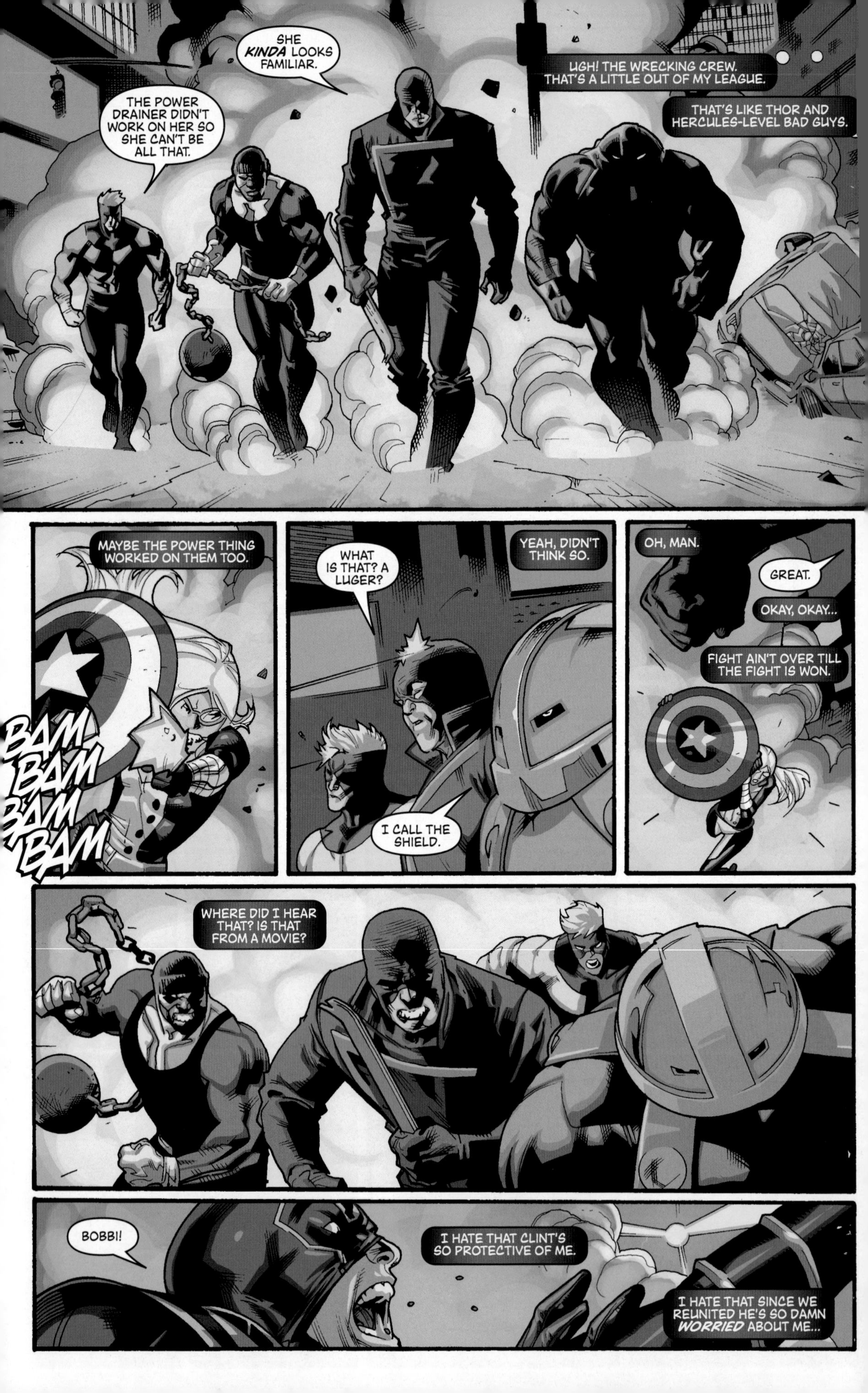
THE POWER DRAINER DIDN'T WORK ON HER SO SHE CAN'T BE ALL THAT.
SHE *KINDA* LOOKS FAMILIAR.
UGH! THE WRECKING CREW. THAT'S A LITTLE OUT OF MY LEAGUE.
THAT'S LIKE THOR AND HERCULES-LEVEL BAD GUYS.
MAYBE THE POWER THING WORKED ON THEM TOO.
BAM BAM BAM BAM
WHAT IS THAT? A LUGER?
YEAH, DIDN'T THINK SO.
I CALL THE SHIELD.
OH, MAN.
GREAT.
OKAY, OKAY...
FIGHT AIN'T OVER TILL THE FIGHT IS WON.
WHERE DID I HEAR THAT? IS THAT FROM A MOVIE?
BOBBI!
I HATE THAT CLINT'S SO PROTECTIVE OF ME.
I HATE THAT SINCE WE REUNITED HE'S SO DAMN *WORRIED* ABOUT ME...

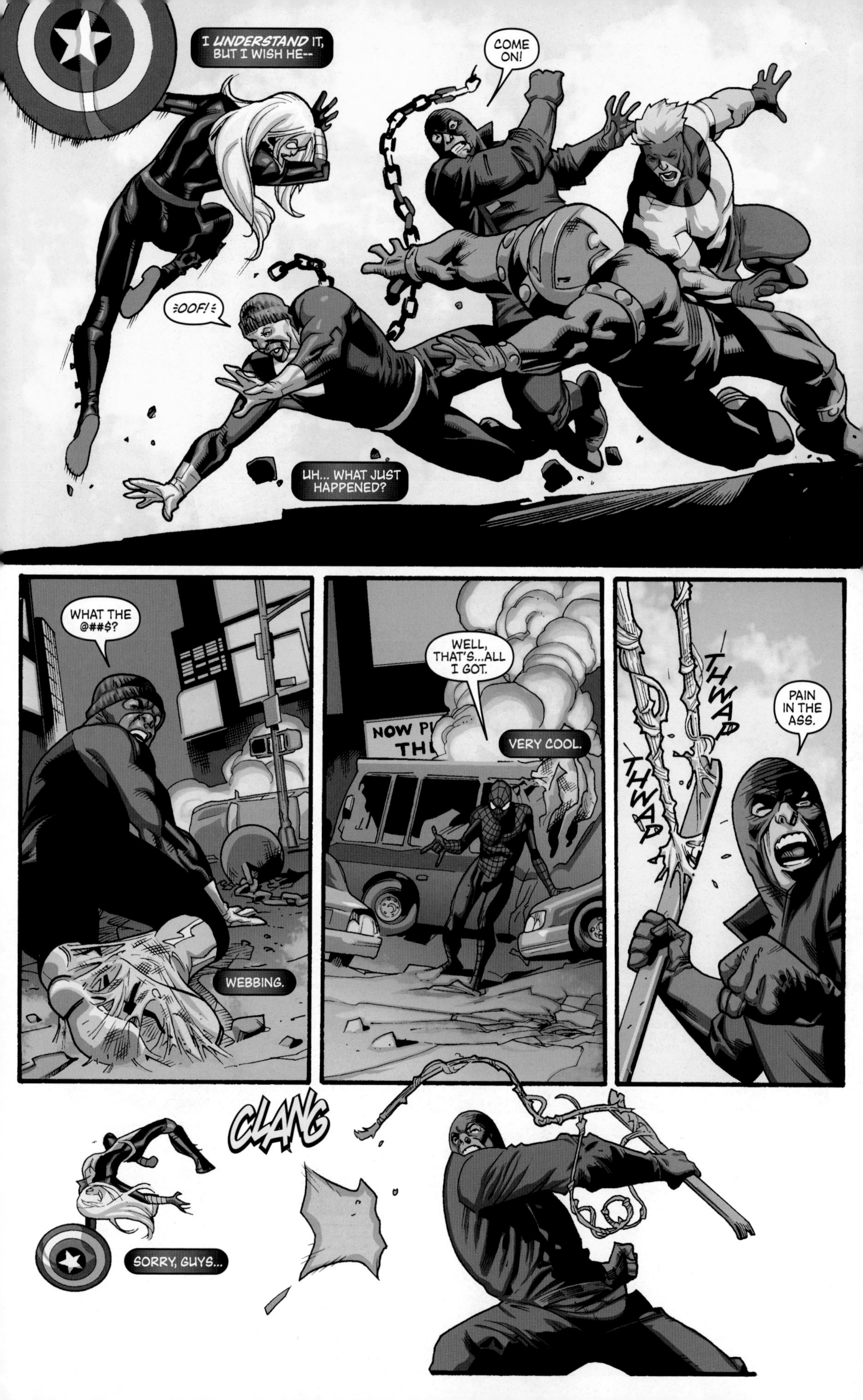
I UNDERSTAND IT, BUT I WISH HE--
COME ON!
OOF!
UH... WHAT JUST HAPPENED?
WHAT THE @##$?
WEBBING.
WELL, THAT'S...ALL I GOT.
VERY COOL.
NOW P
TH
THWAP
THWAP
PAIN IN THE ASS.
CLANG
SORRY, GUYS...

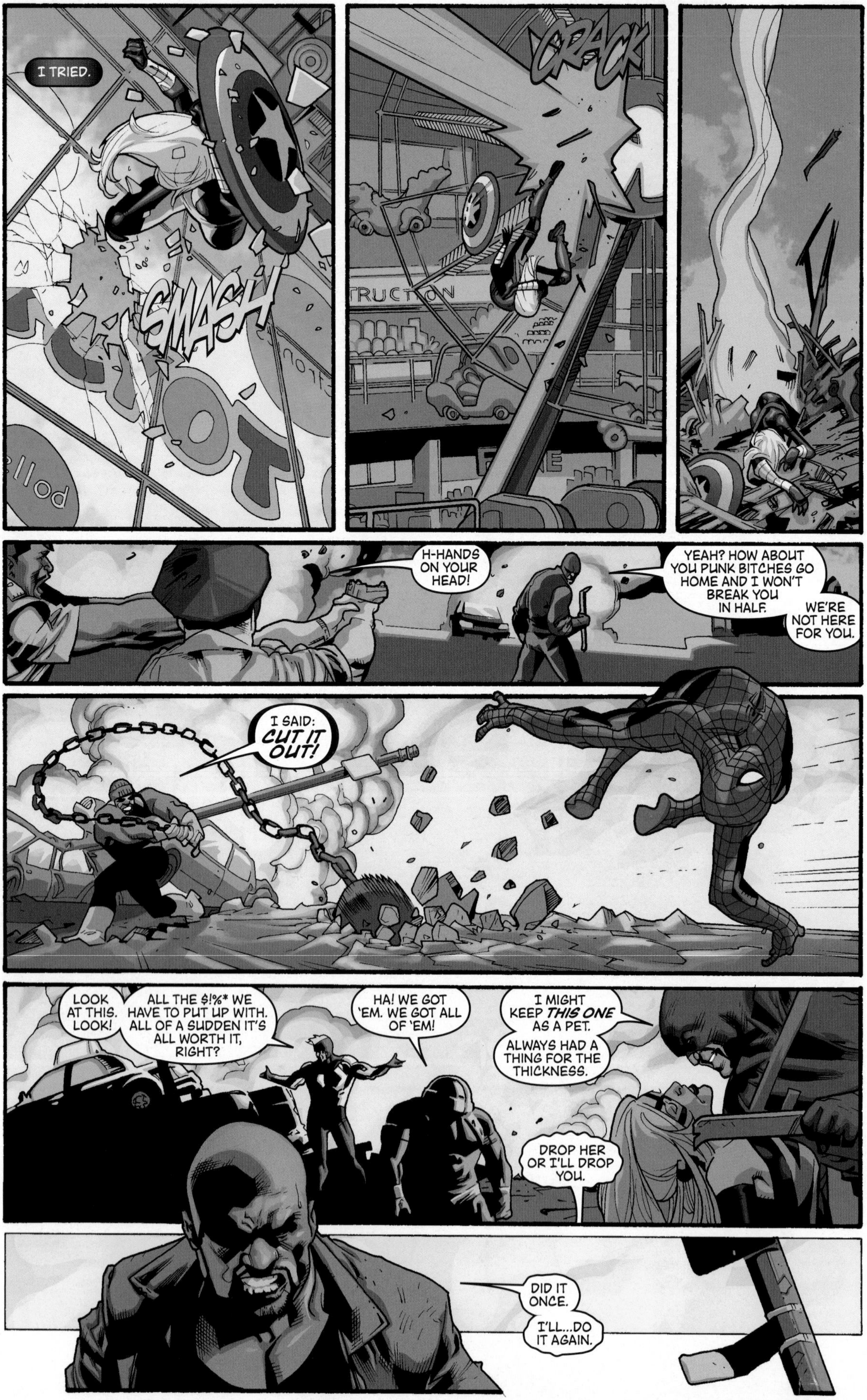
I TRIED.
SMASH
CRACK
TRUCTION
H-HANDS ON YOUR HEAD!
YEAH? HOW ABOUT YOU PUNK BITCHES GO HOME AND I WON'T BREAK YOU IN HALF.
WE'RE NOT HERE FOR YOU.
I SAID: CUT IT OUT!
LOOK AT THIS. LOOK!
ALL THE $!%* WE HAVE TO PUT UP WITH. ALL OF A SUDDEN IT'S ALL WORTH IT, RIGHT?
HA! WE GOT 'EM. WE GOT ALL OF 'EM!
I MIGHT KEEP THIS ONE AS A PET.
ALWAYS HAD A THING FOR THE THICKNESS.
DROP HER OR I'LL DROP YOU.
DID IT ONCE.
I'LL...DO IT AGAIN.

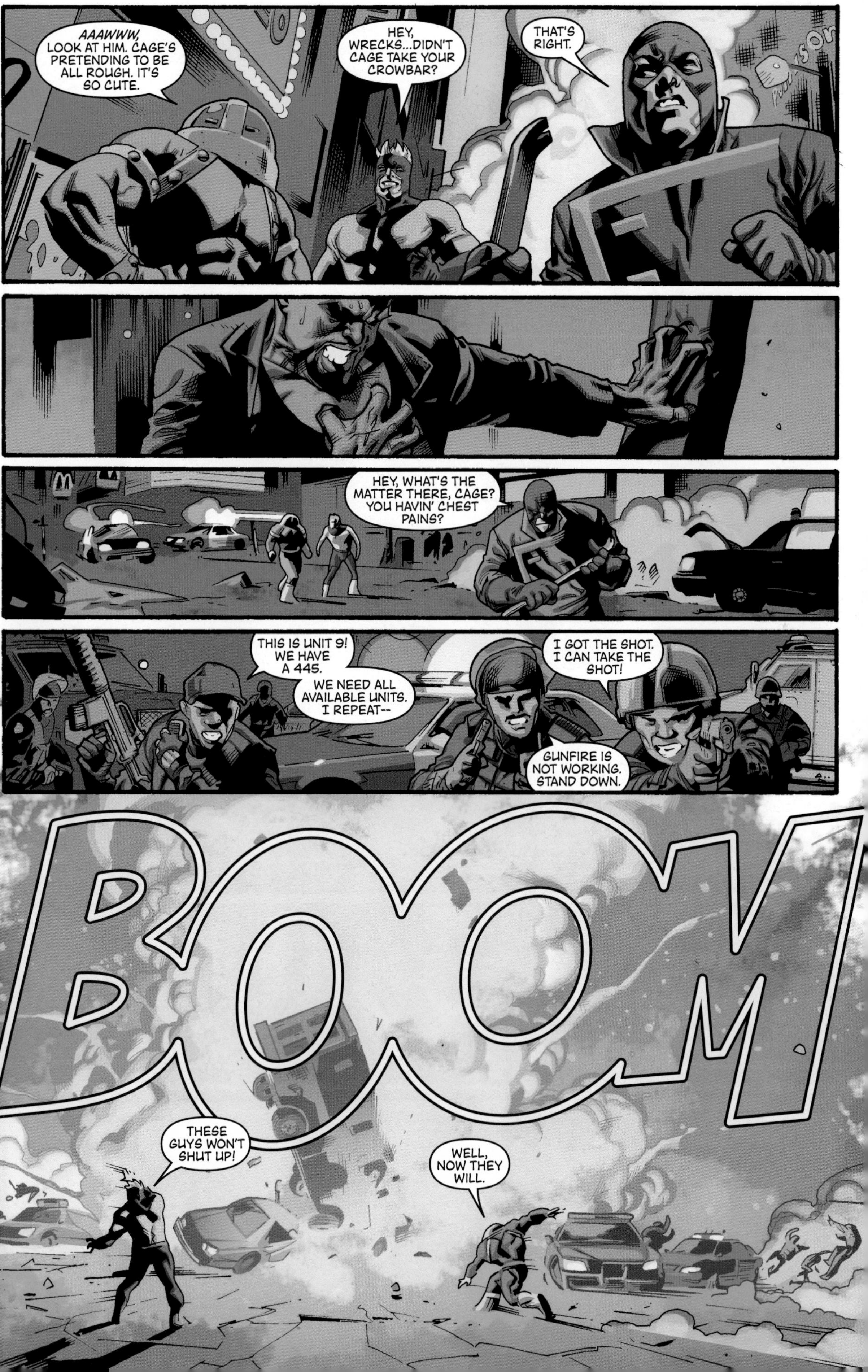
AAAWWW, LOOK AT HIM. CAGE'S PRETENDING TO BE ALL ROUGH. IT'S SO CUTE.
HEY, WRECKS...DIDN'T CAGE TAKE YOUR CROWBAR?
THAT'S RIGHT.
HEY, WHAT'S THE MATTER THERE, CAGE? YOU HAVIN' CHEST PAINS?
THIS IS UNIT 9! WE HAVE A 445.
WE NEED ALL AVAILABLE UNITS. I REPEAT--
I GOT THE SHOT. I CAN TAKE THE SHOT!
GUNFIRE IS NOT WORKING. STAND DOWN.
BOOM
THESE GUYS WON'T SHUT UP!
WELL, NOW THEY WILL.

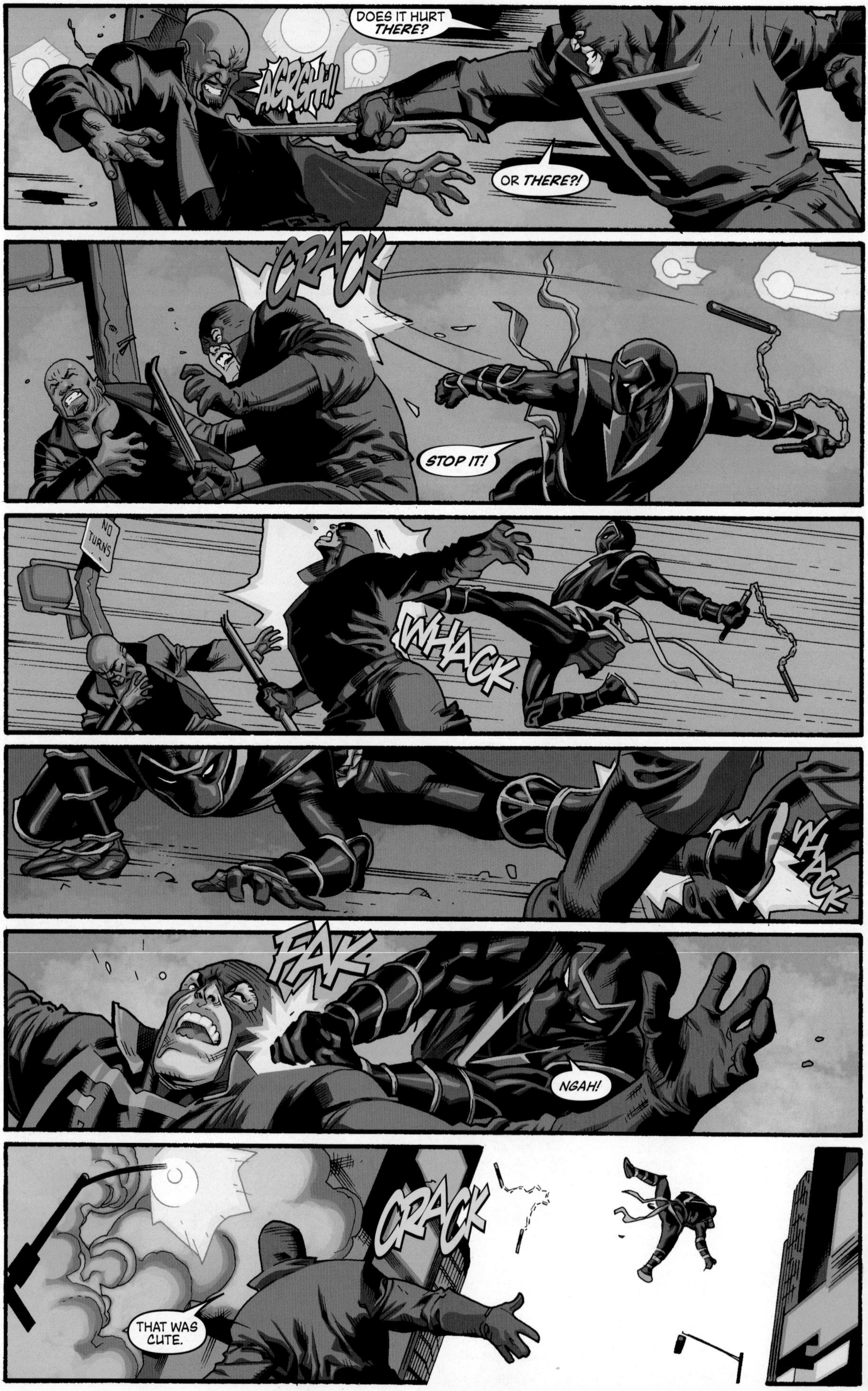
DOES IT HURT THERE?
AGRGH!!
OR THERE?!
CRACK
STOP IT!
NO TURNS
WHACK
WHACK
FAK
NGAH!
CRACK
THAT WAS CUTE.

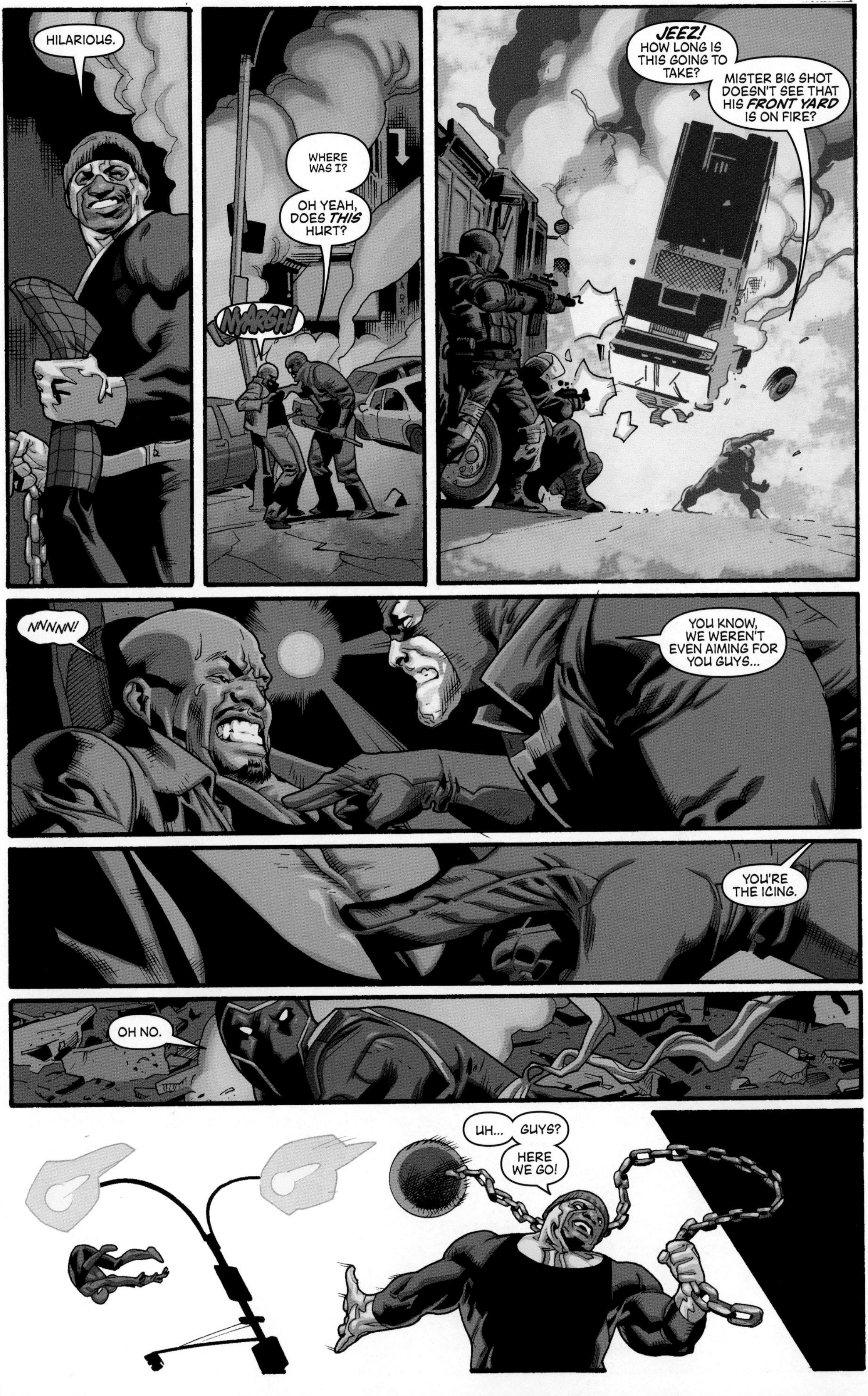
HILARIOUS.
WHERE WAS I?
OH YEAH, DOES *THIS* HURT?
NYARSH!
JEEZ! HOW LONG IS THIS GOING TO TAKE?
MISTER BIG SHOT DOESN'T SEE THAT HIS *FRONT YARD* IS ON FIRE?
NNNNN!
YOU KNOW, WE WEREN'T EVEN AIMING FOR YOU GUYS...
YOU'RE THE ICING.
OH NO.
UH... GUYS?
HERE WE GO!

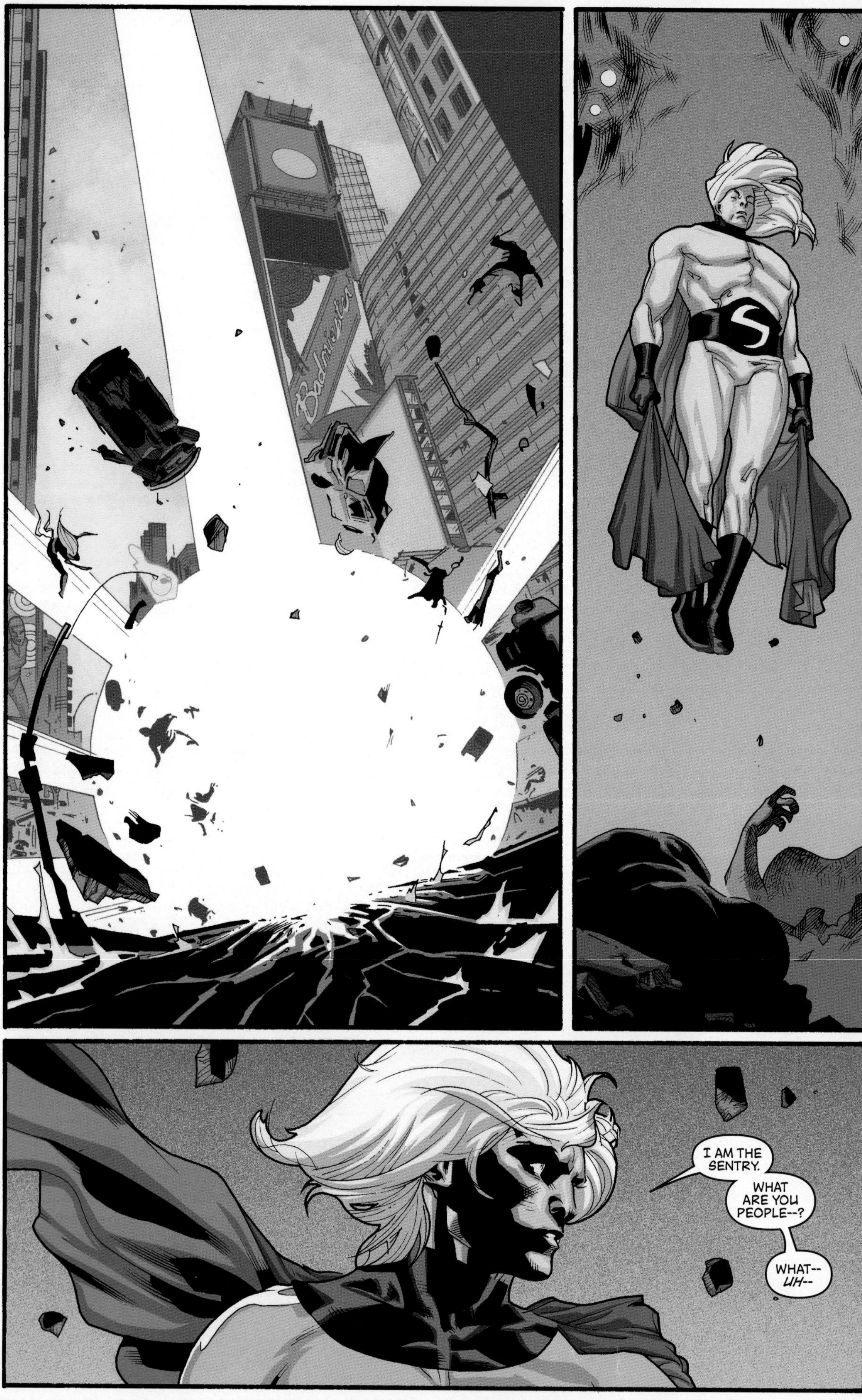
I AM THE SENTRY.
WHAT ARE YOU PEOPLE--?
WHAT-- *UH--*

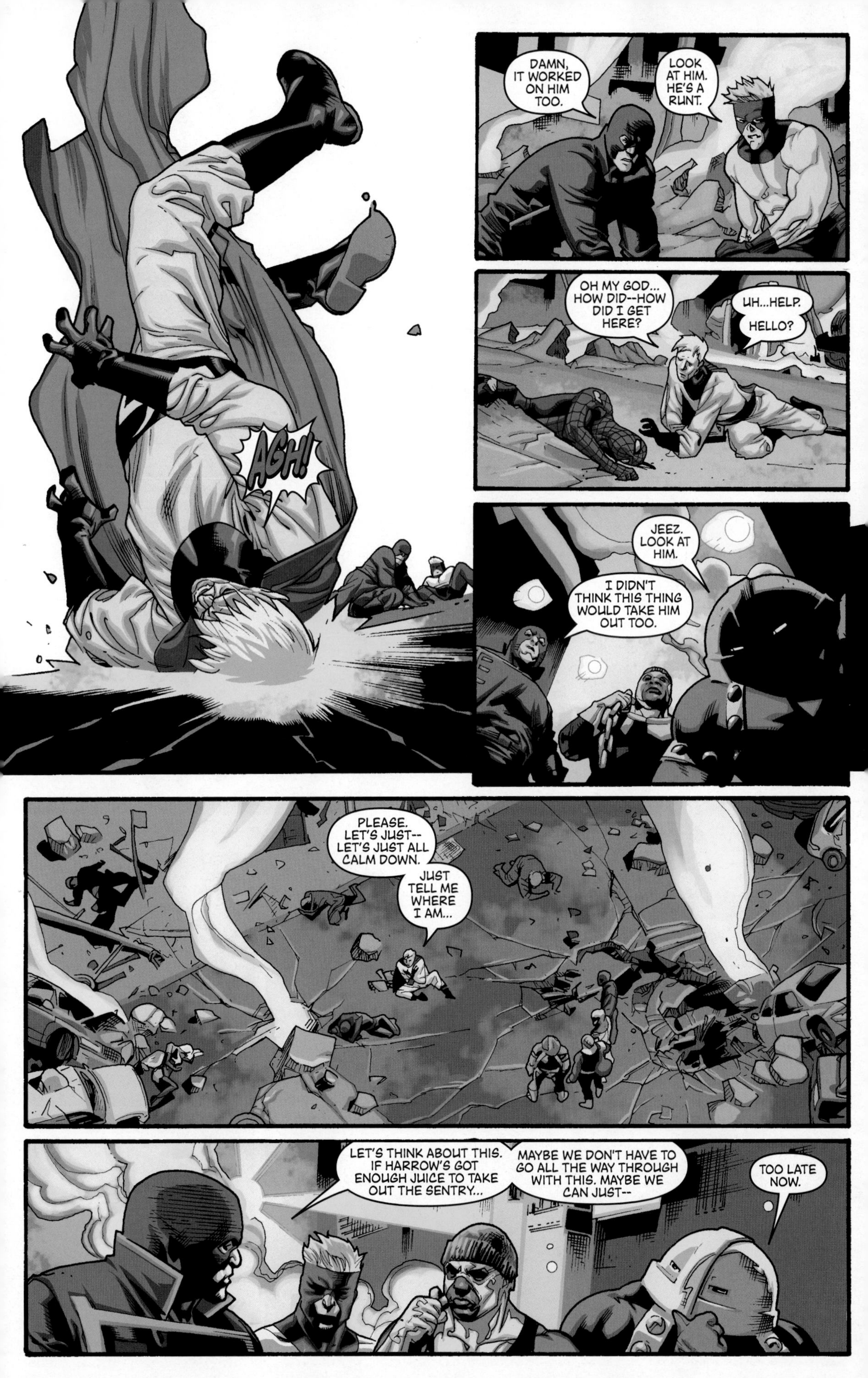
AGH!
DAMN, IT WORKED ON HIM TOO.
LOOK AT HIM. HE'S A RUNT.
OH MY GOD... HOW DID--HOW DID I GET HERE?
UH...HELP.
HELLO?
JEEZ. LOOK AT HIM.
I DIDN'T THINK THIS THING WOULD TAKE HIM OUT TOO.
PLEASE. LET'S JUST-- LET'S JUST ALL CALM DOWN.
JUST TELL ME WHERE I AM...
LET'S THINK ABOUT THIS. IF HARROW'S GOT ENOUGH JUICE TO TAKE OUT THE SENTRY...
MAYBE WE DON'T HAVE TO GO ALL THE WAY THROUGH WITH THIS. MAYBE WE CAN JUST--
TOO LATE NOW.

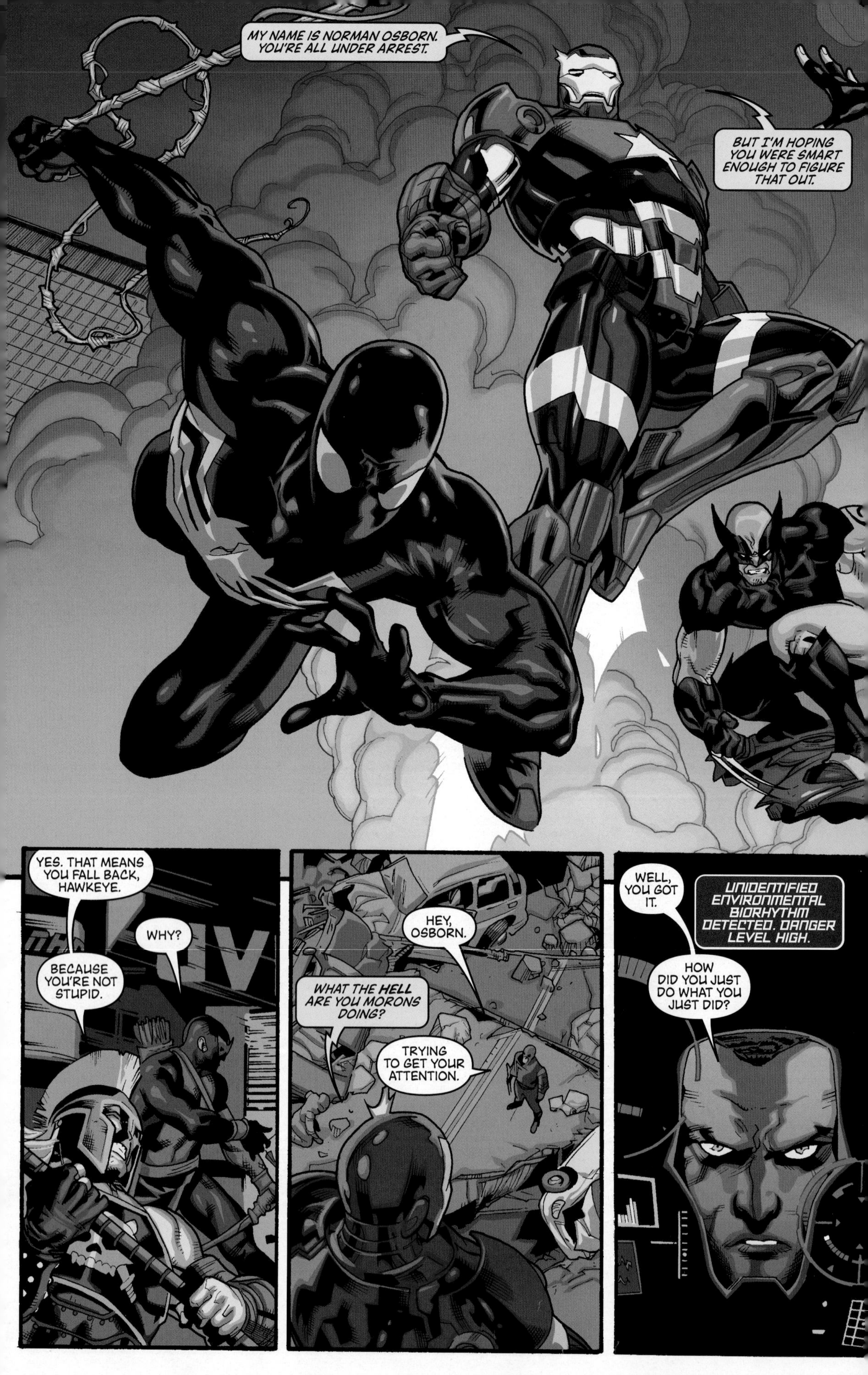
MY NAME IS NORMAN OSBORN. YOU'RE ALL UNDER ARREST.
BUT I'M HOPING YOU WERE SMART ENOUGH TO FIGURE THAT OUT.
YES. THAT MEANS YOU FALL BACK, HAWKEYE.
WHY?
BECAUSE YOU'RE NOT STUPID.
HEY, OSBORN.
WHAT THE **HELL** ARE YOU MORONS DOING?
TRYING TO GET YOUR ATTENTION.
WELL, YOU GOT IT.
UNIDENTIFIED ENVIRONMENTAL BIORHYTHM DETECTED. DANGER LEVEL HIGH.
HOW DID YOU JUST DO WHAT YOU JUST DID?

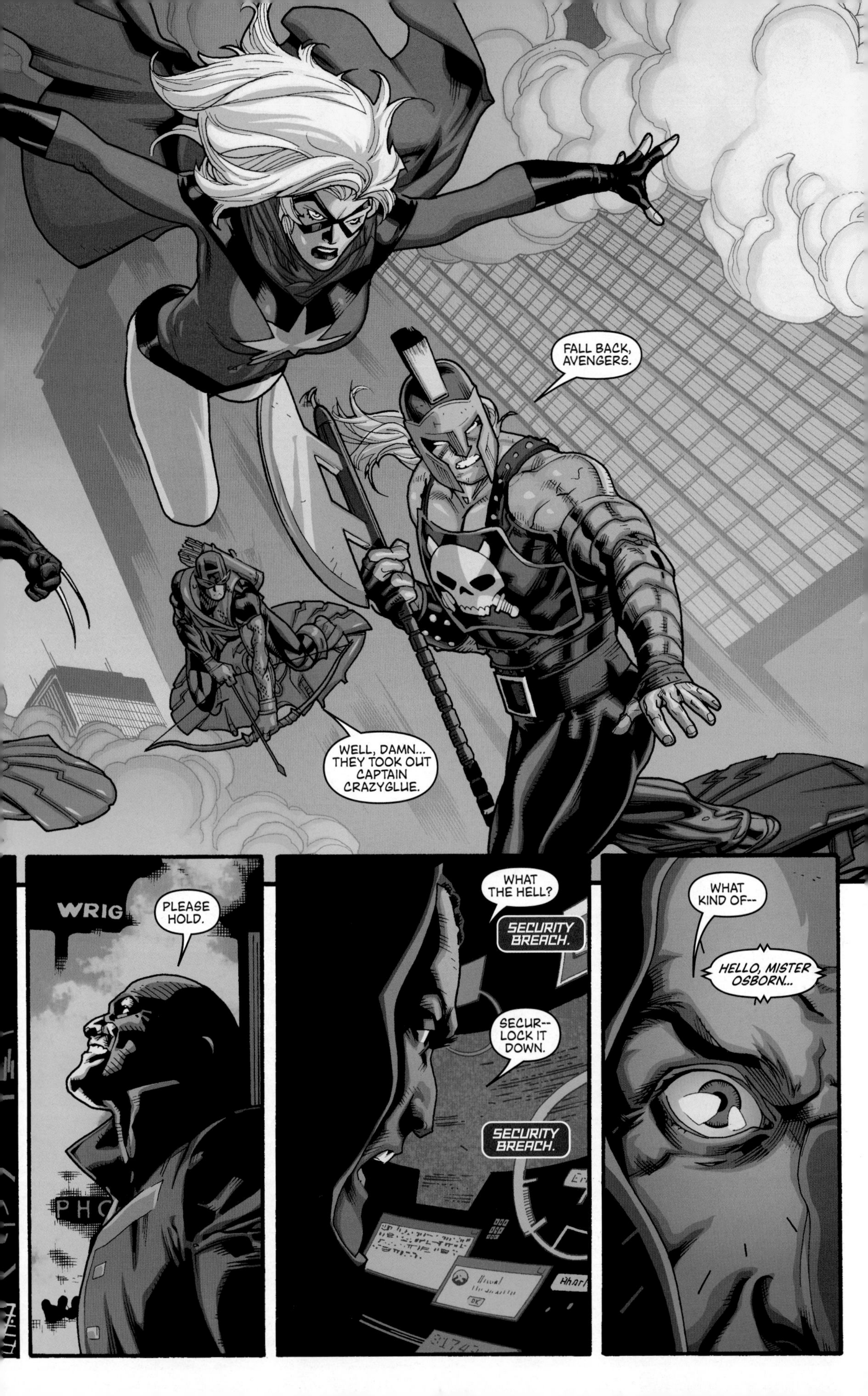
FALL BACK, AVENGERS.
WELL, DAMN... THEY TOOK OUT CAPTAIN CRAZYGLUE.
WRIG
PLEASE HOLD.
PHO
WHAT THE HELL?
SECURITY BREACH.
SECUR-- LOCK IT DOWN.
SECURITY BREACH.
WHAT KIND OF--
HELLO, MISTER OSBORN...

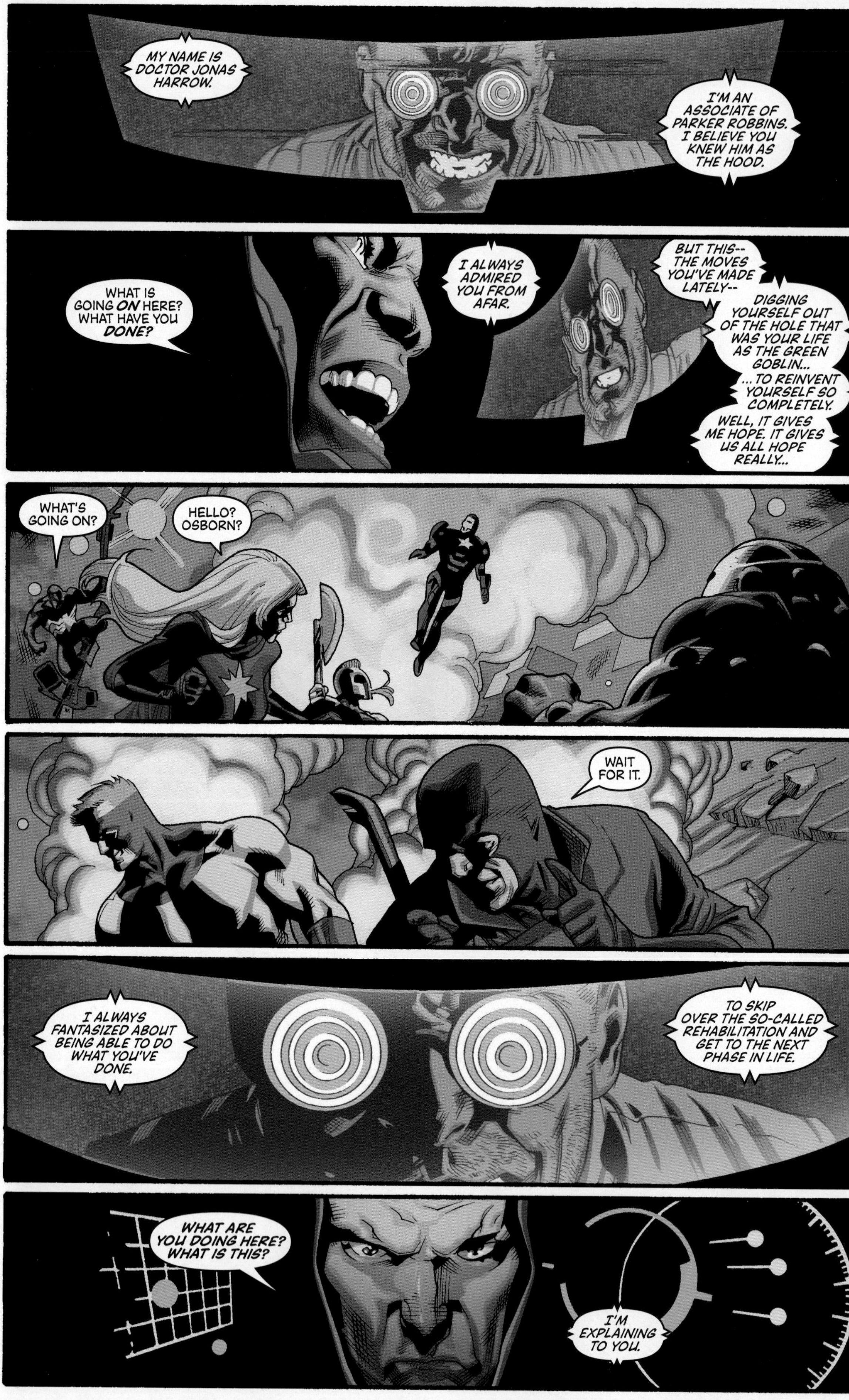

MY NAME IS DOCTOR JONAS HARROW.
I'M AN ASSOCIATE OF PARKER ROBBINS. I BELIEVE YOU KNEW HIM AS THE HOOD.
WHAT IS GOING ON HERE? WHAT HAVE YOU DONE?
I ALWAYS ADMIRED YOU FROM AFAR.
BUT THIS-- THE MOVES YOU'VE MADE LATELY--
DIGGING YOURSELF OUT OF THE HOLE THAT WAS YOUR LIFE AS THE GREEN GOBLIN...
...TO REINVENT YOURSELF SO COMPLETELY.
WELL, IT GIVES ME HOPE. IT GIVES US ALL HOPE REALLY...
WHAT'S GOING ON?
HELLO? OSBORN?
WAIT FOR IT.
I ALWAYS FANTASIZED ABOUT BEING ABLE TO DO WHAT YOU'VE DONE.
TO SKIP OVER THE SO-CALLED REHABILITATION AND GET TO THE NEXT PHASE IN LIFE.
WHAT ARE YOU DOING HERE? WHAT IS THIS?
I'M EXPLAINING TO YOU.

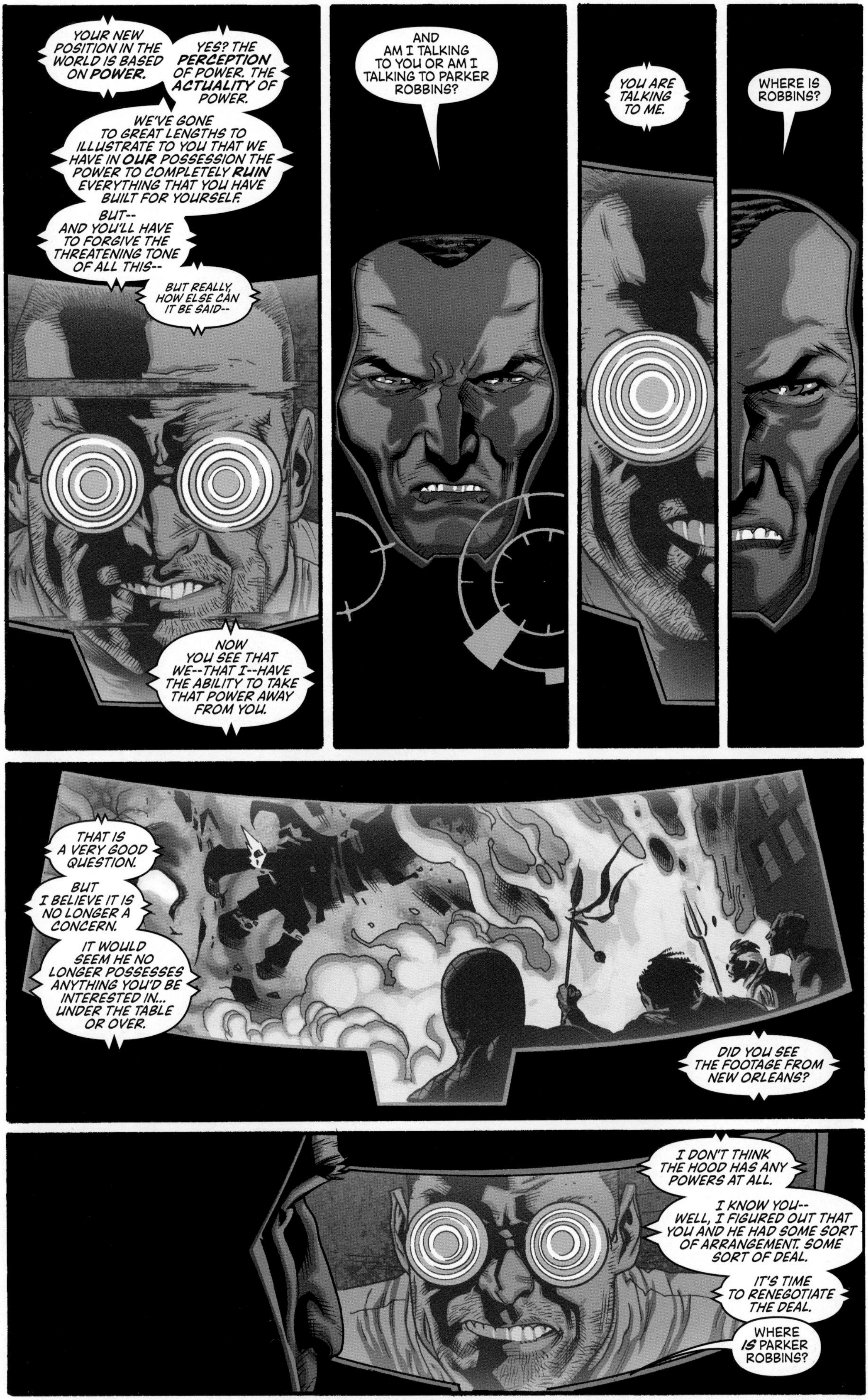

YOUR NEW POSITION IN THE WORLD IS BASED ON POWER.
YES? THE PERCEPTION OF POWER. THE ACTUALITY OF POWER.
WE'VE GONE TO GREAT LENGTHS TO ILLUSTRATE TO YOU THAT WE HAVE IN OUR POSSESSION THE POWER TO COMPLETELY RUIN EVERYTHING THAT YOU HAVE BUILT FOR YOURSELF.
BUT-- AND YOU'LL HAVE TO FORGIVE THE THREATENING TONE OF ALL THIS--
BUT REALLY, HOW ELSE CAN IT BE SAID--
NOW YOU SEE THAT WE--THAT I--HAVE THE ABILITY TO TAKE THAT POWER AWAY FROM YOU.
AND AM I TALKING TO YOU OR AM I TALKING TO PARKER ROBBINS?
YOU ARE TALKING TO ME.
WHERE IS ROBBINS?
THAT IS A VERY GOOD QUESTION.
BUT I BELIEVE IT IS NO LONGER A CONCERN.
IT WOULD SEEM HE NO LONGER POSSESSES ANYTHING YOU'D BE INTERESTED IN... UNDER THE TABLE OR OVER.
DID YOU SEE THE FOOTAGE FROM NEW ORLEANS?
I DON'T THINK THE HOOD HAS ANY POWERS AT ALL.
I KNOW YOU-- WELL, I FIGURED OUT THAT YOU AND HE HAD SOME SORT OF ARRANGEMENT. SOME SORT OF DEAL.
IT'S TIME TO RENEGOTIATE THE DEAL.
WHERE IS PARKER ROBBINS?

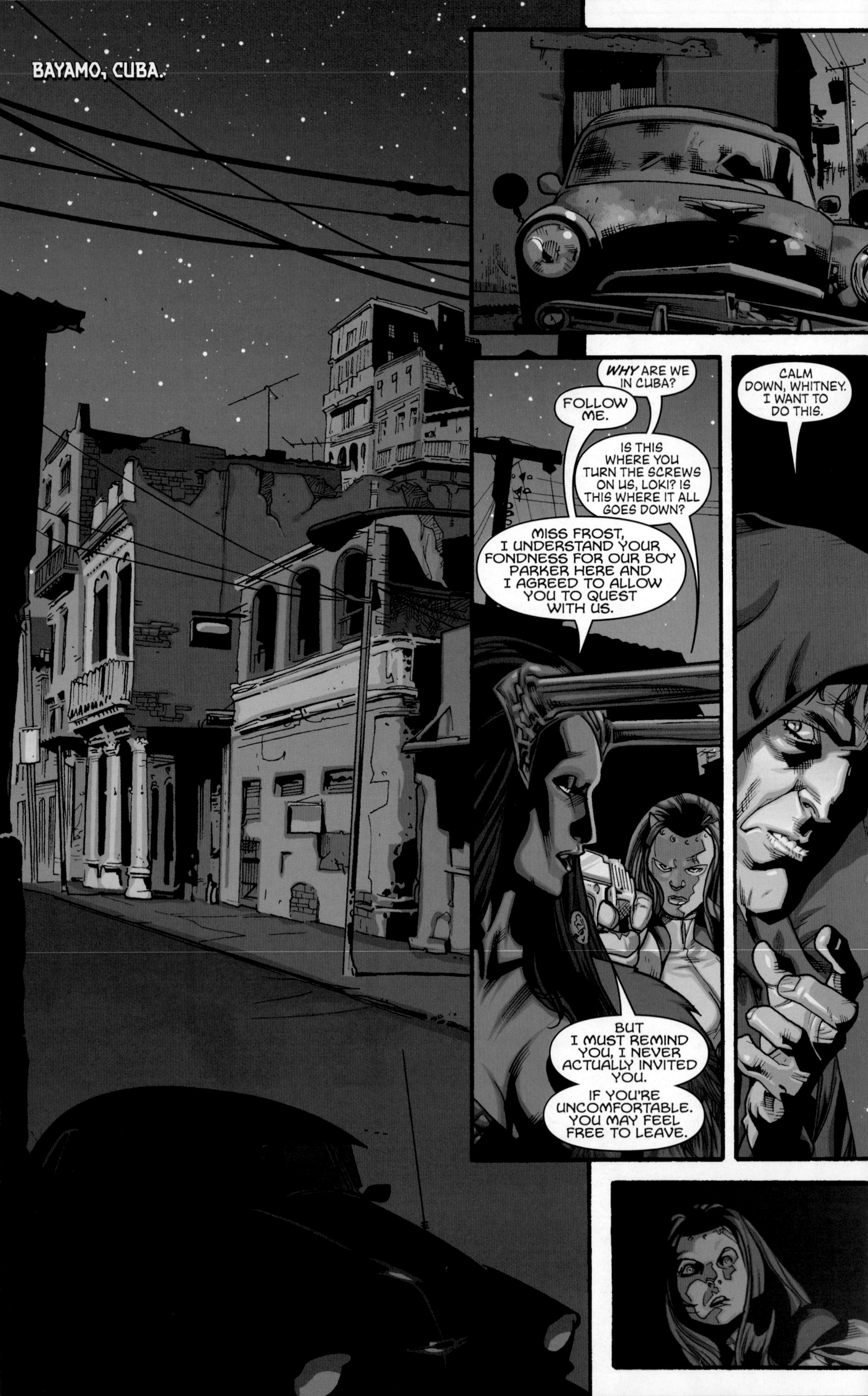
BAYAMO, CUBA.
WHY ARE WE IN CUBA?
FOLLOW ME.
IS THIS WHERE YOU TURN THE SCREWS ON US, LOKI? IS THIS WHERE IT ALL GOES DOWN?
MISS FROST, I UNDERSTAND YOUR FONDNESS FOR OUR BOY PARKER HERE AND I AGREED TO ALLOW YOU TO QUEST WITH US.
BUT I MUST REMIND YOU, I NEVER ACTUALLY INVITED YOU.
IF YOU'RE UNCOMFORTABLE. YOU MAY FEEL FREE TO LEAVE.
CALM DOWN, WHITNEY. I WANT TO DO THIS.

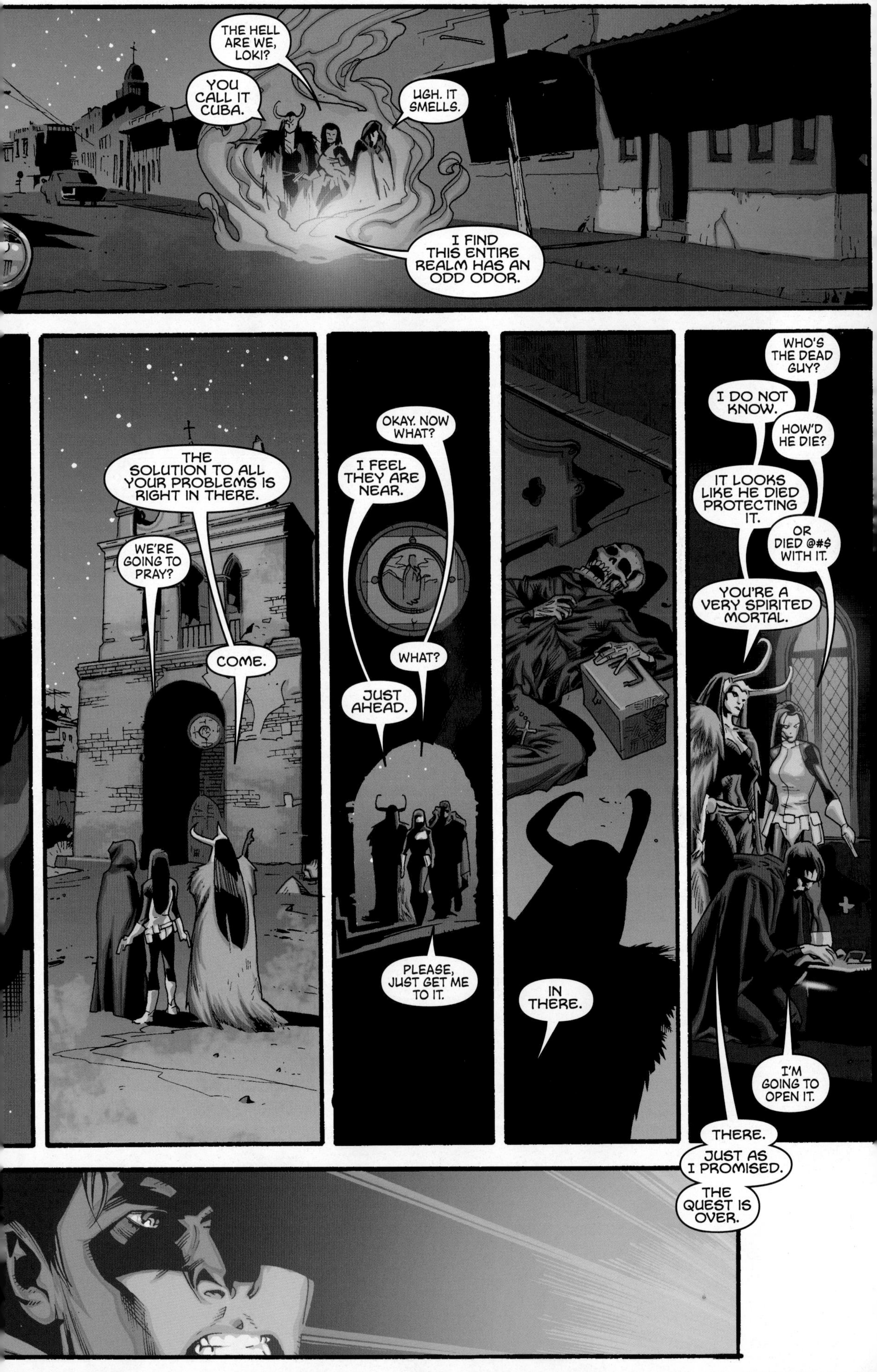
THE HELL ARE WE, LOKI?
YOU CALL IT CUBA.
UGH. IT SMELLS.
I FIND THIS ENTIRE REALM HAS AN ODD ODOR.
THE SOLUTION TO ALL YOUR PROBLEMS IS RIGHT IN THERE.
WE'RE GOING TO PRAY?
COME.
OKAY. NOW WHAT?
I FEEL THEY ARE NEAR.
WHAT?
JUST AHEAD.
PLEASE, JUST GET ME TO IT.
IN THERE.
WHO'S THE DEAD GUY?
I DO NOT KNOW.
HOW'D HE DIE?
IT LOOKS LIKE HE DIED PROTECTING IT.
OR DIED @#$ WITH IT.
YOU'RE A VERY SPIRITED MORTAL.
I'M GOING TO OPEN IT.
THERE.
JUST AS I PROMISED.
THE QUEST IS OVER.

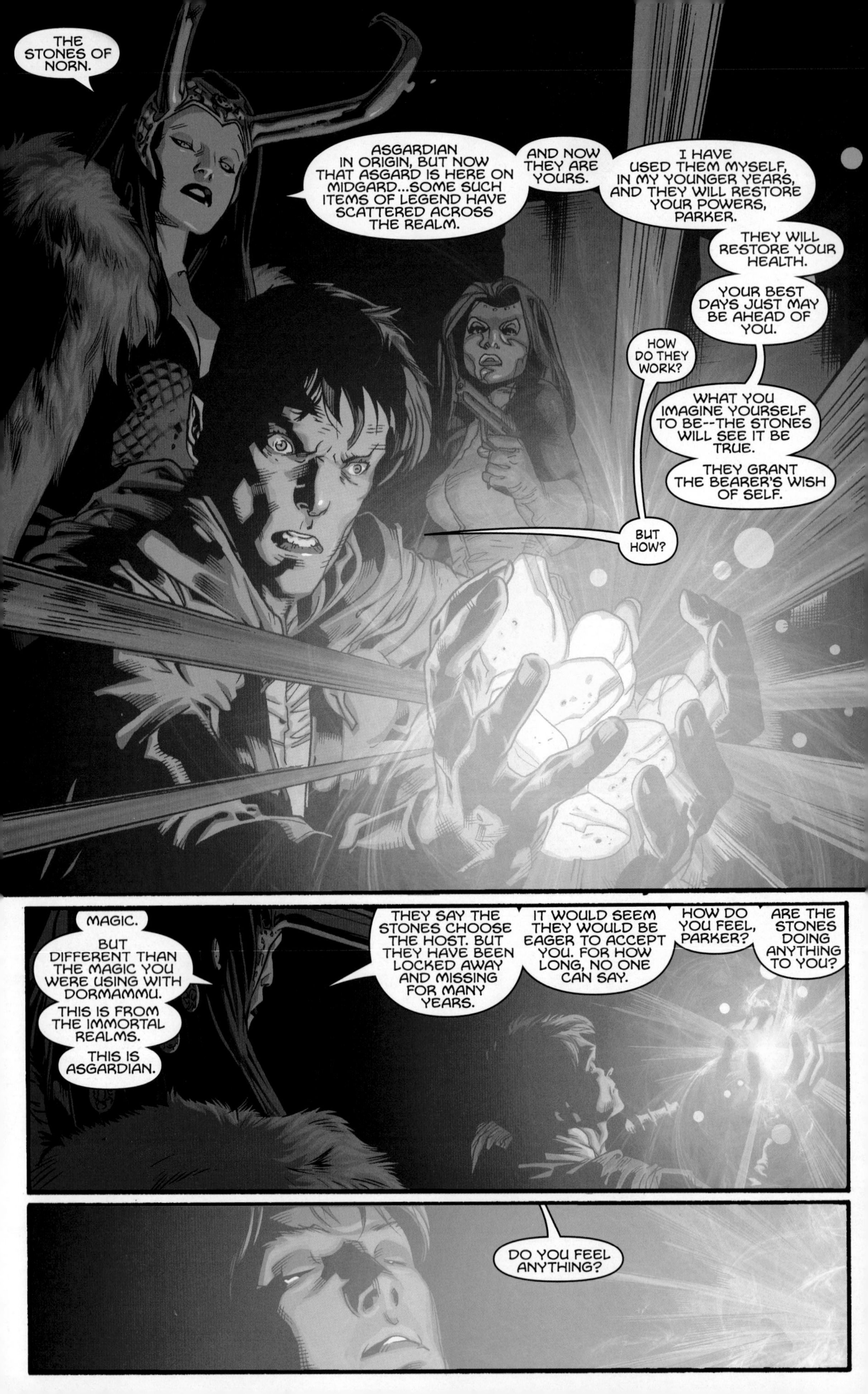
THE STONES OF NORN.
ASGARDIAN IN ORIGIN, BUT NOW THAT ASGARD IS HERE ON MIDGARD...SOME SUCH ITEMS OF LEGEND HAVE SCATTERED ACROSS THE REALM.
AND NOW THEY ARE YOURS.
I HAVE USED THEM MYSELF, IN MY YOUNGER YEARS, AND THEY WILL RESTORE YOUR POWERS, PARKER.
THEY WILL RESTORE YOUR HEALTH.
YOUR BEST DAYS JUST MAY BE AHEAD OF YOU.
HOW DO THEY WORK?
WHAT YOU IMAGINE YOURSELF TO BE--THE STONES WILL SEE IT BE TRUE.
THEY GRANT THE BEARER'S WISH OF SELF.
BUT HOW?
MAGIC.
BUT DIFFERENT THAN THE MAGIC YOU WERE USING WITH DORMAMMU.
THIS IS FROM THE IMMORTAL REALMS.
THIS IS ASGARDIAN.
THEY SAY THE STONES CHOOSE THE HOST. BUT THEY HAVE BEEN LOCKED AWAY AND MISSING FOR MANY YEARS.
IT WOULD SEEM THEY WOULD BE EAGER TO ACCEPT YOU. FOR HOW LONG, NO ONE CAN SAY.
HOW DO YOU FEEL, PARKER?
ARE THE STONES DOING ANYTHING TO YOU?
DO YOU FEEL ANYTHING?

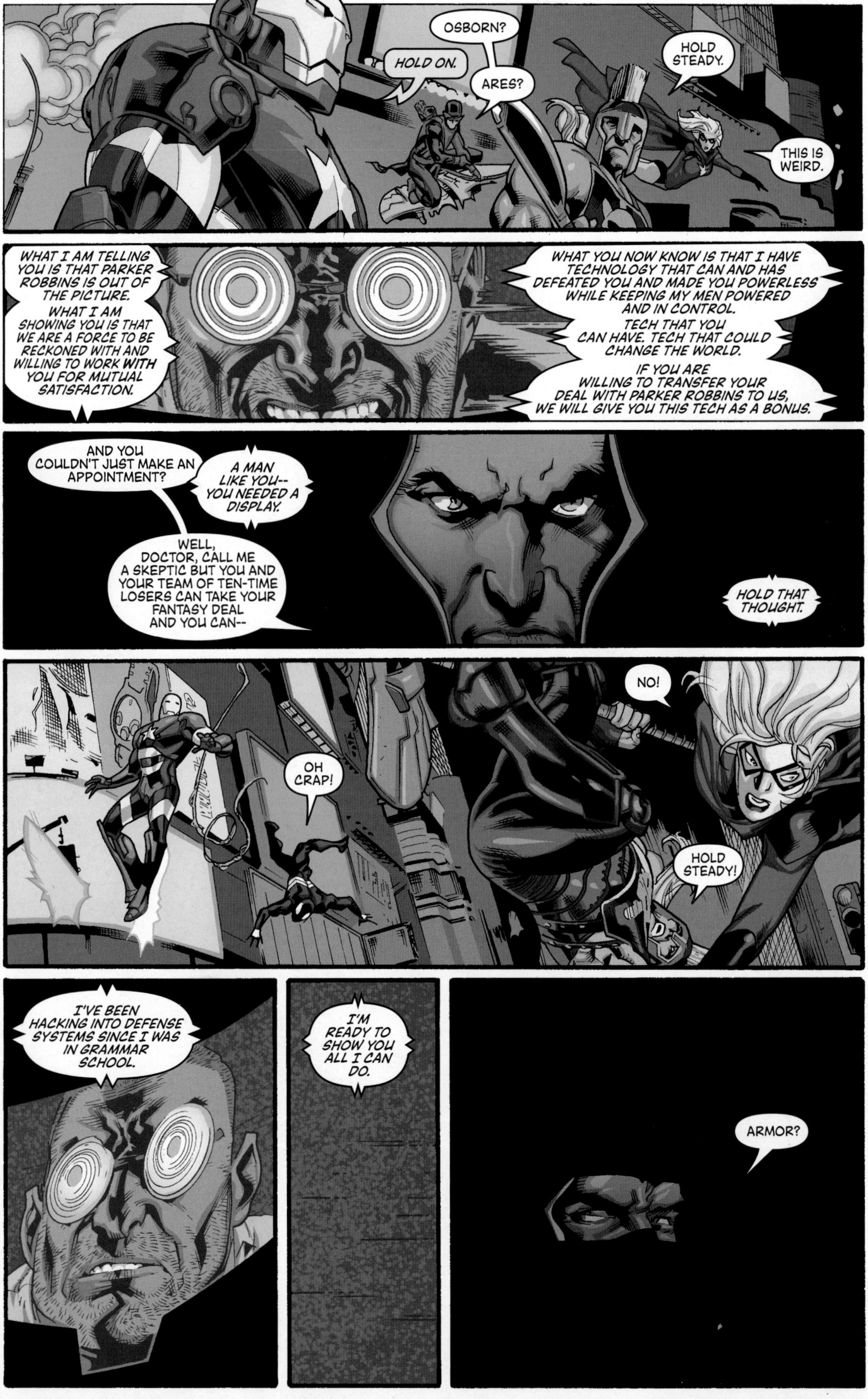
OSBORN?
HOLD ON.
ARES?
HOLD STEADY.
THIS IS WEIRD.
WHAT I AM TELLING YOU IS THAT PARKER ROBBINS IS OUT OF THE PICTURE.
WHAT I AM SHOWING YOU IS THAT WE ARE A FORCE TO BE RECKONED WITH AND WILLING TO WORK WITH YOU FOR MUTUAL SATISFACTION.
WHAT YOU NOW KNOW IS THAT I HAVE TECHNOLOGY THAT CAN AND HAS DEFEATED YOU AND MADE YOU POWERLESS WHILE KEEPING MY MEN POWERED AND IN CONTROL.
TECH THAT YOU CAN HAVE. TECH THAT COULD CHANGE THE WORLD.
IF YOU ARE WILLING TO TRANSFER YOUR DEAL WITH PARKER ROBBINS TO US, WE WILL GIVE YOU THIS TECH AS A BONUS.
AND YOU COULDN'T JUST MAKE AN APPOINTMENT?
A MAN LIKE YOU-- YOU NEEDED A DISPLAY.
WELL, DOCTOR, CALL ME A SKEPTIC BUT YOU AND YOUR TEAM OF TEN-TIME LOSERS CAN TAKE YOUR FANTASY DEAL AND YOU CAN--
HOLD THAT THOUGHT.
NO!
OH CRAP!
HOLD STEADY!
I'VE BEEN HACKING INTO DEFENSE SYSTEMS SINCE I WAS IN GRAMMAR SCHOOL.
I'M READY TO SHOW YOU ALL I CAN DO.
ARMOR?

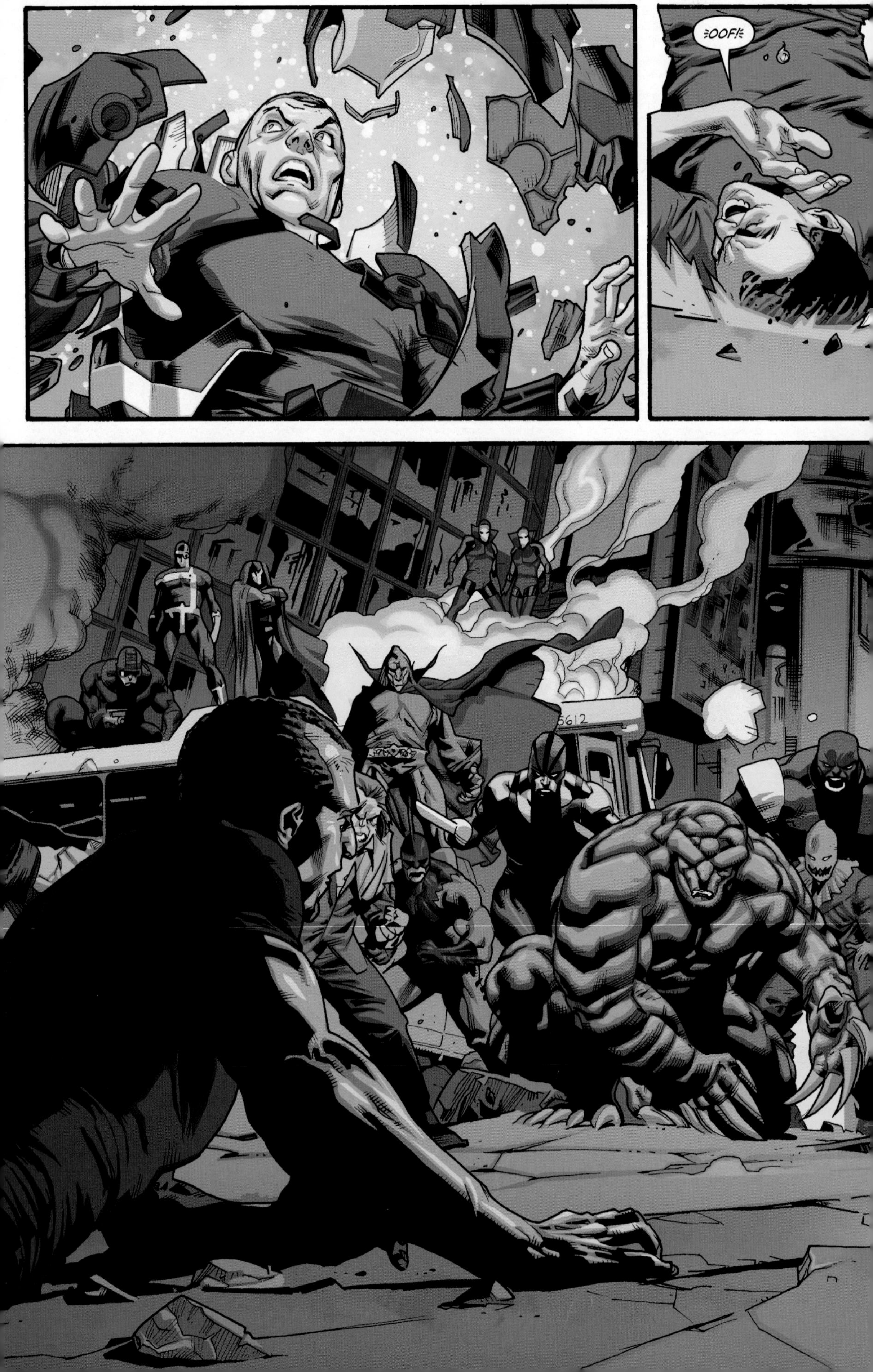
OOF!

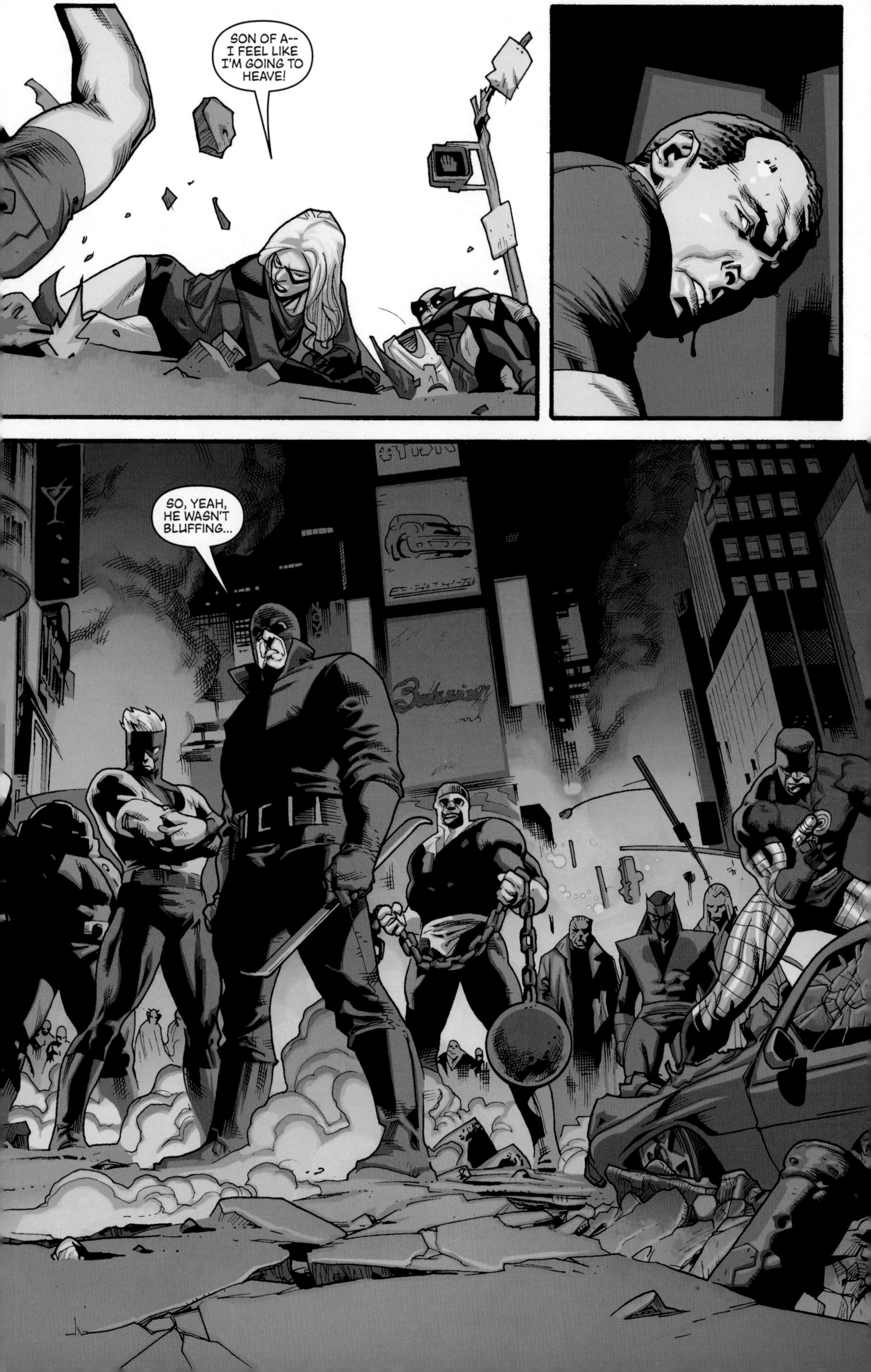
SON OF A-- I FEEL LIKE I'M GOING TO HEAVE!
SO, YEAH, HE WASN'T BLUFFING...

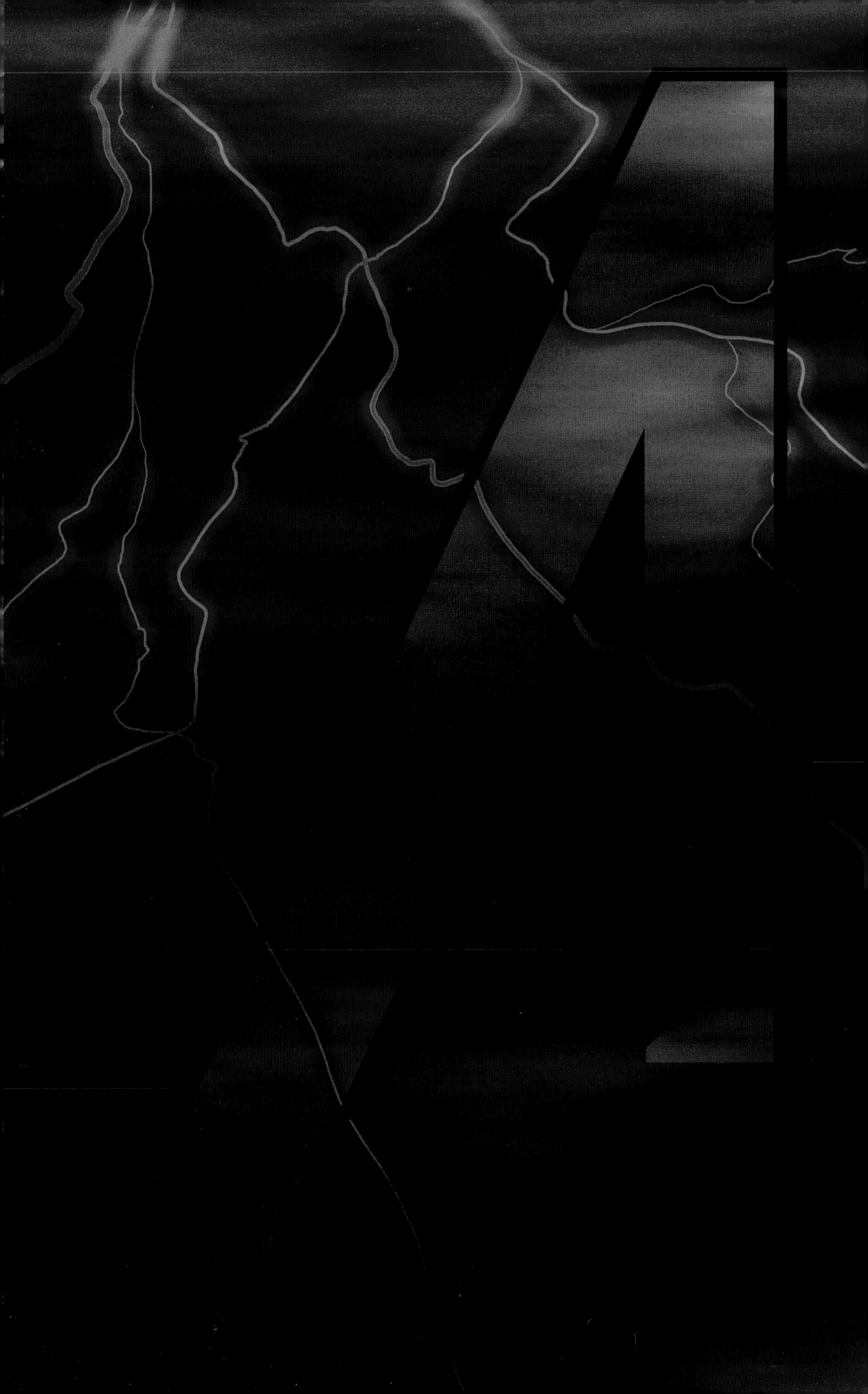

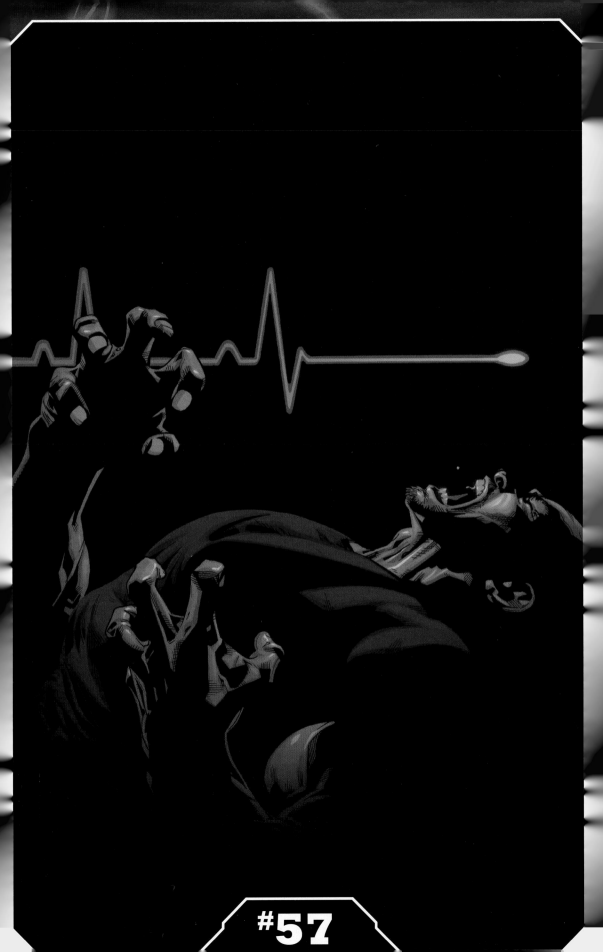

#57

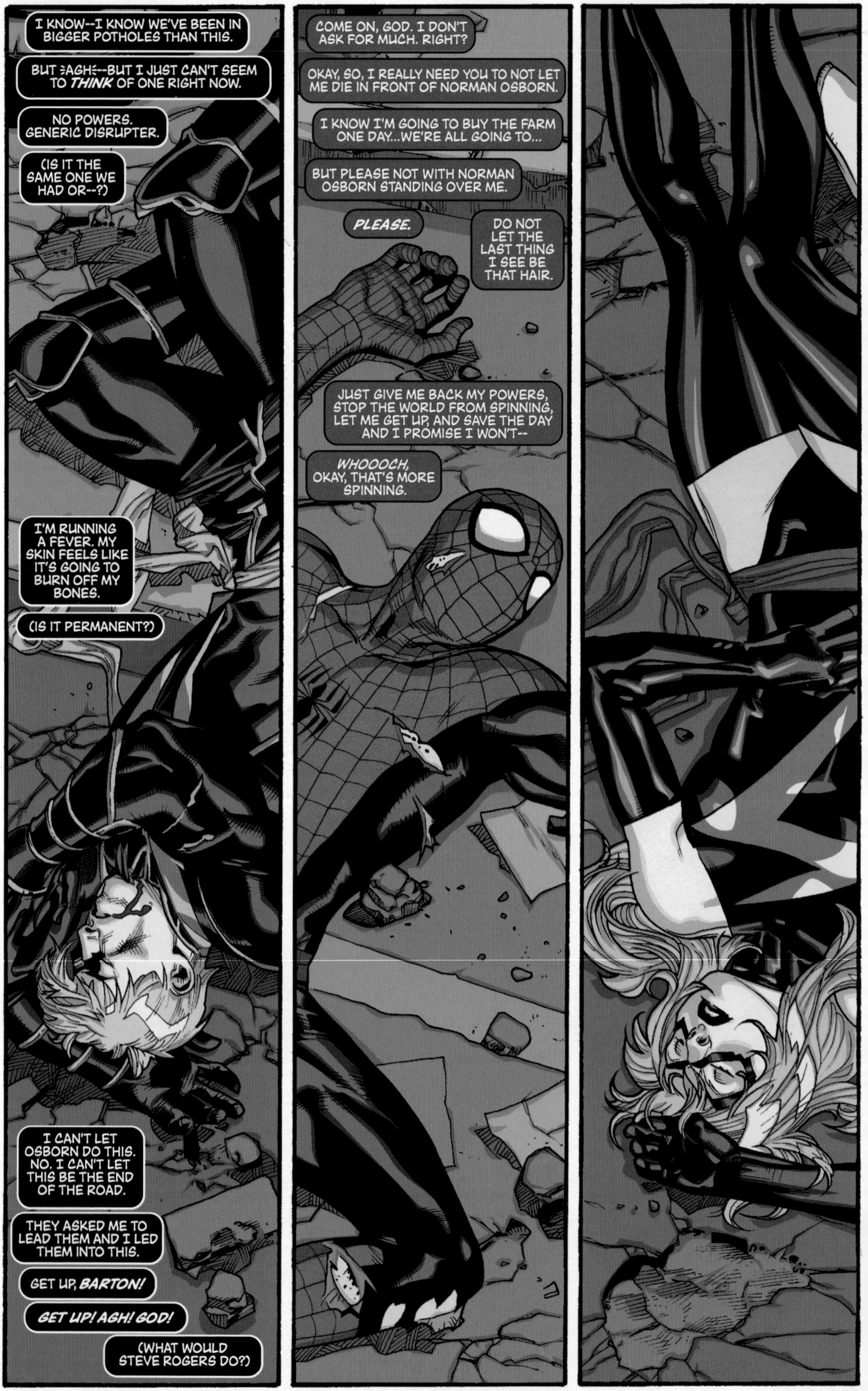

I KNOW--I KNOW WE'VE BEEN IN BIGGER POTHOLES THAN THIS.
BUT ≷AGH≶--BUT I JUST CAN'T SEEM TO *THINK* OF ONE RIGHT NOW.
NO POWERS. GENERIC DISRUPTER.
(IS IT THE SAME ONE WE HAD OR--?)
I'M RUNNING A FEVER. MY SKIN FEELS LIKE IT'S GOING TO BURN OFF MY BONES.
(IS IT PERMANENT?)
I CAN'T LET OSBORN DO THIS. NO. I CAN'T LET THIS BE THE END OF THE ROAD.
THEY ASKED ME TO LEAD THEM AND I LED THEM INTO THIS.
GET UP, *BARTON!*
GET UP! AGH! GOD!
(WHAT WOULD STEVE ROGERS DO?)
COME ON, GOD. I DON'T ASK FOR MUCH. RIGHT?
OKAY, SO, I REALLY NEED YOU TO NOT LET ME DIE IN FRONT OF NORMAN OSBORN.
I KNOW I'M GOING TO BUY THE FARM ONE DAY...WE'RE ALL GOING TO...
BUT PLEASE NOT WITH NORMAN OSBORN STANDING OVER ME.
PLEASE.
DO NOT LET THE LAST THING I SEE BE THAT HAIR.
JUST GIVE ME BACK MY POWERS, STOP THE WORLD FROM SPINNING, LET ME GET UP, AND SAVE THE DAY AND I PROMISE I WON'T--
WHOOOCH, OKAY, THAT'S MORE SPINNING.

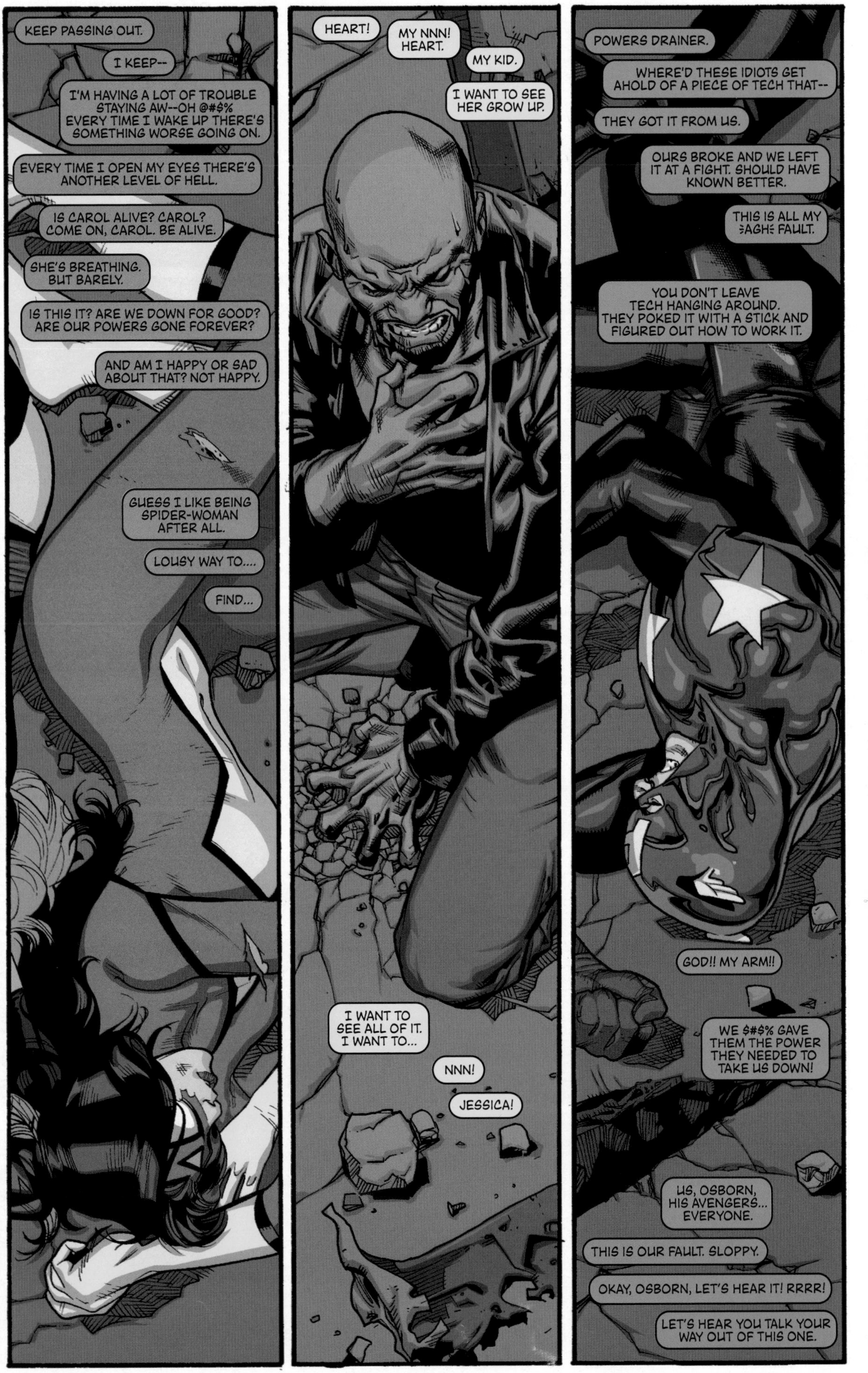
KEEP PASSING OUT.
I KEEP--
I'M HAVING A LOT OF TROUBLE STAYING AW--OH @#$% EVERY TIME I WAKE UP THERE'S SOMETHING WORSE GOING ON.
EVERY TIME I OPEN MY EYES THERE'S ANOTHER LEVEL OF HELL.
IS CAROL ALIVE? CAROL? COME ON, CAROL. BE ALIVE.
SHE'S BREATHING. BUT BARELY.
IS THIS IT? ARE WE DOWN FOR GOOD? ARE OUR POWERS GONE FOREVER?
AND AM I HAPPY OR SAD ABOUT THAT? NOT HAPPY.
GUESS I LIKE BEING SPIDER-WOMAN AFTER ALL.
LOUSY WAY TO....
FIND...
HEART!
MY NNN! HEART.
MY KID.
I WANT TO SEE HER GROW UP.
I WANT TO SEE ALL OF IT. I WANT TO...
NNN!
JESSICA!
POWERS DRAINER.
WHERE'D THESE IDIOTS GET AHOLD OF A PIECE OF TECH THAT--
THEY GOT IT FROM US.
OURS BROKE AND WE LEFT IT AT A FIGHT. SHOULD HAVE KNOWN BETTER.
THIS IS ALL MY AGH FAULT.
YOU DON'T LEAVE TECH HANGING AROUND. THEY POKED IT WITH A STICK AND FIGURED OUT HOW TO WORK IT.
GOD!! MY ARM!!
WE $#$% GAVE THEM THE POWER THEY NEEDED TO TAKE US DOWN!
US, OSBORN, HIS AVENGERS... EVERYONE.
THIS IS OUR FAULT. SLOPPY.
OKAY, OSBORN, LET'S HEAR IT! RRRR!
LET'S HEAR YOU TALK YOUR WAY OUT OF THIS ONE.

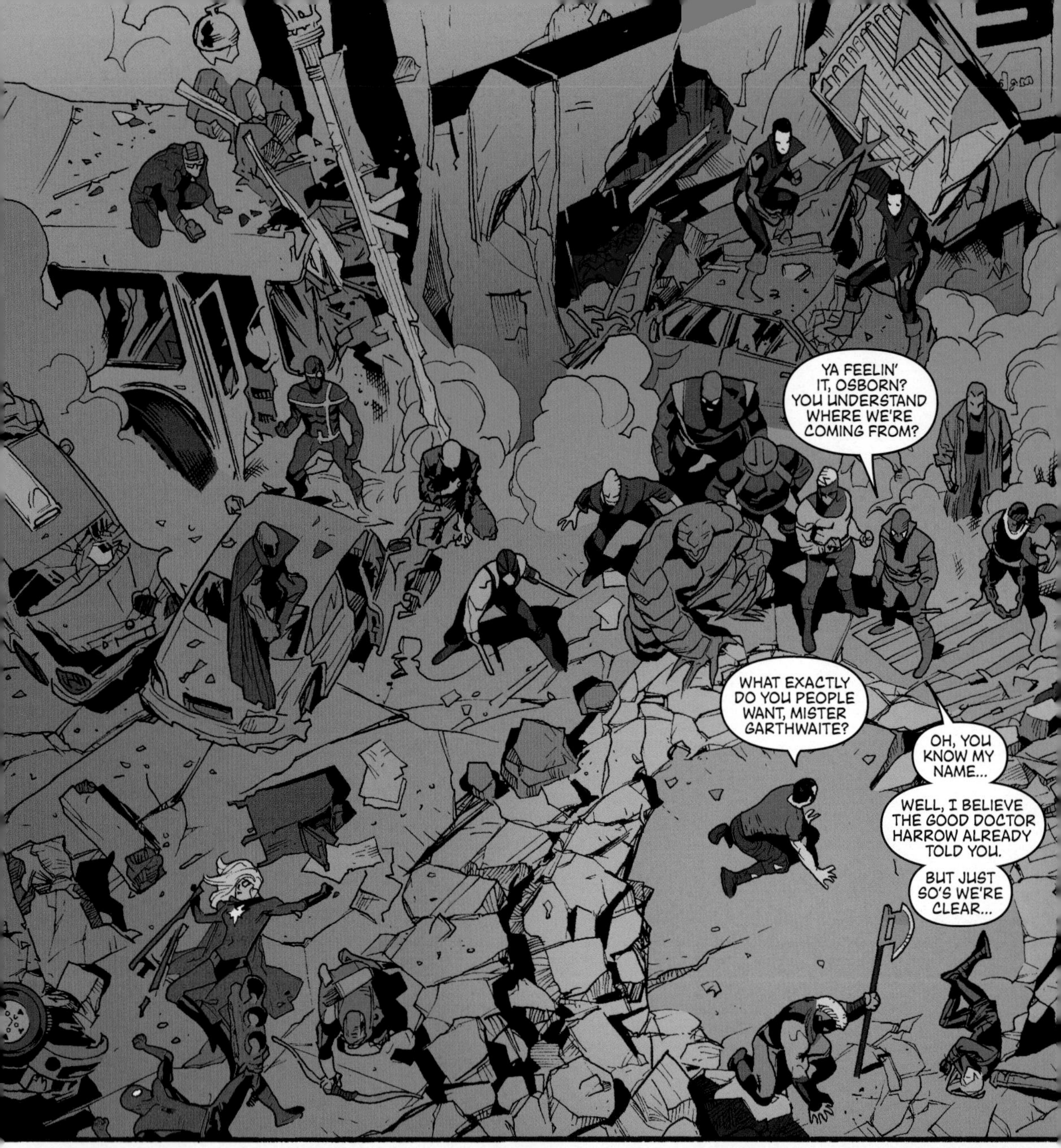
YA FEELIN' IT, OSBORN? YOU UNDERSTAND WHERE WE'RE COMING FROM?
WHAT EXACTLY DO YOU PEOPLE WANT, MISTER GARTHWAITE?
OH, YOU KNOW MY NAME...
WELL, I BELIEVE THE GOOD DOCTOR HARROW ALREADY TOLD YOU.
BUT JUST SO'S WE'RE CLEAR...

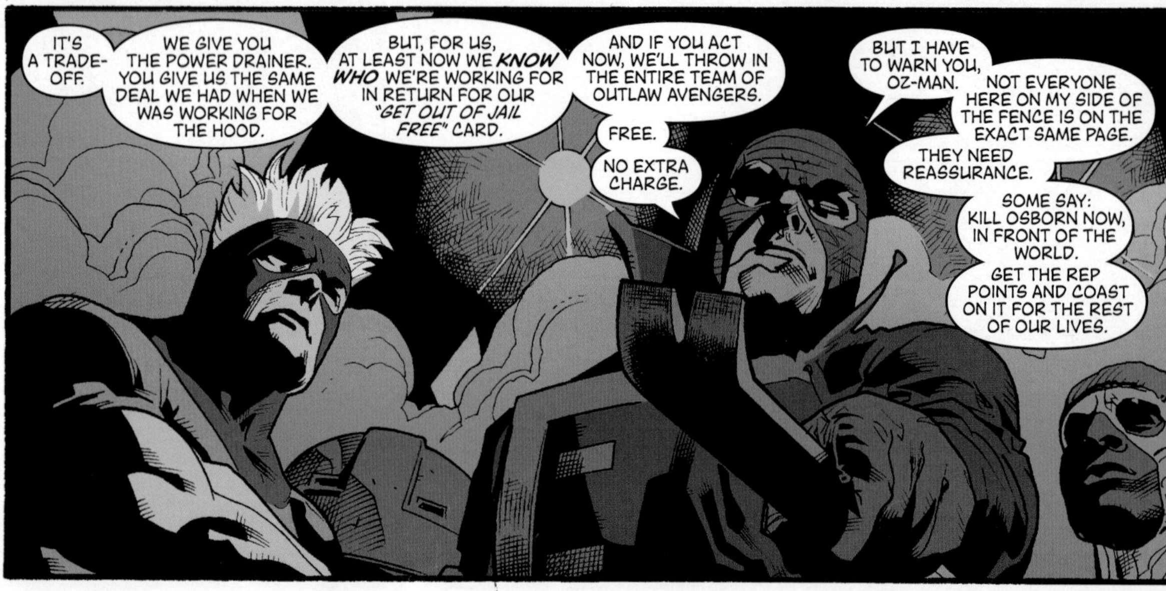
IT'S A TRADE-OFF.
WE GIVE YOU THE POWER DRAINER. YOU GIVE US THE SAME DEAL WE HAD WHEN WE WAS WORKING FOR THE HOOD.
BUT, FOR US, AT LEAST NOW WE *KNOW WHO* WE'RE WORKING FOR IN RETURN FOR OUR *"GET OUT OF JAIL FREE"* CARD.
AND IF YOU ACT NOW, WE'LL THROW IN THE ENTIRE TEAM OF OUTLAW AVENGERS.
FREE.
NO EXTRA CHARGE.
BUT I HAVE TO WARN YOU, OZ-MAN.
NOT EVERYONE HERE ON MY SIDE OF THE FENCE IS ON THE EXACT SAME PAGE.
THEY NEED REASSURANCE.
SOME SAY: KILL OSBORN NOW, IN FRONT OF THE WORLD.
GET THE REP POINTS AND COAST ON IT FOR THE REST OF OUR LIVES.

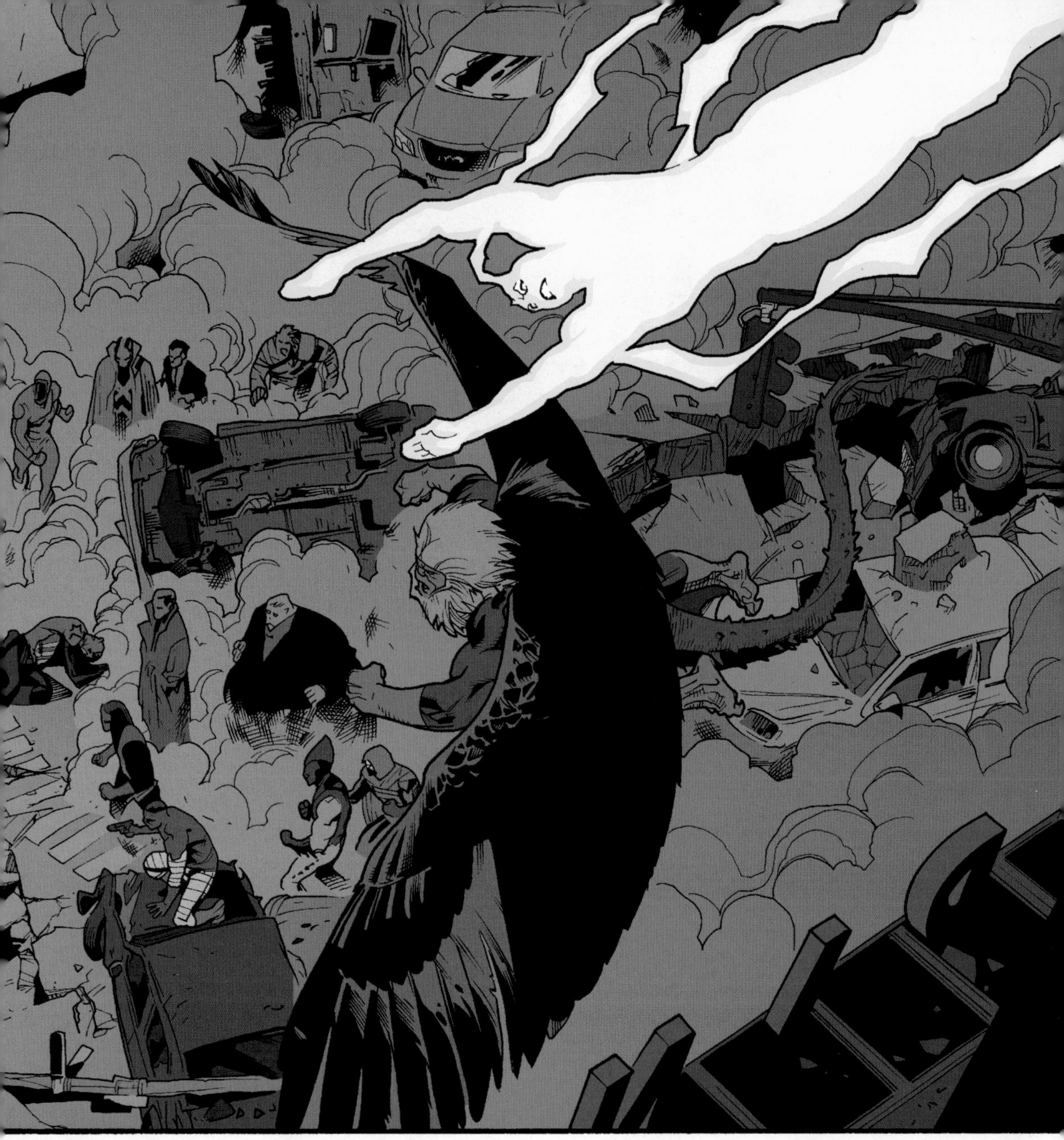

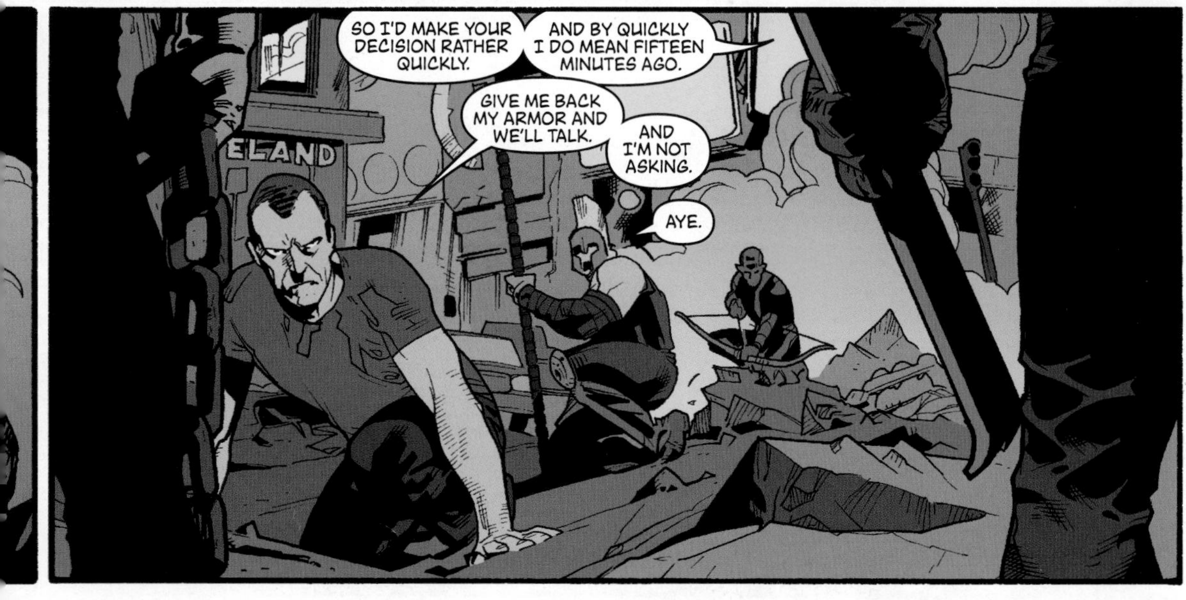

SO I'D MAKE YOUR DECISION RATHER QUICKLY.
AND BY QUICKLY I DO MEAN FIFTEEN MINUTES AGO.
GIVE ME BACK MY ARMOR AND WE'LL TALK.
AND I'M NOT ASKING.
AYE.
ELAND

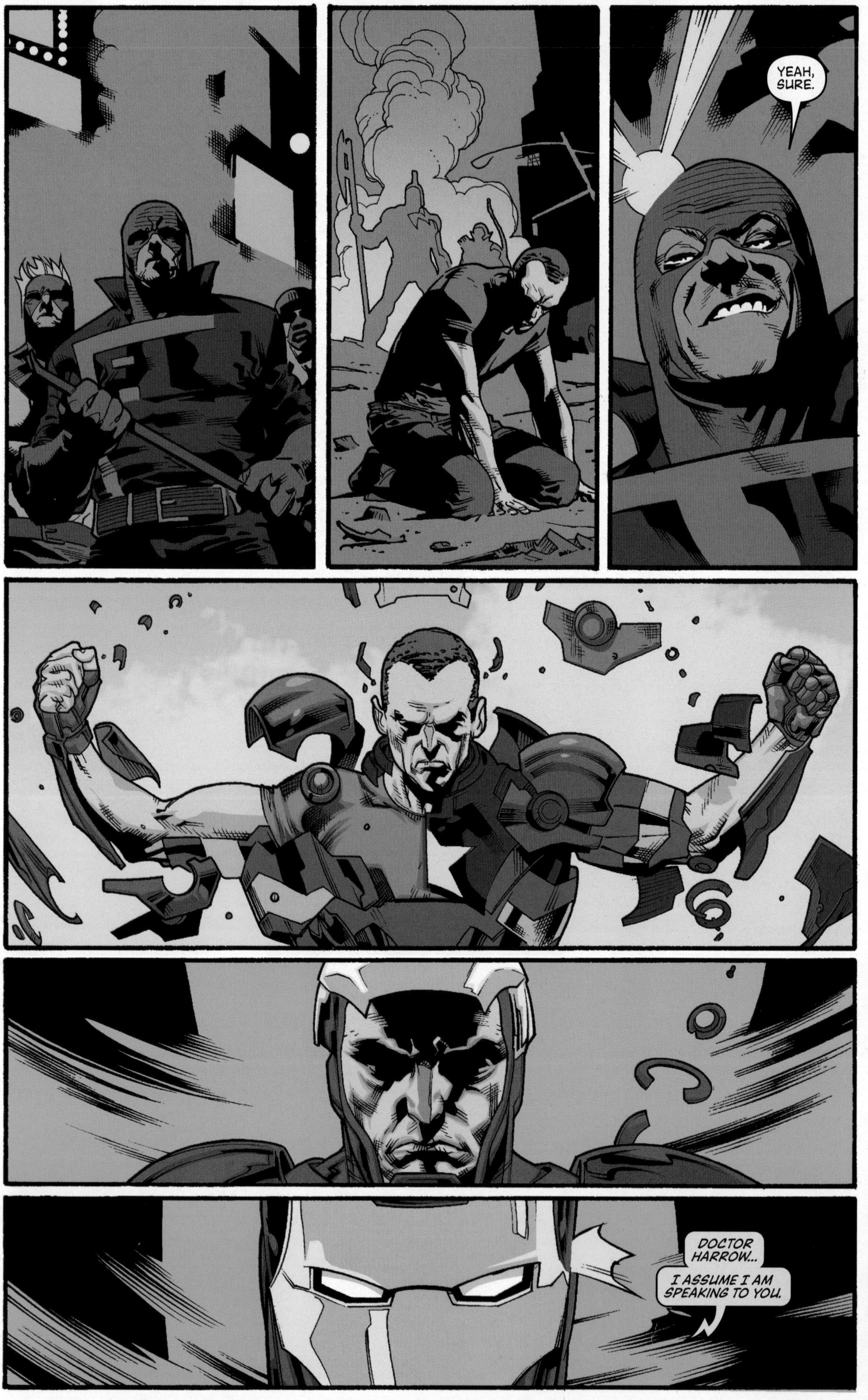
YEAH, SURE.
DOCTOR HARROW...
I ASSUME I AM SPEAKING TO YOU.

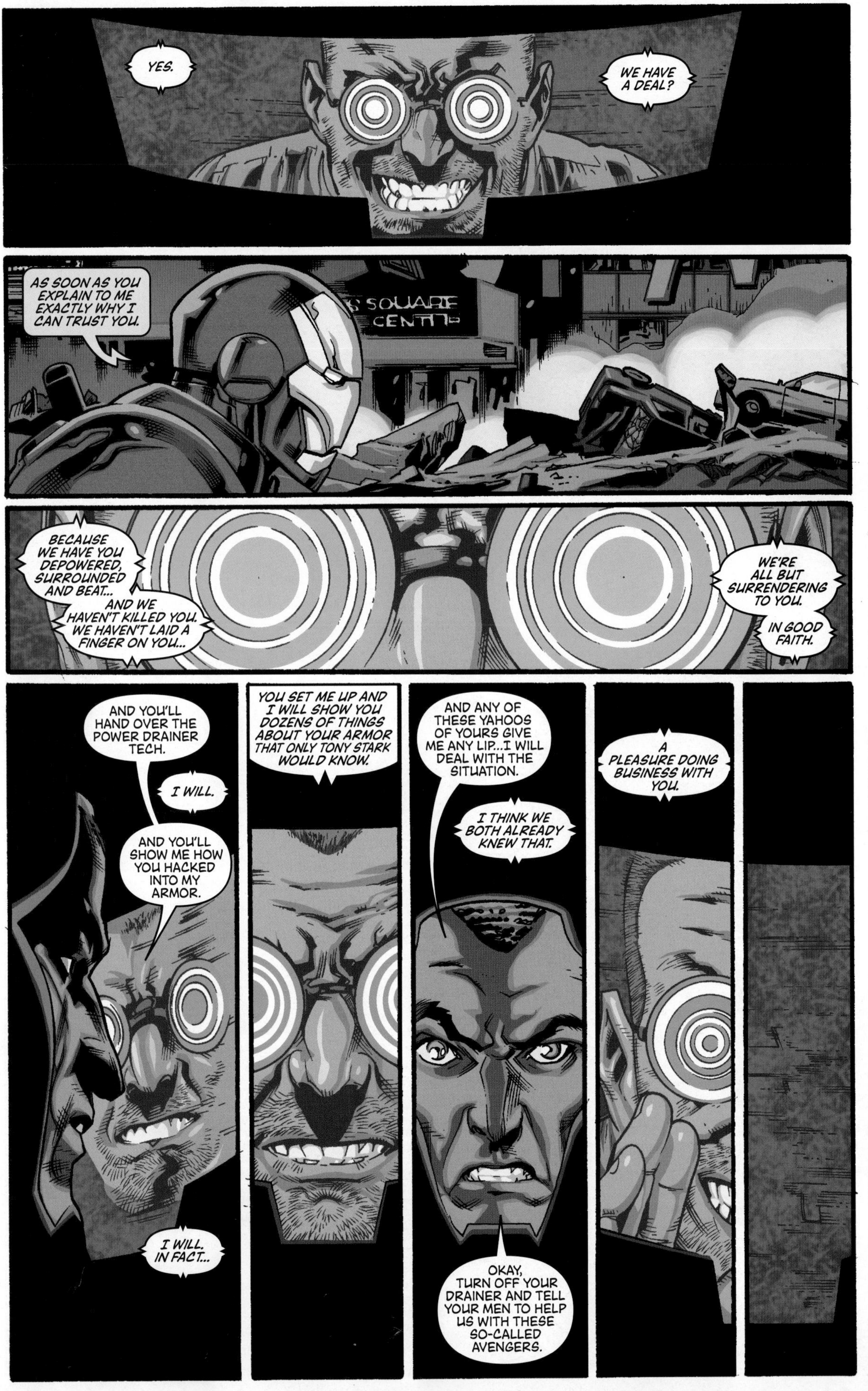
YES.
WE HAVE A DEAL?
AS SOON AS YOU EXPLAIN TO ME EXACTLY WHY I CAN TRUST YOU.
S SQUARE CENT
BECAUSE WE HAVE YOU DEPOWERED, SURROUNDED AND BEAT...
AND WE HAVEN'T KILLED YOU. WE HAVEN'T LAID A FINGER ON YOU...
WE'RE ALL BUT SURRENDERING TO YOU.
IN GOOD FAITH.
AND YOU'LL HAND OVER THE POWER DRAINER TECH.
I WILL.
AND YOU'LL SHOW ME HOW YOU HACKED INTO MY ARMOR.
I WILL. IN FACT...
YOU SET ME UP AND I WILL SHOW YOU DOZENS OF THINGS ABOUT YOUR ARMOR THAT ONLY TONY STARK WOULD KNOW.
AND ANY OF THESE YAHOOS OF YOURS GIVE ME ANY LIP...I WILL DEAL WITH THE SITUATION.
I THINK WE BOTH ALREADY KNEW THAT.
OKAY, TURN OFF YOUR DRAINER AND TELL YOUR MEN TO HELP US WITH THESE SO-CALLED AVENGERS.
A PLEASURE DOING BUSINESS WITH YOU.

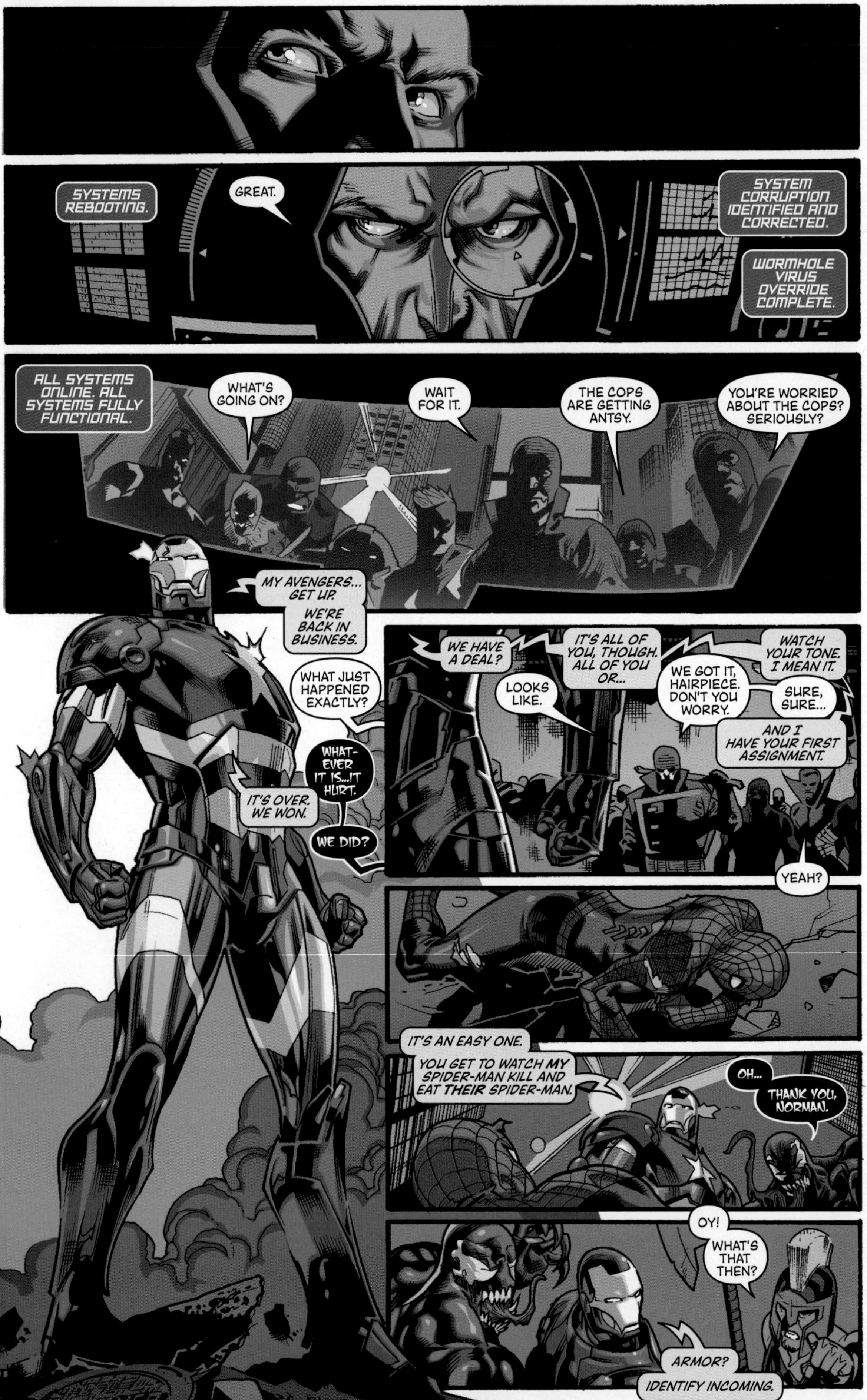

SYSTEMS REBOOTING.
GREAT.
SYSTEM CORRUPTION IDENTIFIED AND CORRECTED.
WORMHOLE VIRUS OVERRIDE COMPLETE.
ALL SYSTEMS ONLINE. ALL SYSTEMS FULLY FUNCTIONAL.
WHAT'S GOING ON?
WAIT FOR IT.
THE COPS ARE GETTING ANTSY.
YOU'RE WORRIED ABOUT THE COPS? SERIOUSLY?
MY AVENGERS... GET UP.
WE'RE BACK IN BUSINESS.
WHAT JUST HAPPENED EXACTLY?
WHAT-EVER IT IS...IT HURT.
IT'S OVER. WE WON.
WE DID?
WE HAVE A DEAL?
LOOKS LIKE.
IT'S ALL OF YOU, THOUGH. ALL OF YOU OR...
WE GOT IT, HAIRPIECE. DON'T YOU WORRY.
WATCH YOUR TONE. I MEAN IT.
SURE, SURE...
AND I HAVE YOUR FIRST ASSIGNMENT.
YEAH?
IT'S AN EASY ONE.
YOU GET TO WATCH MY SPIDER-MAN KILL AND EAT THEIR SPIDER-MAN.
OH...
THANK YOU, NORMAN.
OY!
WHAT'S THAT THEN?
ARMOR?
IDENTIFY INCOMING.

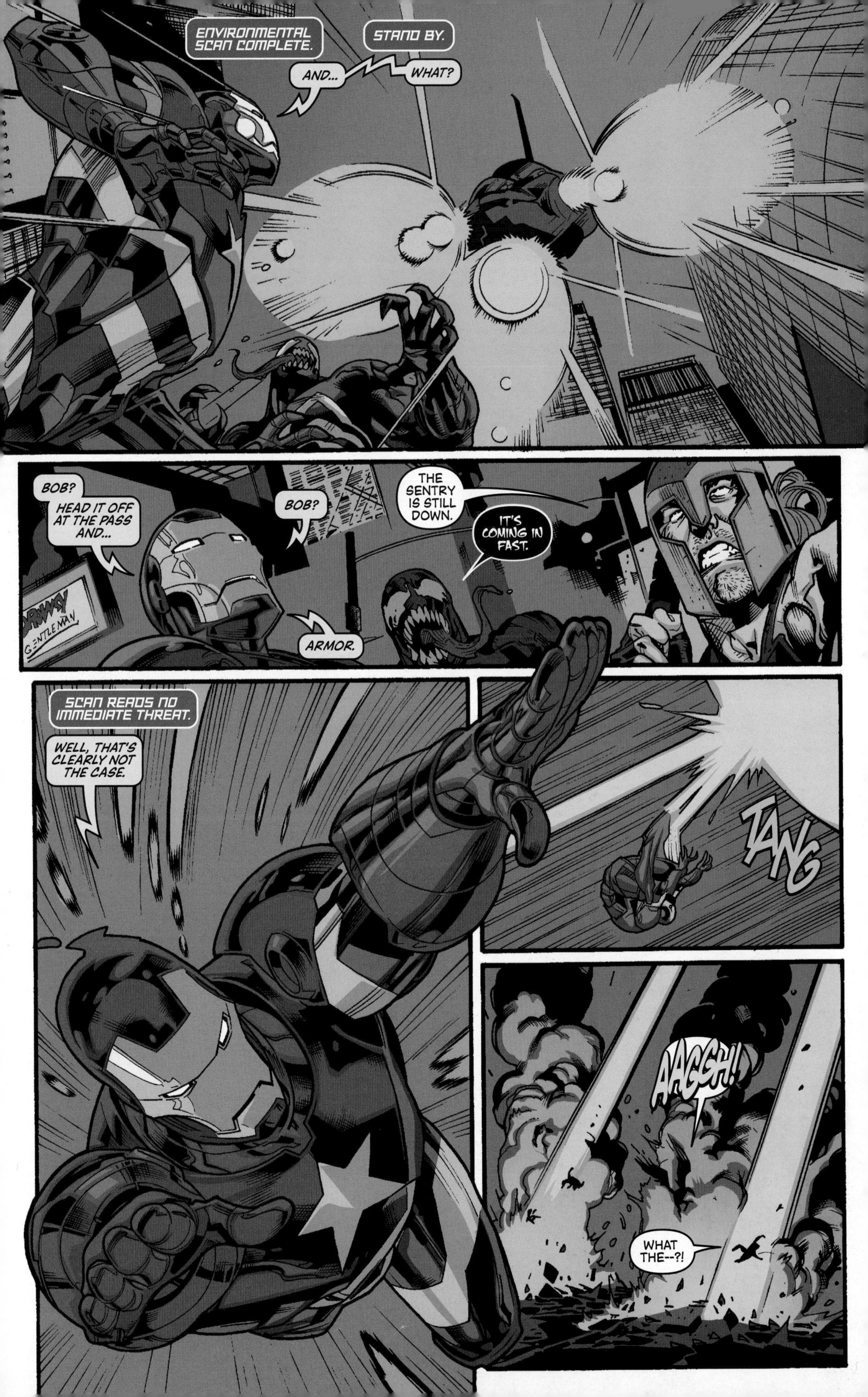
ENVIRONMENTAL SCAN COMPLETE.
AND...
STAND BY.
WHAT?
BOB?
HEAD IT OFF AT THE PASS AND...
BOB?
ARMOR.
THE SENTRY IS STILL DOWN.
IT'S COMING IN FAST.
GENTLEMAN
SCAN READS NO IMMEDIATE THREAT.
WELL, THAT'S CLEARLY NOT THE CASE.
TANG
AAGGH!
WHAT THE--?!

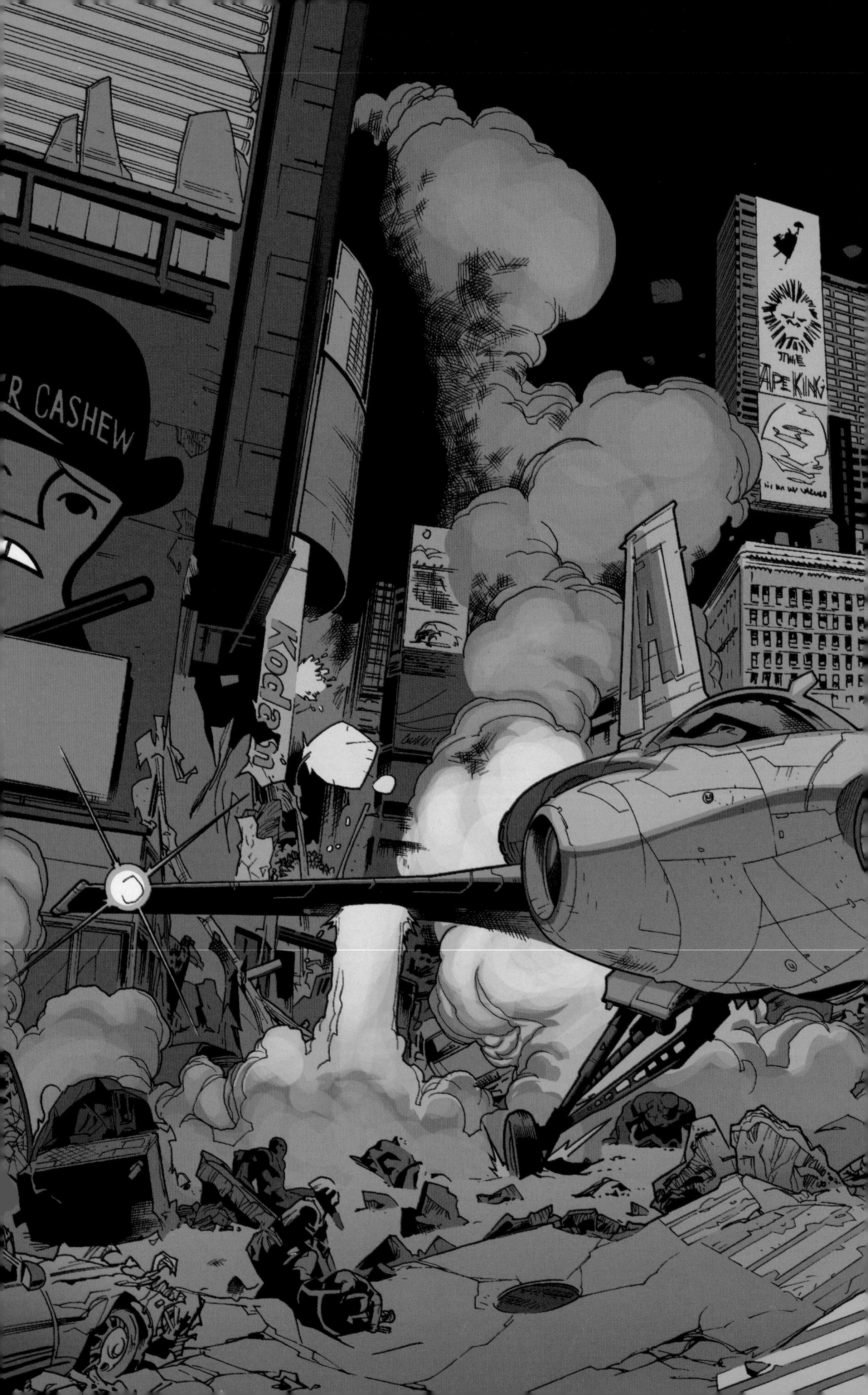
R CASHEW
THE
APE KING

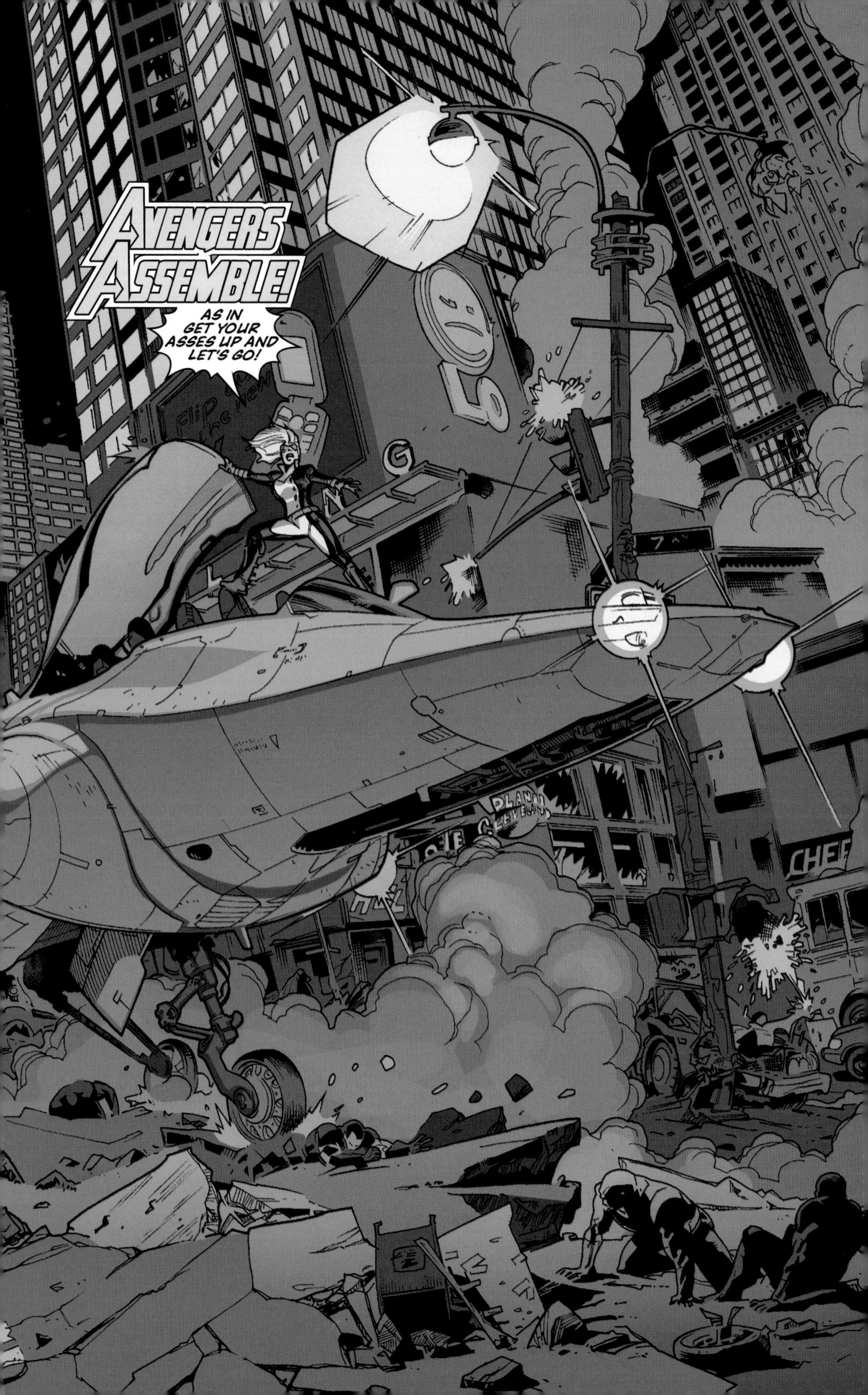
AVENGERS ASSEMBLE!
AS IN GET YOUR ASSES UP AND LET'S GO!
7 AV

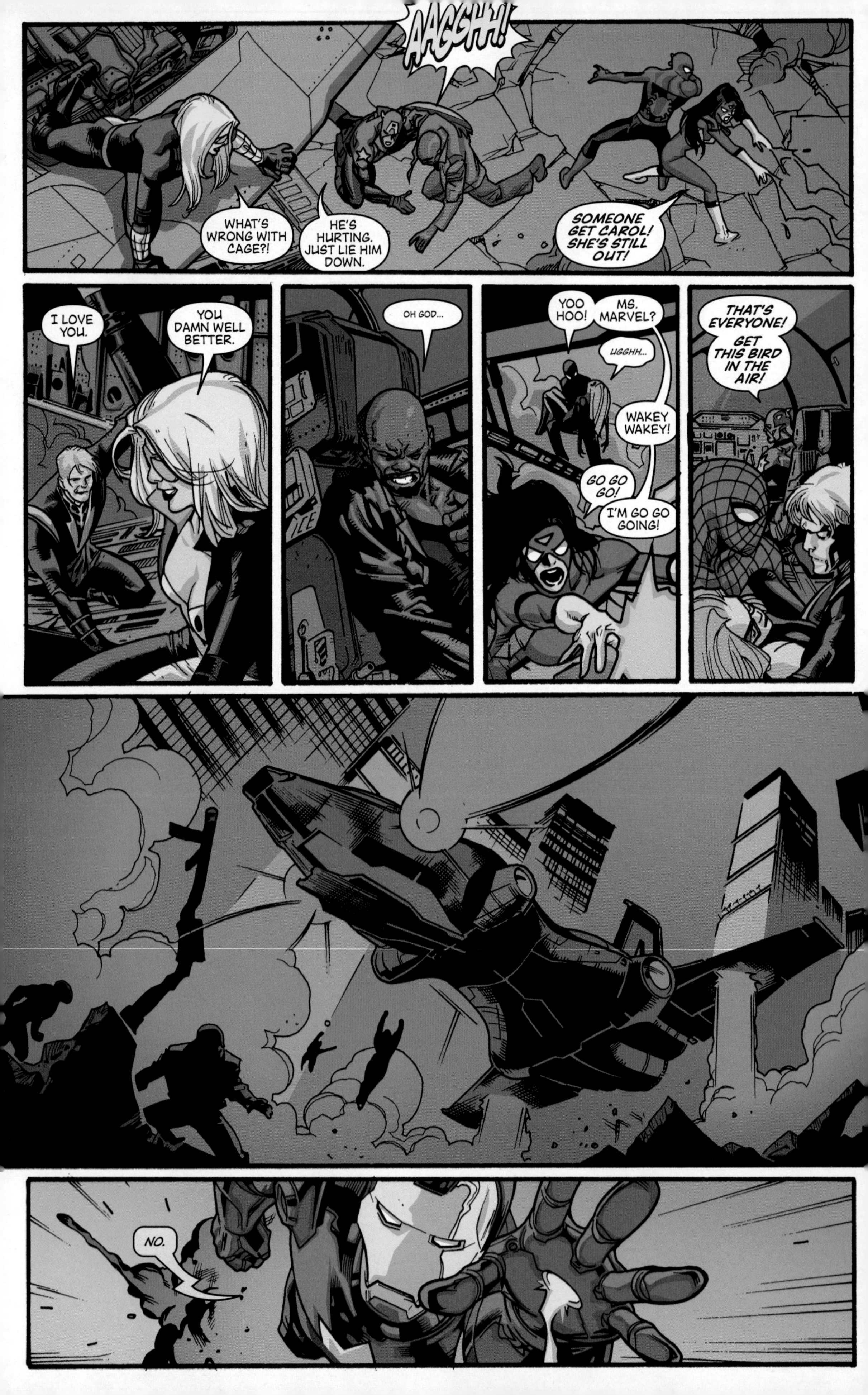
AAGGHH!
WHAT'S WRONG WITH CAGE?!
HE'S HURTING. JUST LIE HIM DOWN.
SOMEONE GET CAROL! SHE'S STILL OUT!
I LOVE YOU.
YOU DAMN WELL BETTER.
OH GOD...
YOO HOO!
MS. MARVEL?
UGGHH...
WAKEY WAKEY!
GO GO GO!
I'M GO GO GOING!
THAT'S EVERYONE! GET THIS BIRD IN THE AIR!
NO.

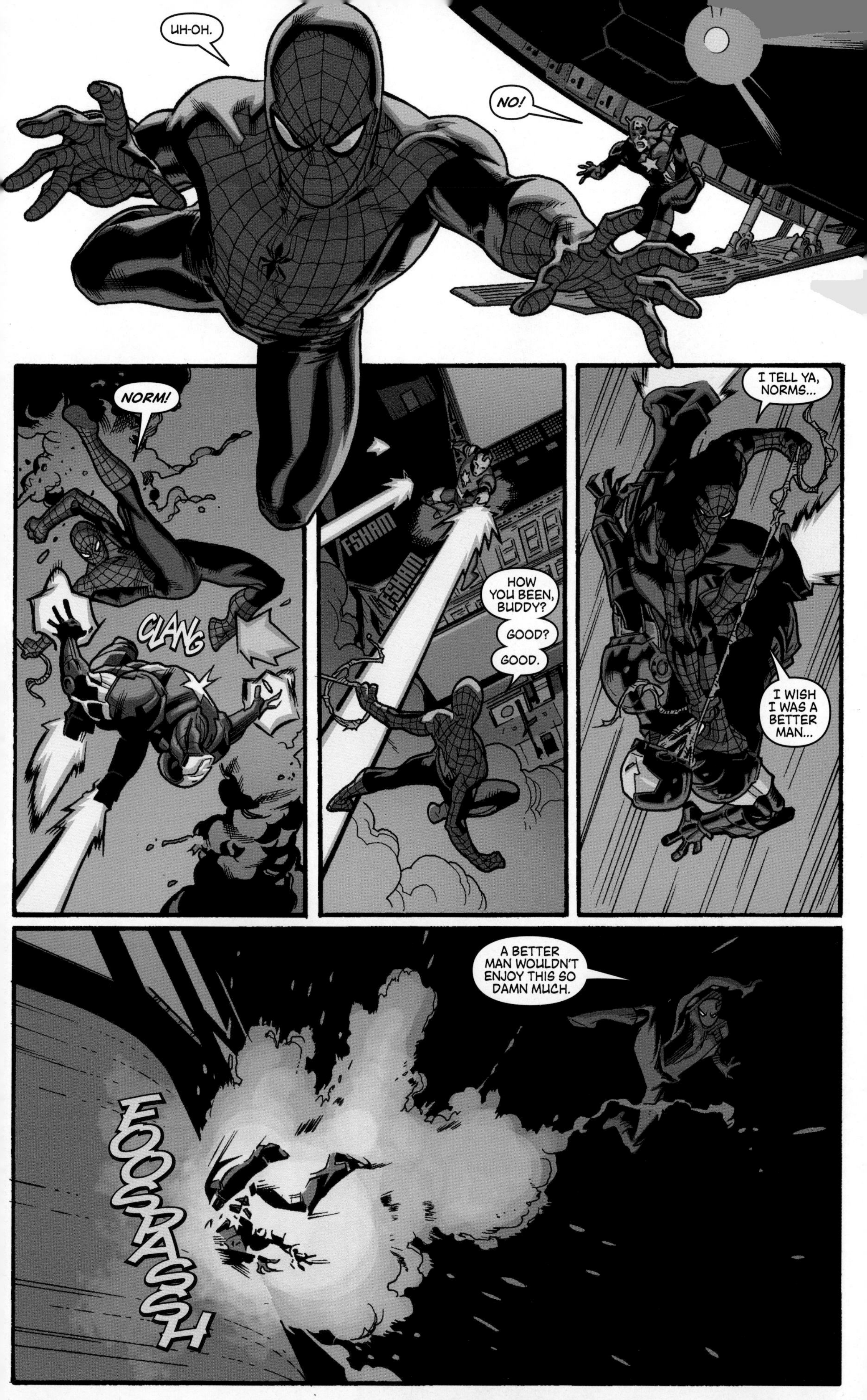
UH-OH.
NO!
NORM!
CLANG
HOW YOU BEEN, BUDDY?
GOOD?
GOOD.
I TELL YA, NORMS...
I WISH I WAS A BETTER MAN...
A BETTER MAN WOULDN'T ENJOY THIS SO DAMN MUCH.
FOOSPASSH

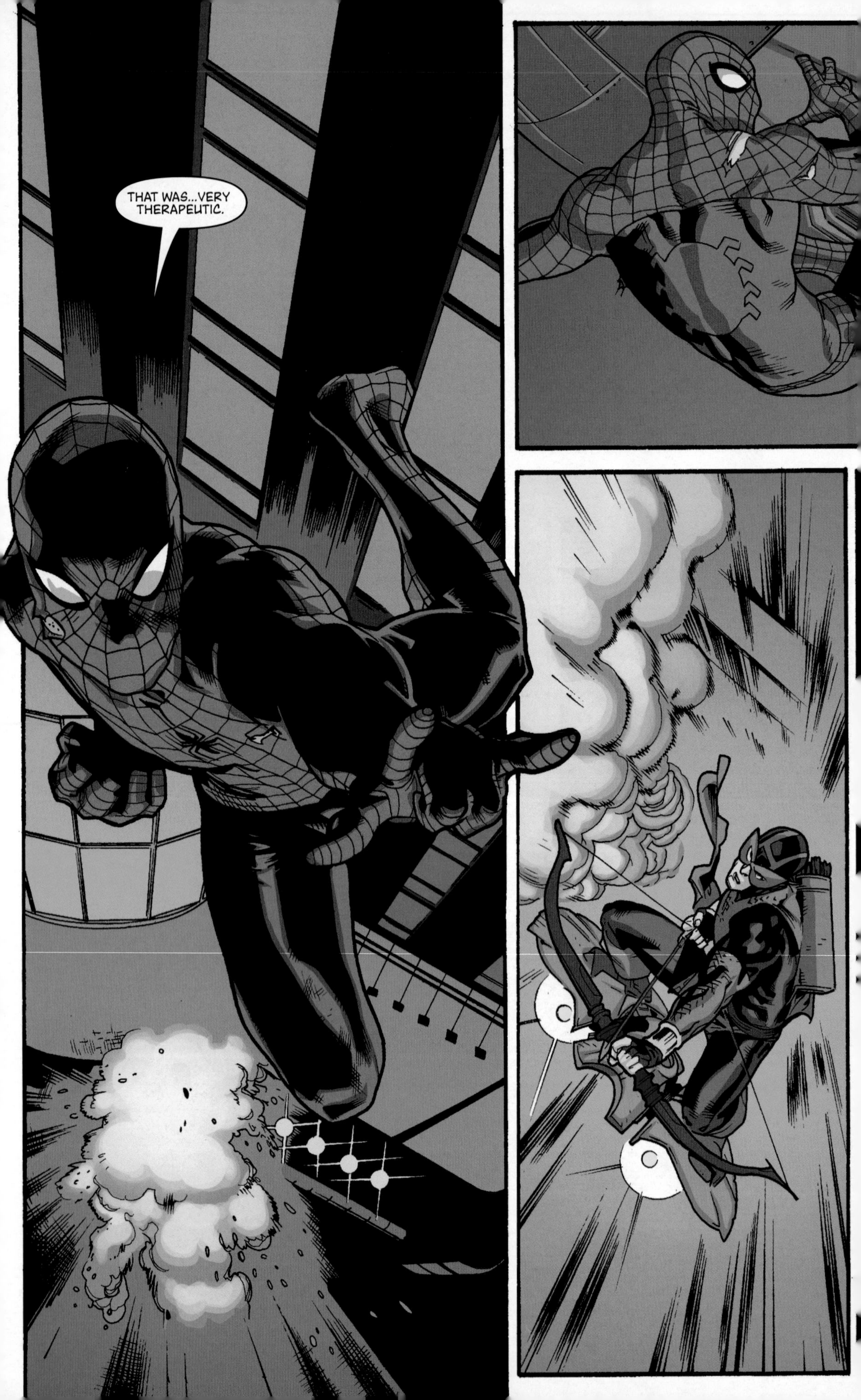
THAT WAS...VERY THERAPEUTIC.

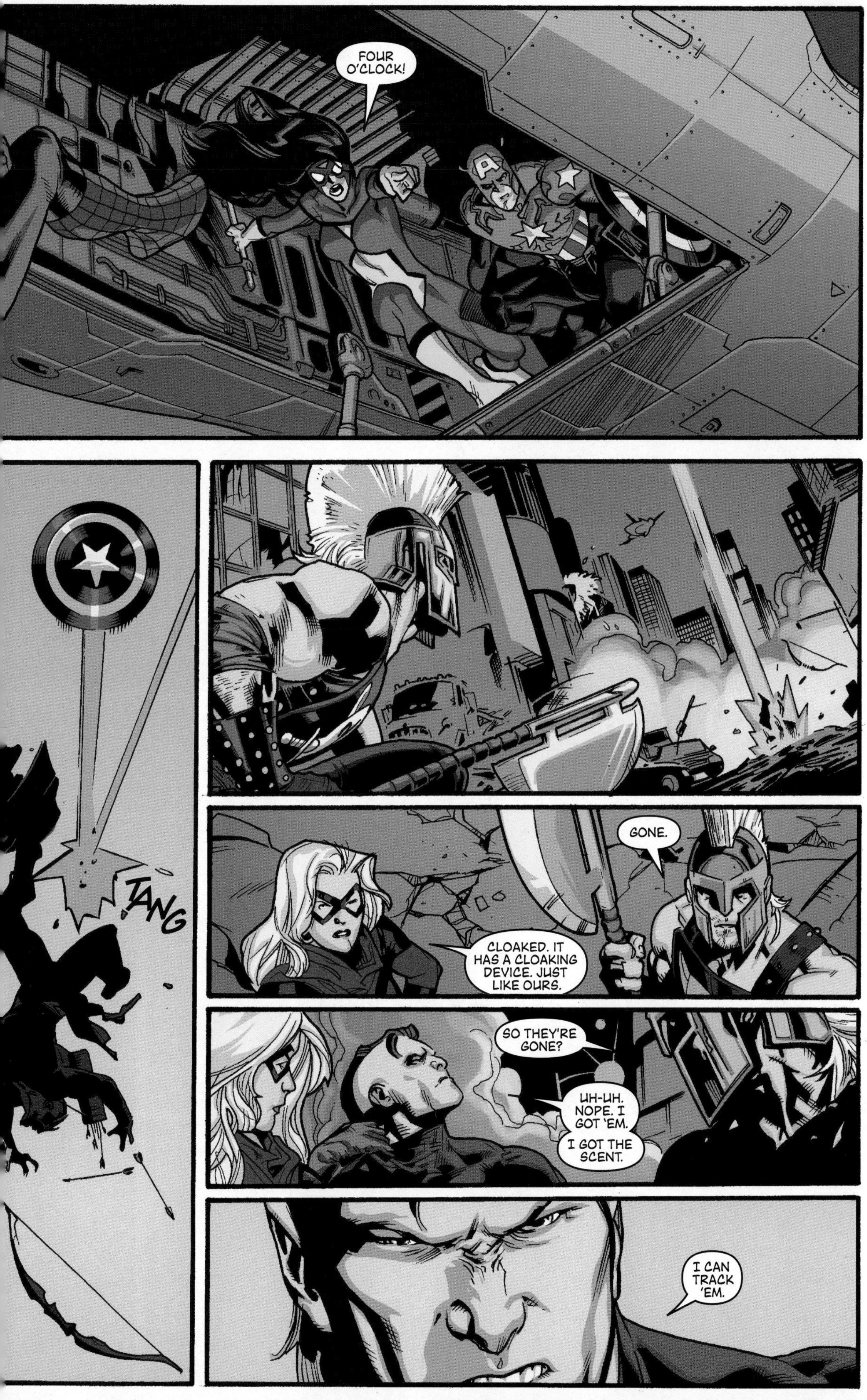

FOUR O'CLOCK!
TANG
GONE.
CLOAKED. IT HAS A CLOAKING DEVICE. JUST LIKE OURS.
SO THEY'RE GONE?
UH-UH. NOPE. I GOT 'EM.
I GOT THE SCENT.
I CAN TRACK 'EM.

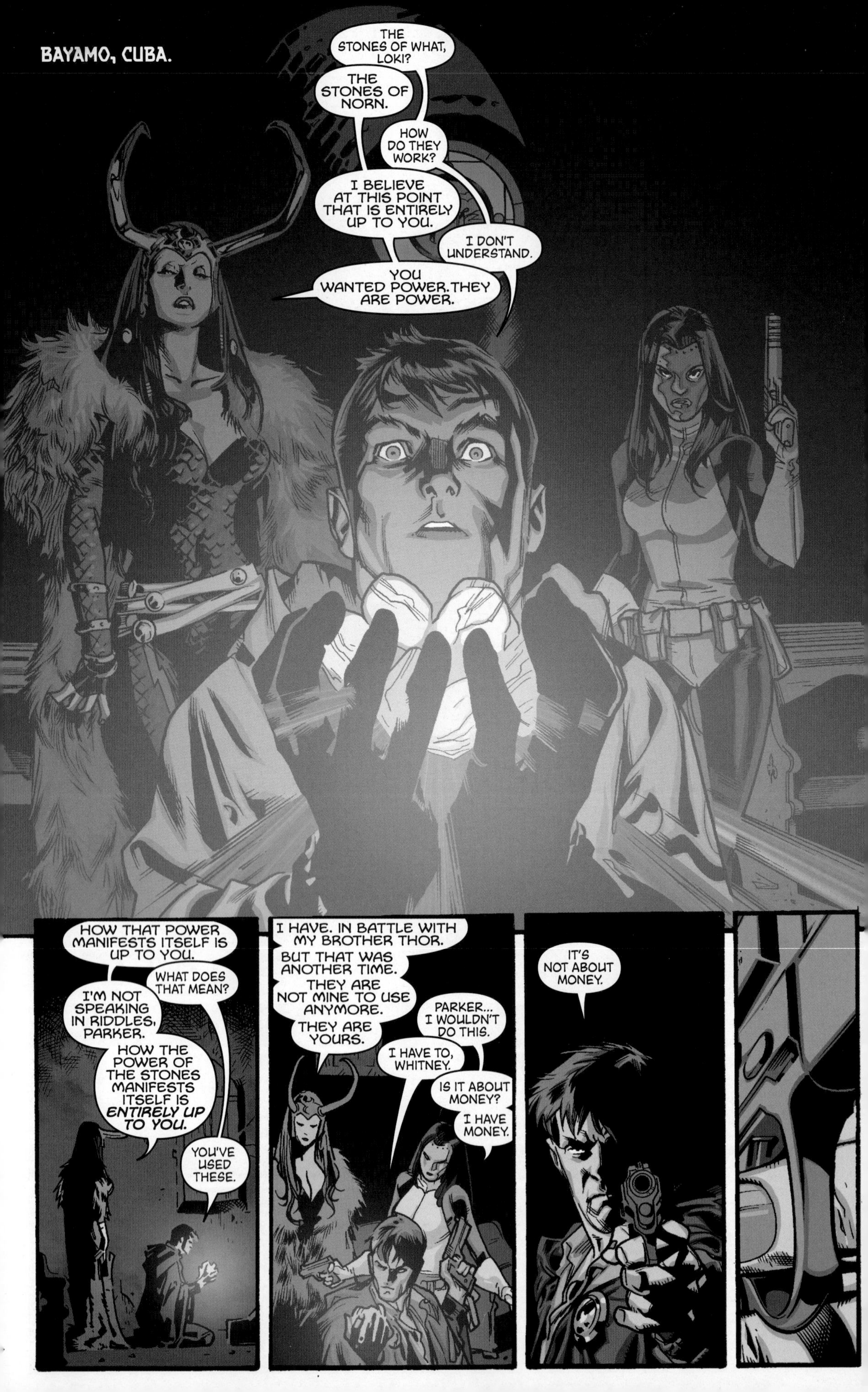
BAYAMO, CUBA.
THE STONES OF WHAT, LOKI?
THE STONES OF NORN.
HOW DO THEY WORK?
I BELIEVE AT THIS POINT THAT IS ENTIRELY UP TO YOU.
I DON'T UNDERSTAND.
YOU WANTED POWER. THEY ARE POWER.
HOW THAT POWER MANIFESTS ITSELF IS UP TO YOU.
WHAT DOES THAT MEAN?
I'M NOT SPEAKING IN RIDDLES, PARKER.
HOW THE POWER OF THE STONES MANIFESTS ITSELF IS *ENTIRELY UP TO YOU.*
YOU'VE USED THESE.
I HAVE. IN BATTLE WITH MY BROTHER THOR.
BUT THAT WAS ANOTHER TIME.
THEY ARE NOT MINE TO USE ANYMORE.
THEY ARE YOURS.
PARKER... I WOULDN'T DO THIS.
I HAVE TO, WHITNEY.
IS IT ABOUT MONEY?
I HAVE MONEY.
IT'S NOT ABOUT MONEY.

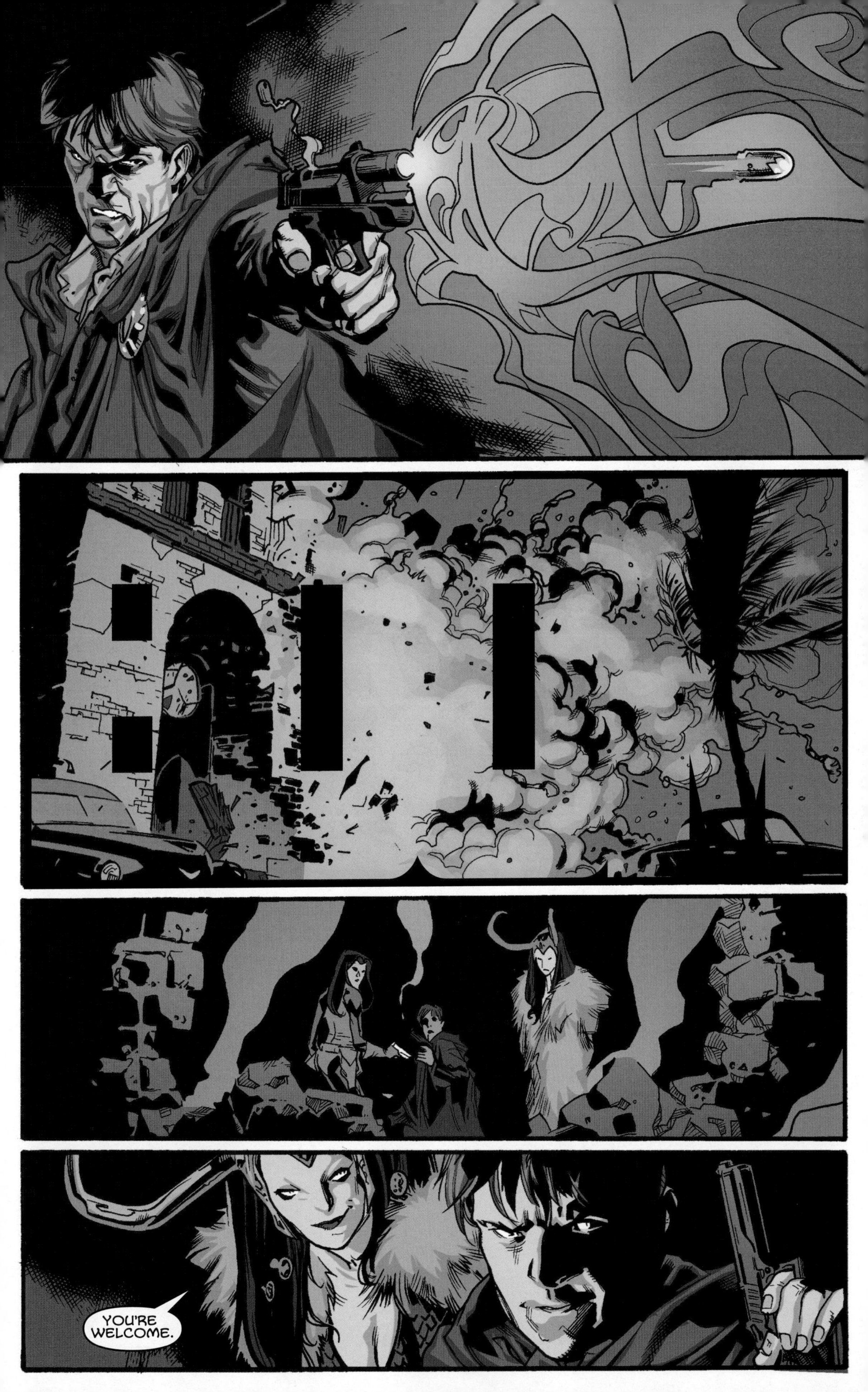
YOU'RE WELCOME.

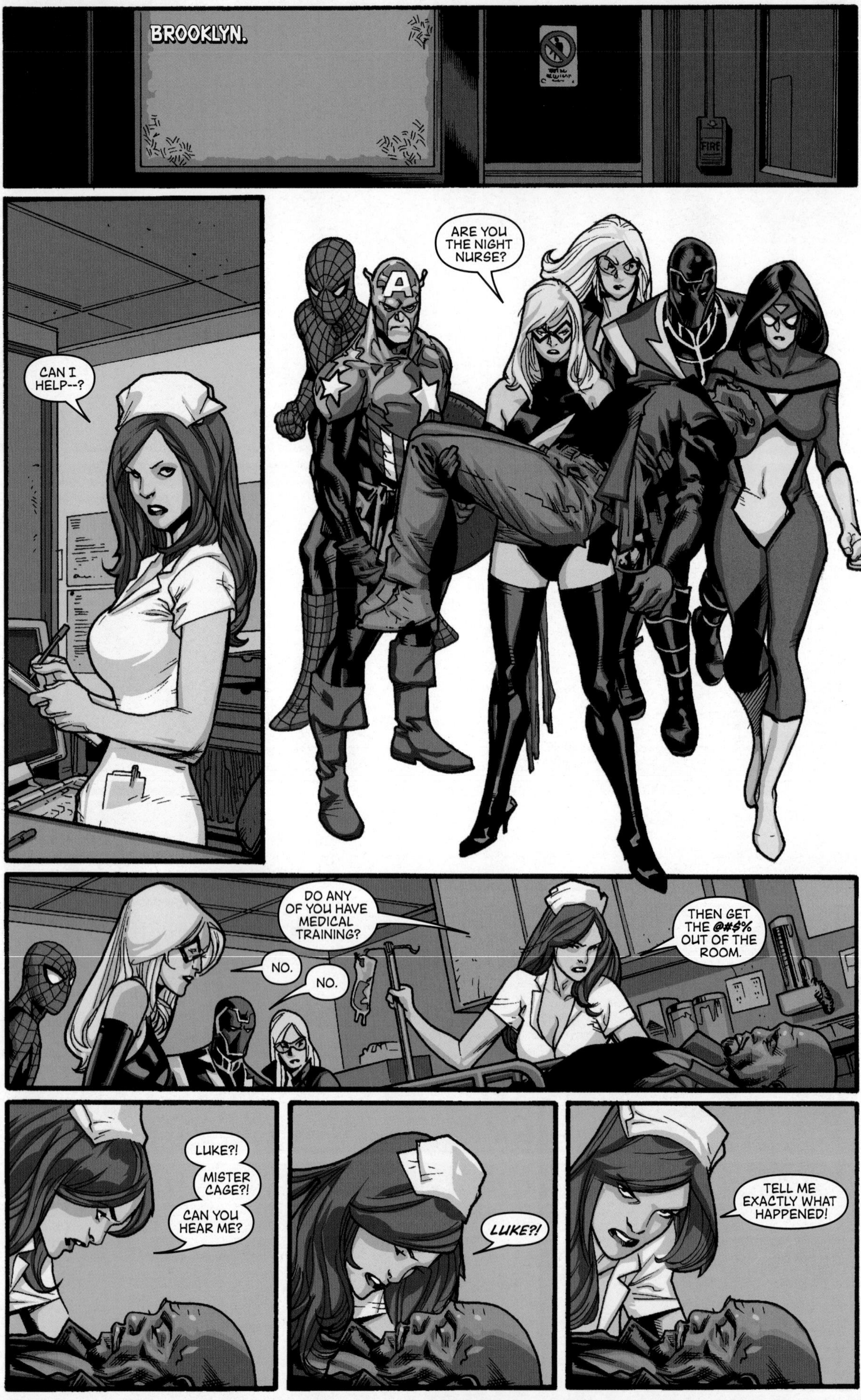
BROOKLYN.
CAN I HELP--?
ARE YOU THE NIGHT NURSE?
DO ANY OF YOU HAVE MEDICAL TRAINING?
NO.
NO.
THEN GET THE @#$% OUT OF THE ROOM.
LUKE?!
MISTER CAGE?!
CAN YOU HEAR ME?
LUKE?!
TELL ME EXACTLY WHAT HAPPENED!

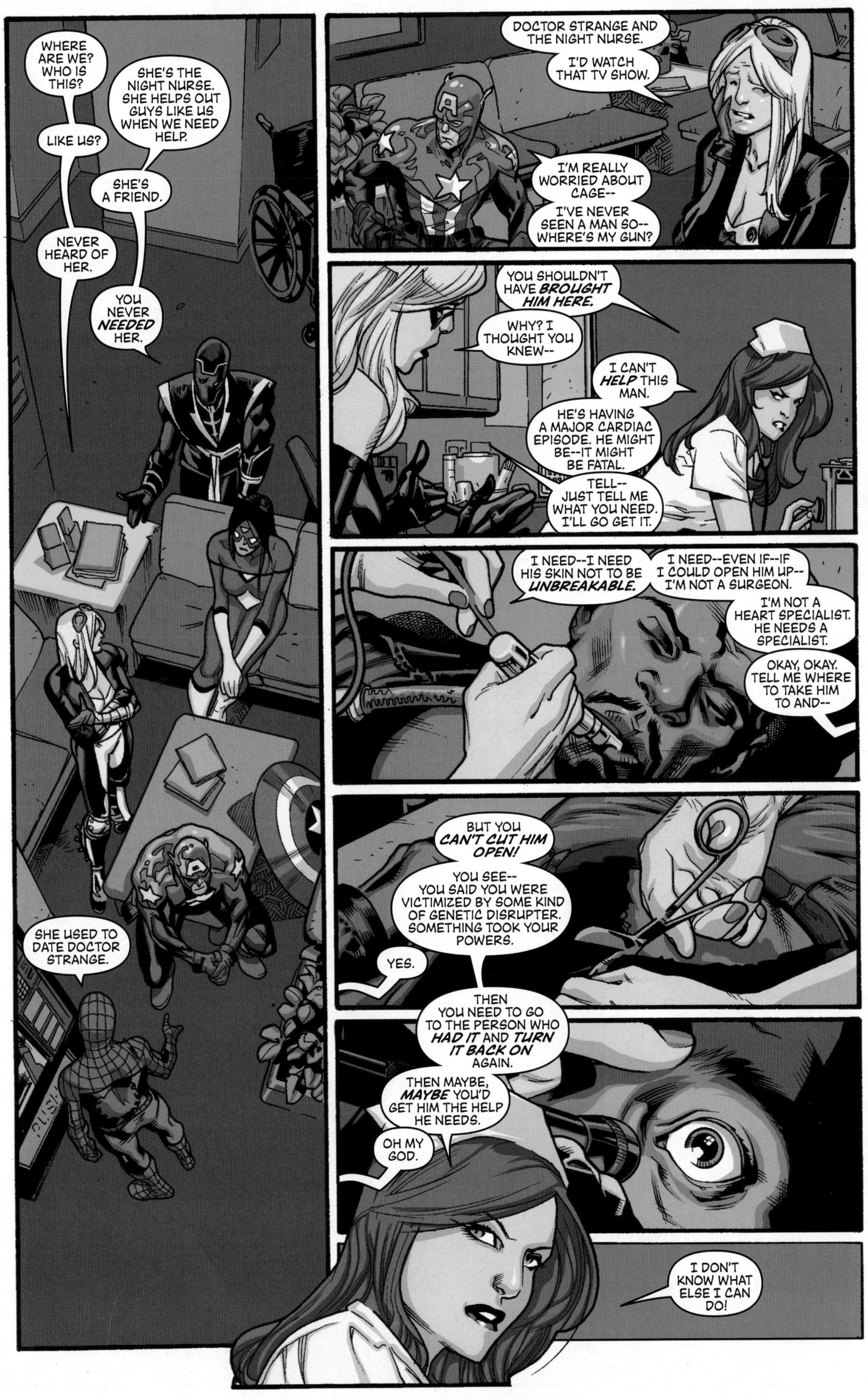
WHERE ARE WE? WHO IS THIS?
SHE'S THE NIGHT NURSE. SHE HELPS OUT GUYS LIKE US WHEN WE NEED HELP.
LIKE US?
SHE'S A FRIEND.
NEVER HEARD OF HER.
YOU NEVER NEEDED HER.
SHE USED TO DATE DOCTOR STRANGE.
DOCTOR STRANGE AND THE NIGHT NURSE.
I'D WATCH THAT TV SHOW.
I'M REALLY WORRIED ABOUT CAGE--
I'VE NEVER SEEN A MAN SO-- WHERE'S MY GUN?
YOU SHOULDN'T HAVE BROUGHT HIM HERE.
WHY? I THOUGHT YOU KNEW--
I CAN'T HELP THIS MAN.
HE'S HAVING A MAJOR CARDIAC EPISODE. HE MIGHT BE--IT MIGHT BE FATAL.
TELL-- JUST TELL ME WHAT YOU NEED. I'LL GO GET IT.
I NEED--I NEED HIS SKIN NOT TO BE UNBREAKABLE.
I NEED--EVEN IF--IF I COULD OPEN HIM UP-- I'M NOT A SURGEON.
I'M NOT A HEART SPECIALIST. HE NEEDS A SPECIALIST.
OKAY, OKAY. TELL ME WHERE TO TAKE HIM TO AND--
BUT YOU CAN'T CUT HIM OPEN!
YOU SEE-- YOU SAID YOU WERE VICTIMIZED BY SOME KIND OF GENETIC DISRUPTER. SOMETHING TOOK YOUR POWERS.
YES.
THEN YOU NEED TO GO TO THE PERSON WHO HAD IT AND TURN IT BACK ON AGAIN.
THEN MAYBE, MAYBE YOU'D GET HIM THE HELP HE NEEDS.
OH MY GOD.
I DON'T KNOW WHAT ELSE I CAN DO!

AVENGERS!

JUST GO IN THERE, OSBORN.

STAND DOWN, KARLA.

WELL, THAT WAS FAST.

I AM NOT GOING TO JAIL.

NO ONE'S GOING TO JAIL.

YOU KNOW WHY I DON'T WANT TO GO TO JAIL? BECAUSE I DIDN'T DO ANYTHING ILLEGAL.

NO ONE'S GOING TO JAIL.

GUYS... WITHOUT OSBORN... CAGE IS GOING TO DIE.

THEN WE GIVE UP.

NO.

WE HAVE TO.

HE'LL DESTROY YOU, MAN.

HE'LL RUIN YOU AND EVERYONE YOU LOVE.

WELL, YEAH...

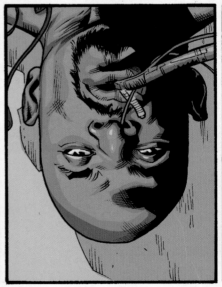

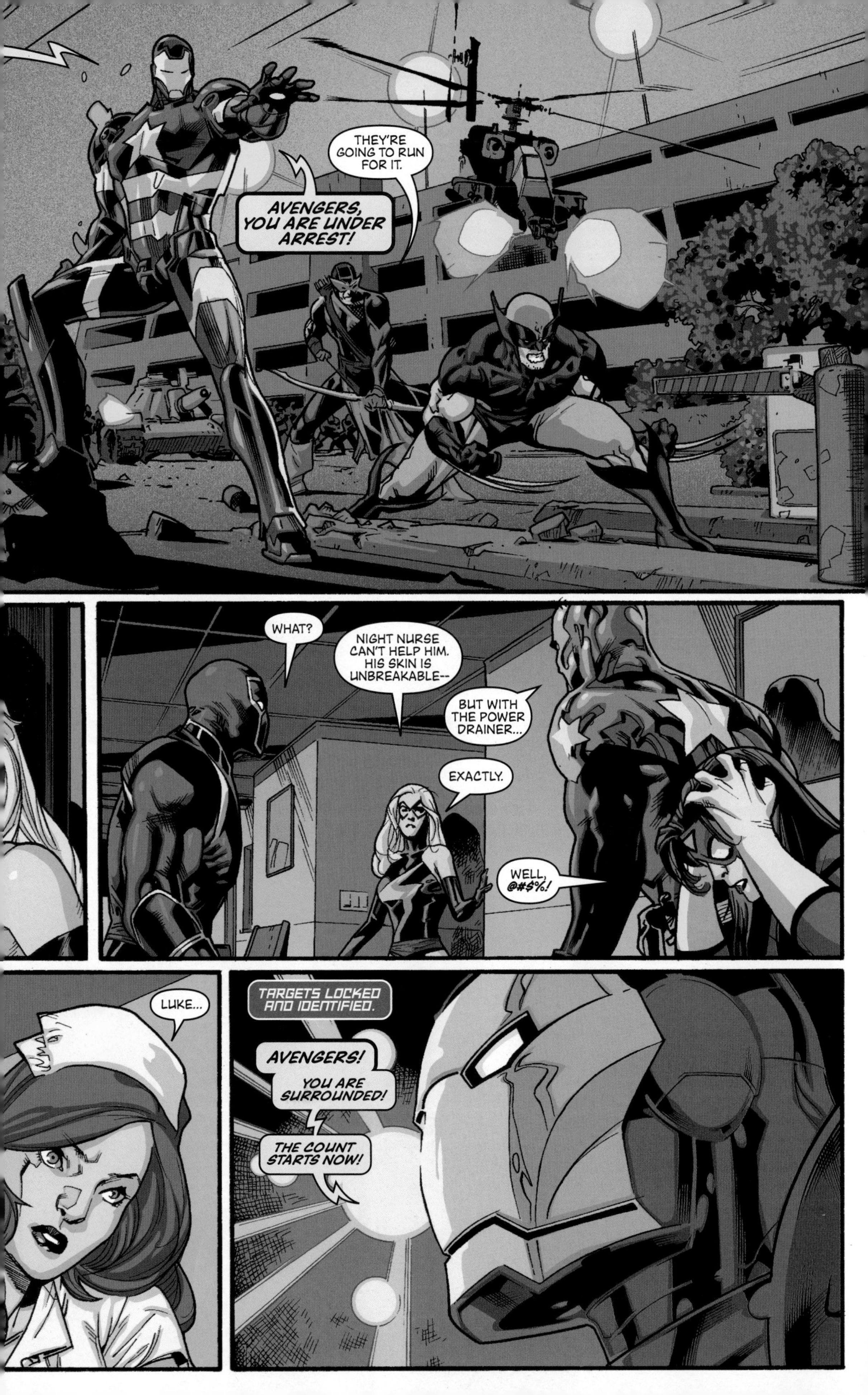
THEY'RE GOING TO RUN FOR IT.
AVENGERS, YOU ARE UNDER ARREST!
WHAT?
NIGHT NURSE CAN'T HELP HIM. HIS SKIN IS UNBREAKABLE--
BUT WITH THE POWER DRAINER...
EXACTLY.
WELL, @#$%!
LUKE...
TARGETS LOCKED AND IDENTIFIED.
AVENGERS!
YOU ARE SURROUNDED!
THE COUNT STARTS NOW!

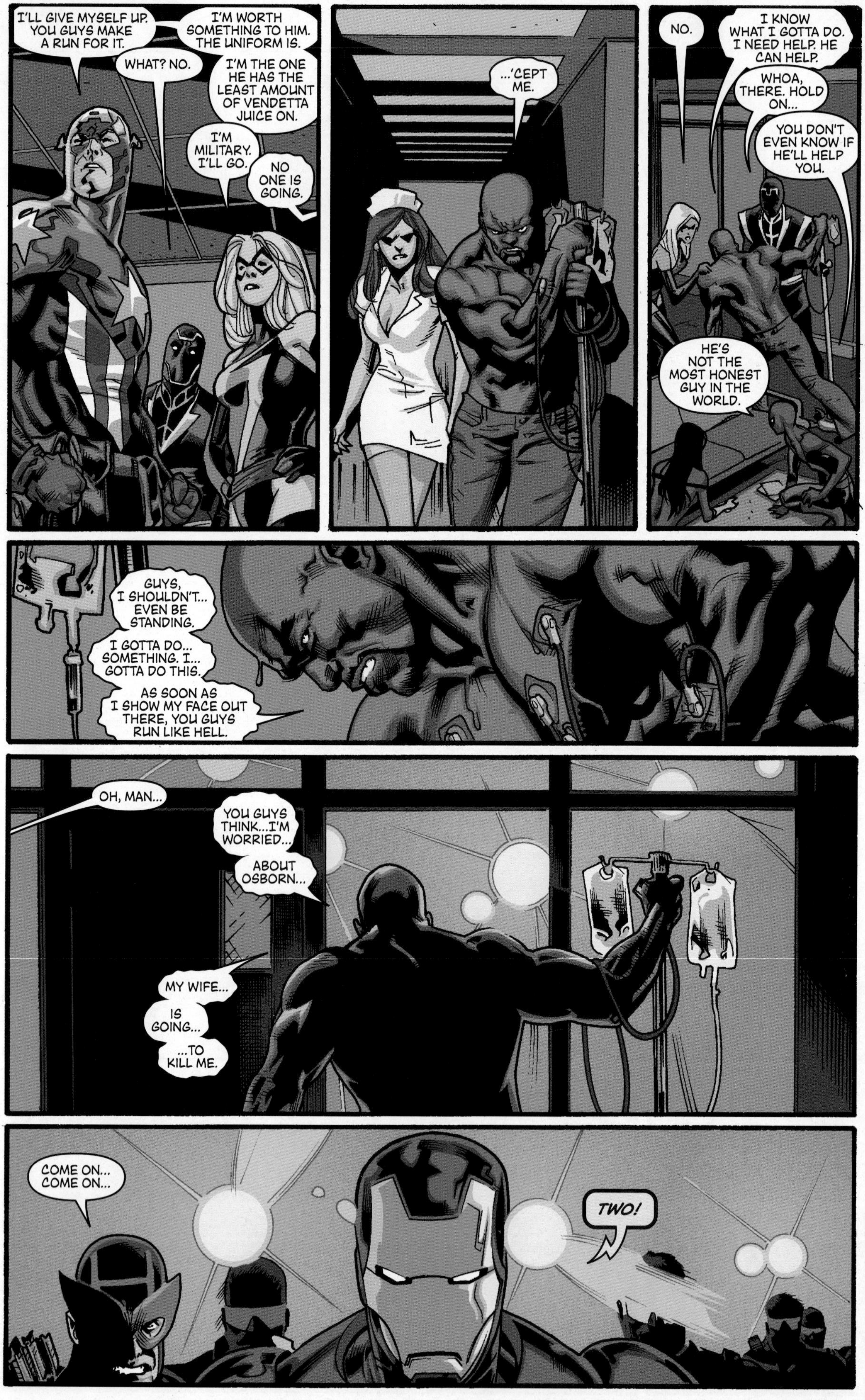
I'LL GIVE MYSELF UP. YOU GUYS MAKE A RUN FOR IT.
I'M WORTH SOMETHING TO HIM. THE UNIFORM IS.
WHAT? NO.
I'M THE ONE HE HAS THE LEAST AMOUNT OF VENDETTA JUICE ON.
I'M MILITARY. I'LL GO.
NO ONE IS GOING.
...'CEPT ME.
NO.
I KNOW WHAT I GOTTA DO. I NEED HELP. HE CAN HELP.
WHOA, THERE. HOLD ON...
YOU DON'T EVEN KNOW IF HE'LL HELP YOU.
HE'S NOT THE MOST HONEST GUY IN THE WORLD.
GUYS, I SHOULDN'T... EVEN BE STANDING.
I GOTTA DO... SOMETHING. I... GOTTA DO THIS.
AS SOON AS I SHOW MY FACE OUT THERE, YOU GUYS RUN LIKE HELL.
OH, MAN...
YOU GUYS THINK...I'M WORRIED...
ABOUT OSBORN...
MY WIFE...
IS GOING...
...TO KILL ME.
COME ON... COME ON...
TWO!

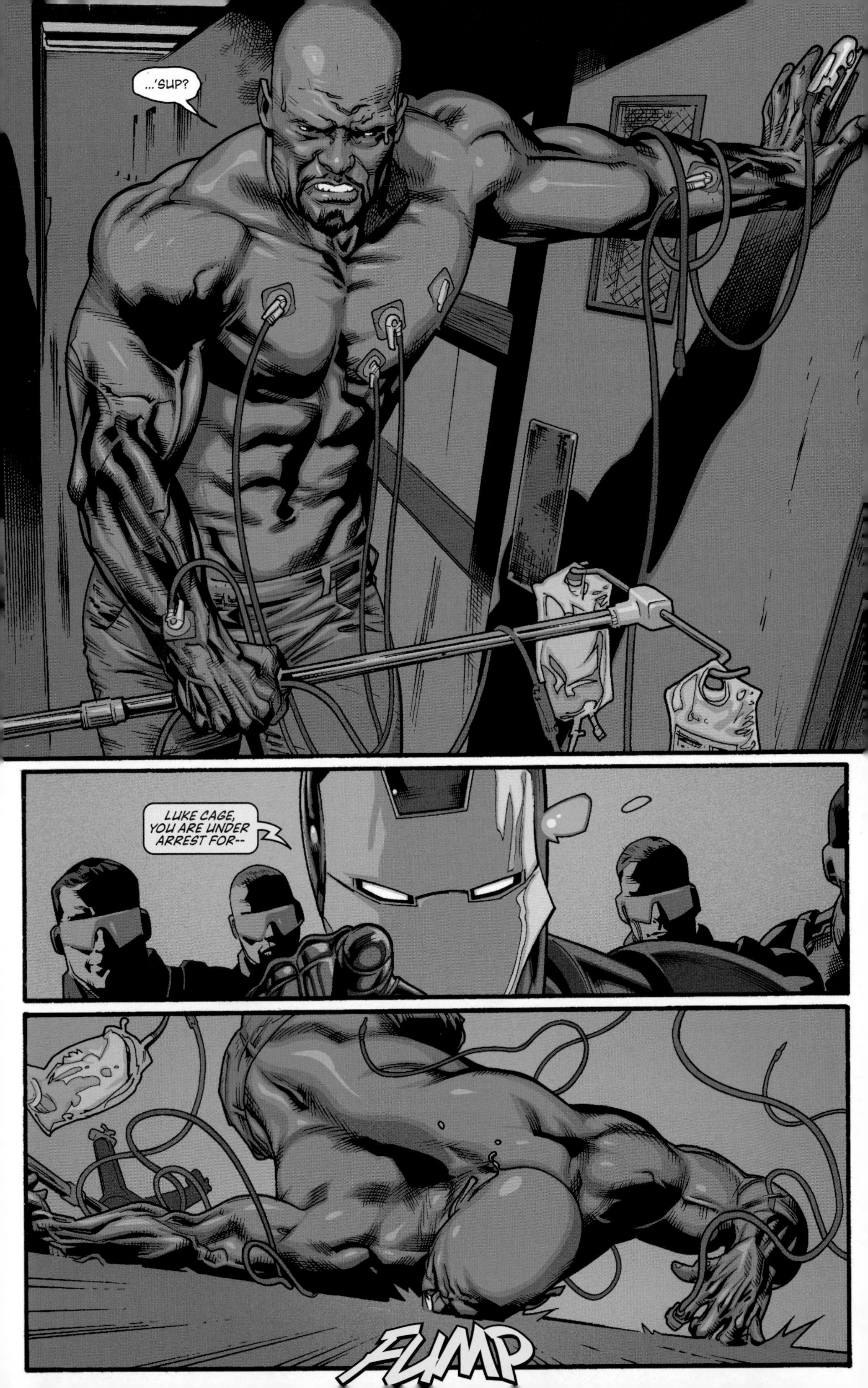
...'SUP?
LUKE CAGE, YOU ARE UNDER ARREST FOR--
FUMP

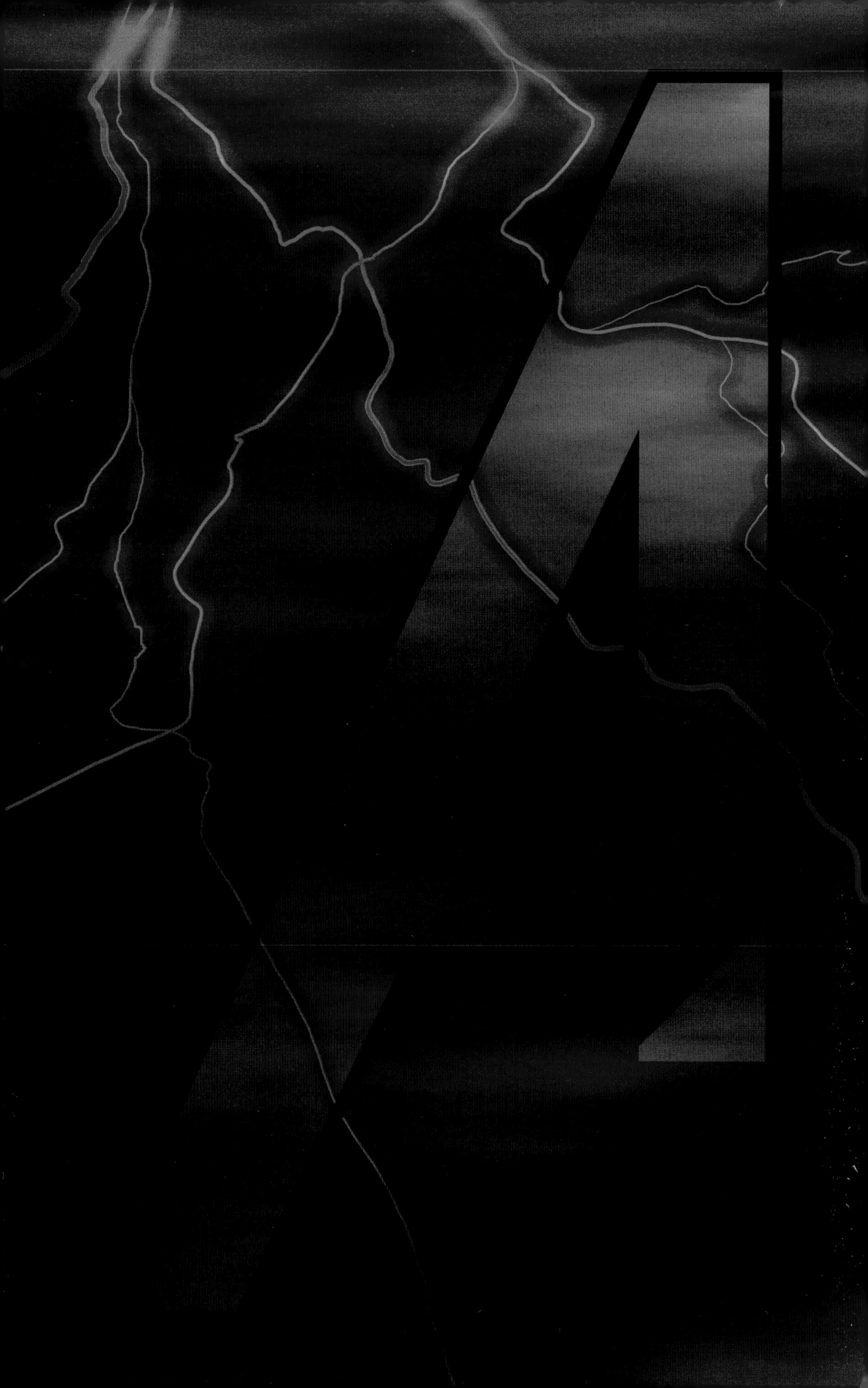
4

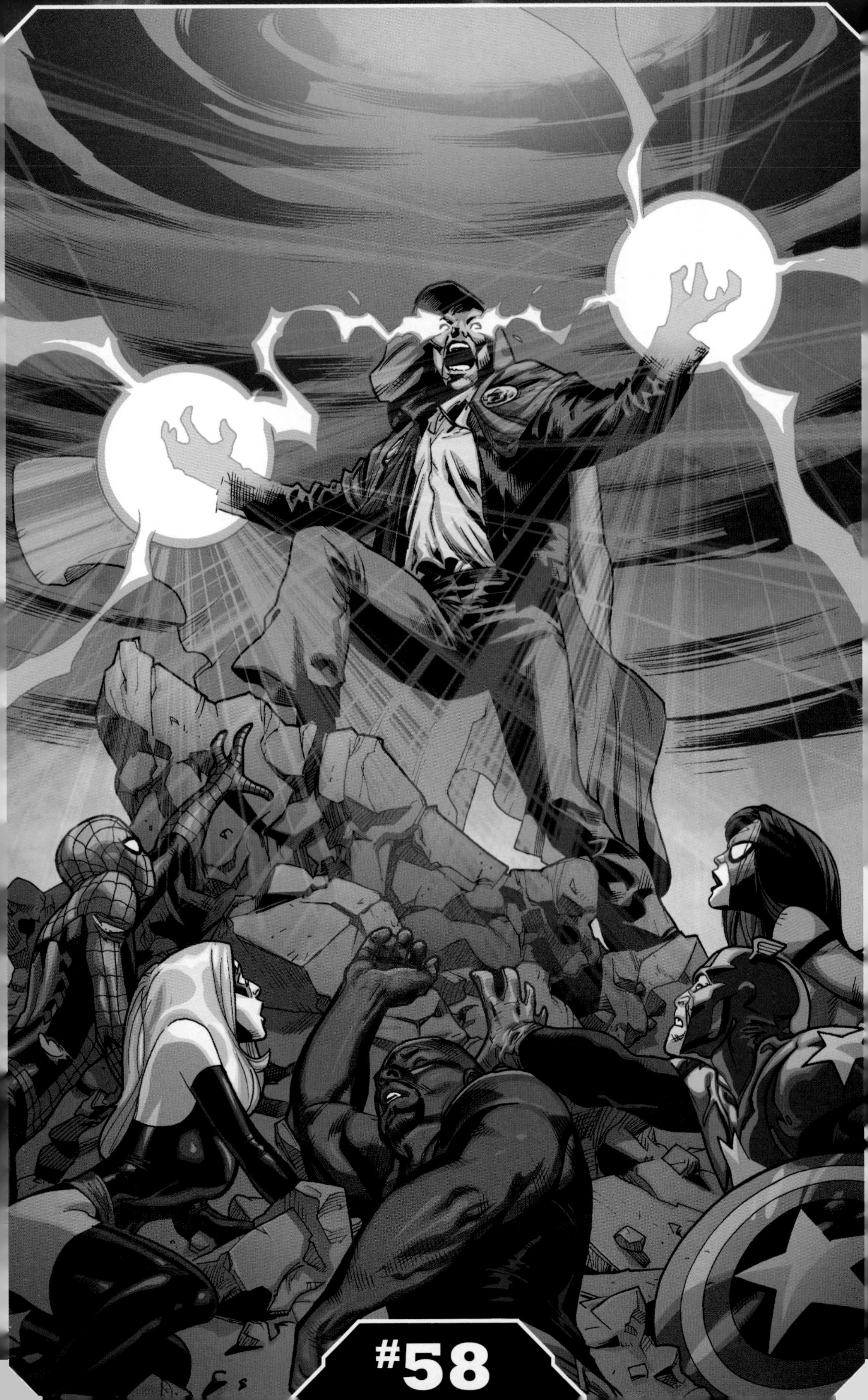
#58

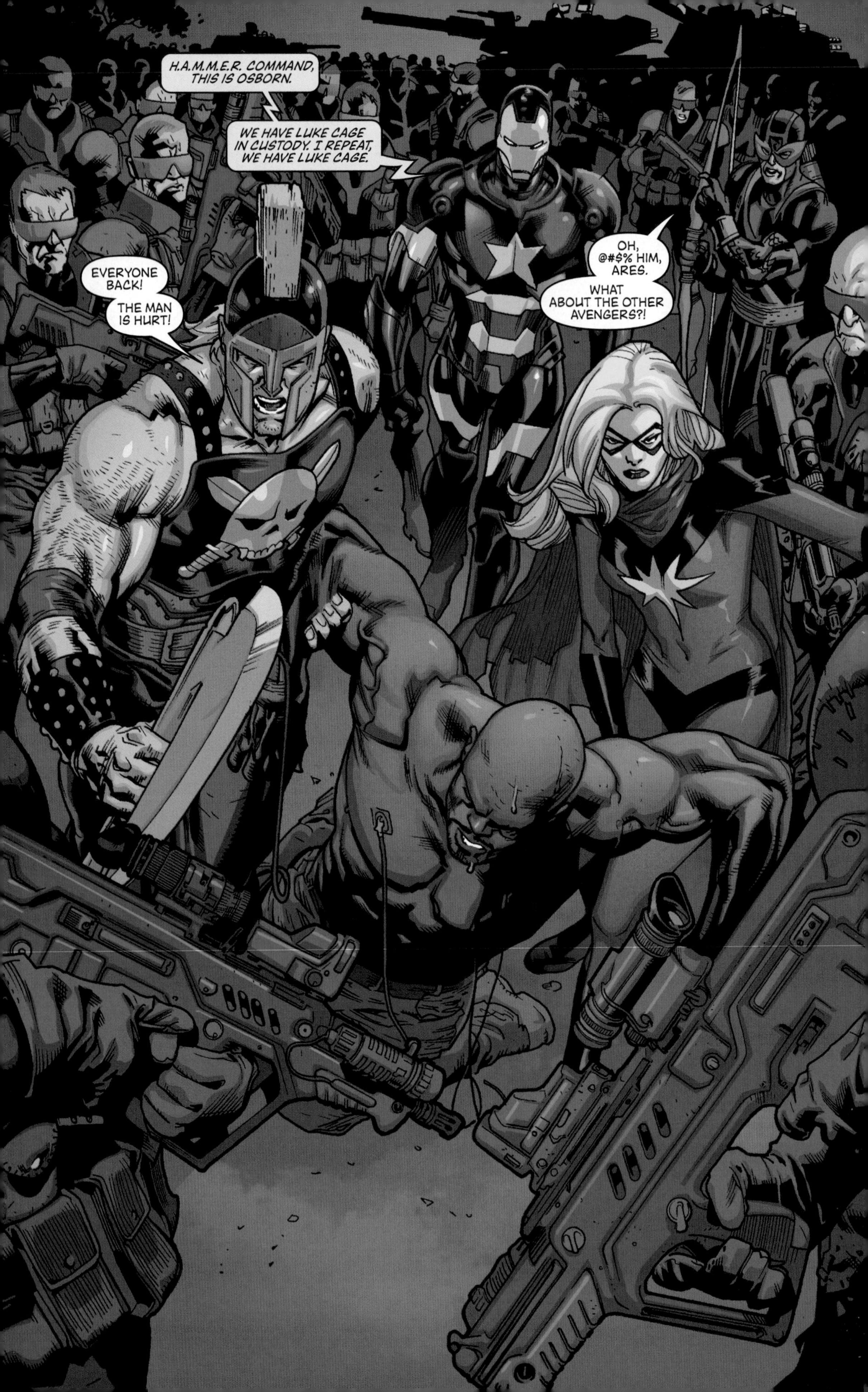

H.A.M.M.E.R. COMMAND, THIS IS OSBORN.
WE HAVE LUKE CAGE IN CUSTODY. I REPEAT, WE HAVE LUKE CAGE.
EVERYONE BACK!
THE MAN IS HURT!
OH, @#$% HIM, ARES.
WHAT ABOUT THE OTHER AVENGERS?!

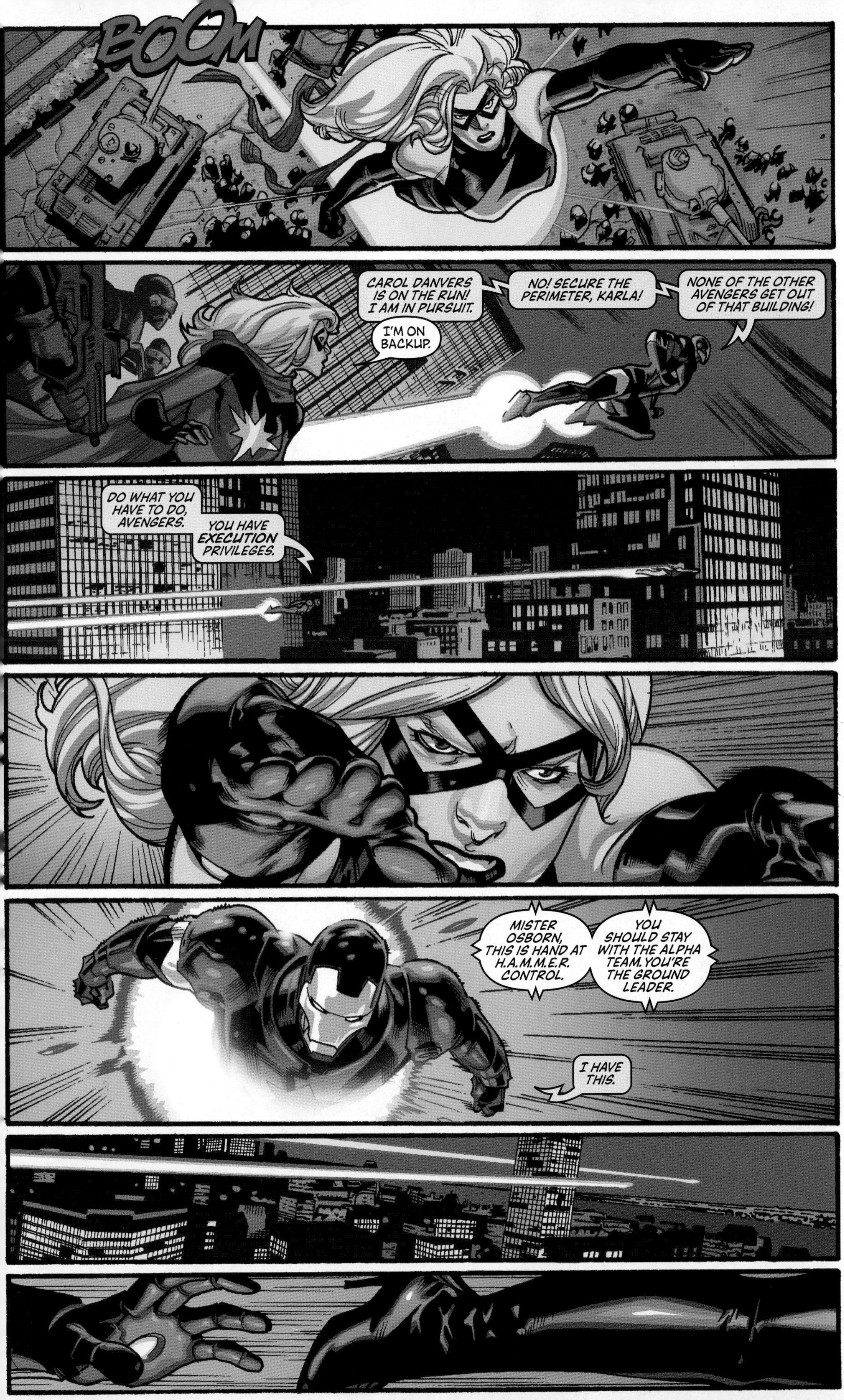
BOOM
CAROL DANVERS IS ON THE RUN! I AM IN PURSUIT.
I'M ON BACKUP.
NO! SECURE THE PERIMETER, KARLA!
NONE OF THE OTHER AVENGERS GET OUT OF THAT BUILDING!
DO WHAT YOU HAVE TO DO, AVENGERS.
YOU HAVE EXECUTION PRIVILEGES.
MISTER OSBORN, THIS IS HAND AT H.A.M.M.E.R. CONTROL.
YOU SHOULD STAY WITH THE ALPHA TEAM. YOU'RE THE GROUND LEADER.
I HAVE THIS.

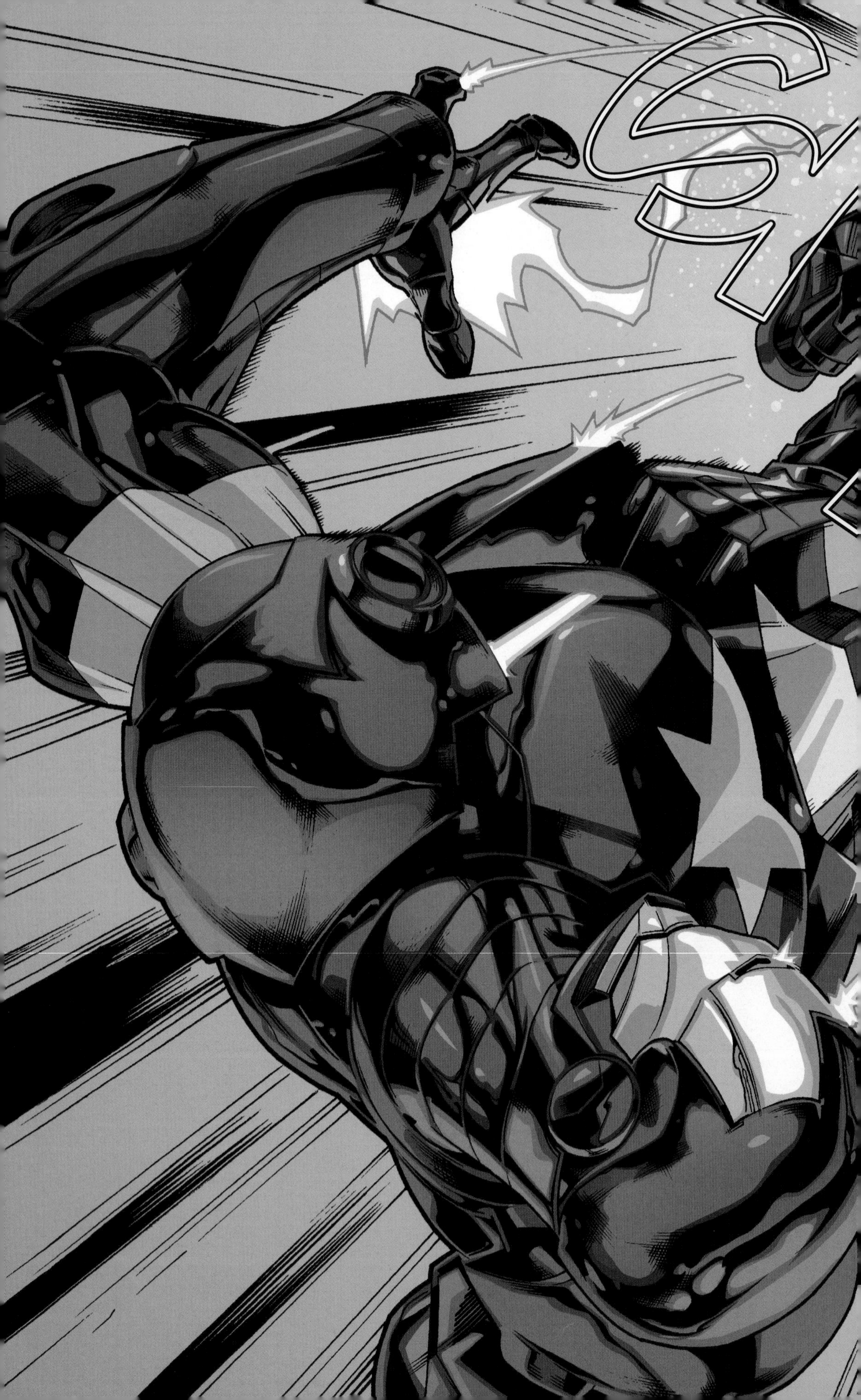

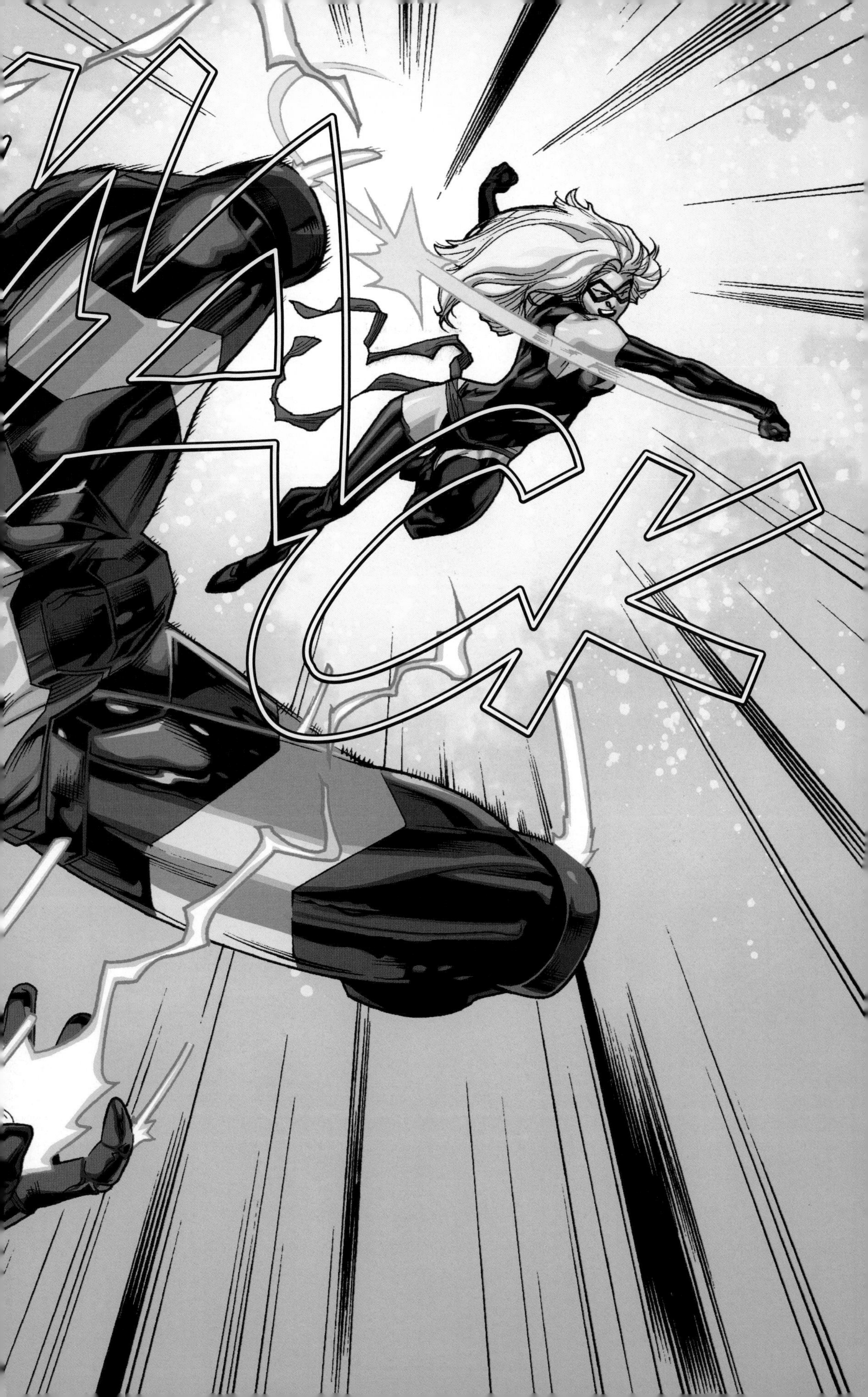
WHACK

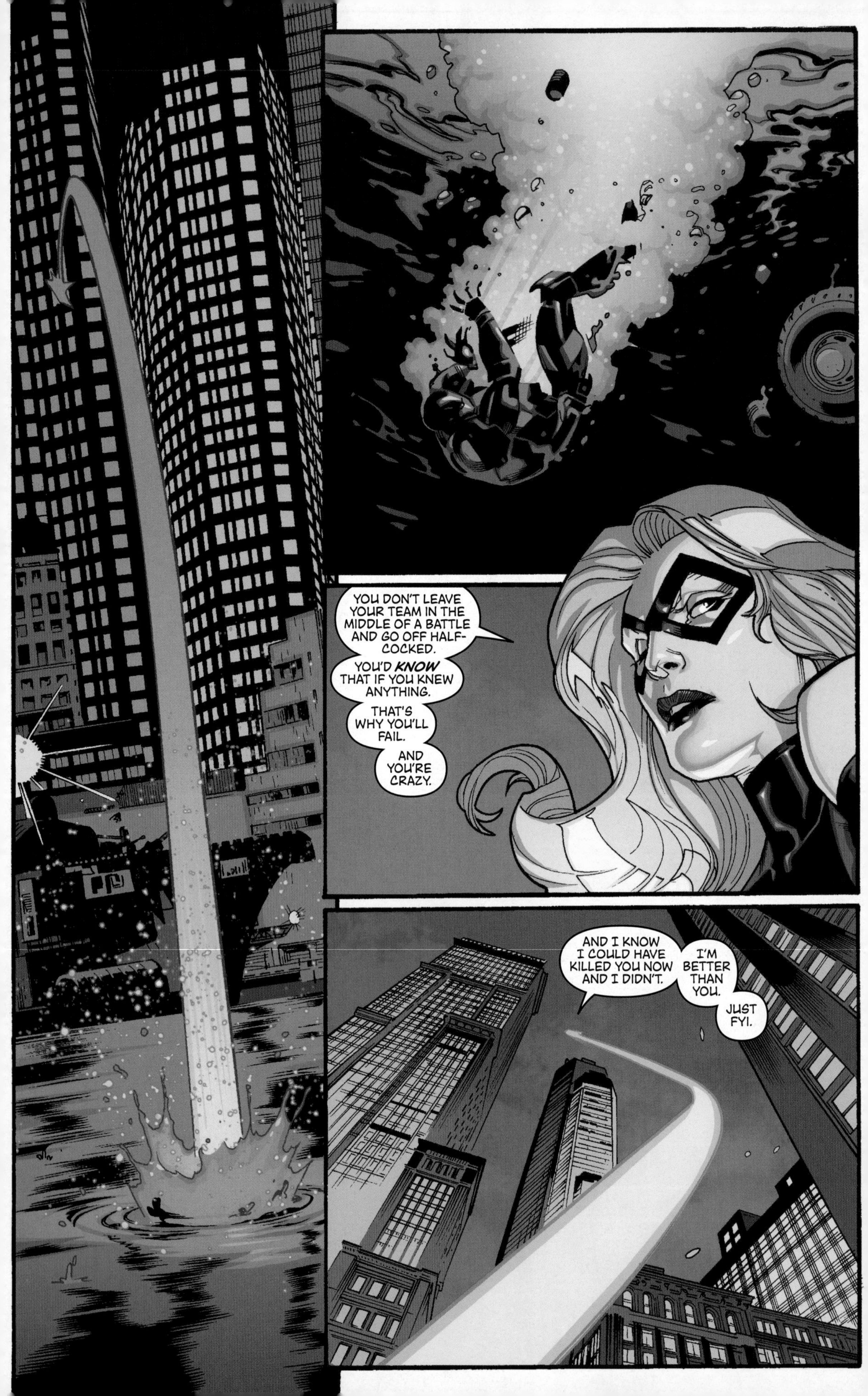
YOU DON'T LEAVE YOUR TEAM IN THE MIDDLE OF A BATTLE AND GO OFF HALF-COCKED.
YOU'D KNOW THAT IF YOU KNEW ANYTHING.
THAT'S WHY YOU'LL FAIL.
AND YOU'RE CRAZY.
AND I KNOW I COULD HAVE KILLED YOU NOW AND I DIDN'T.
I'M BETTER THAN YOU.
JUST FYI.

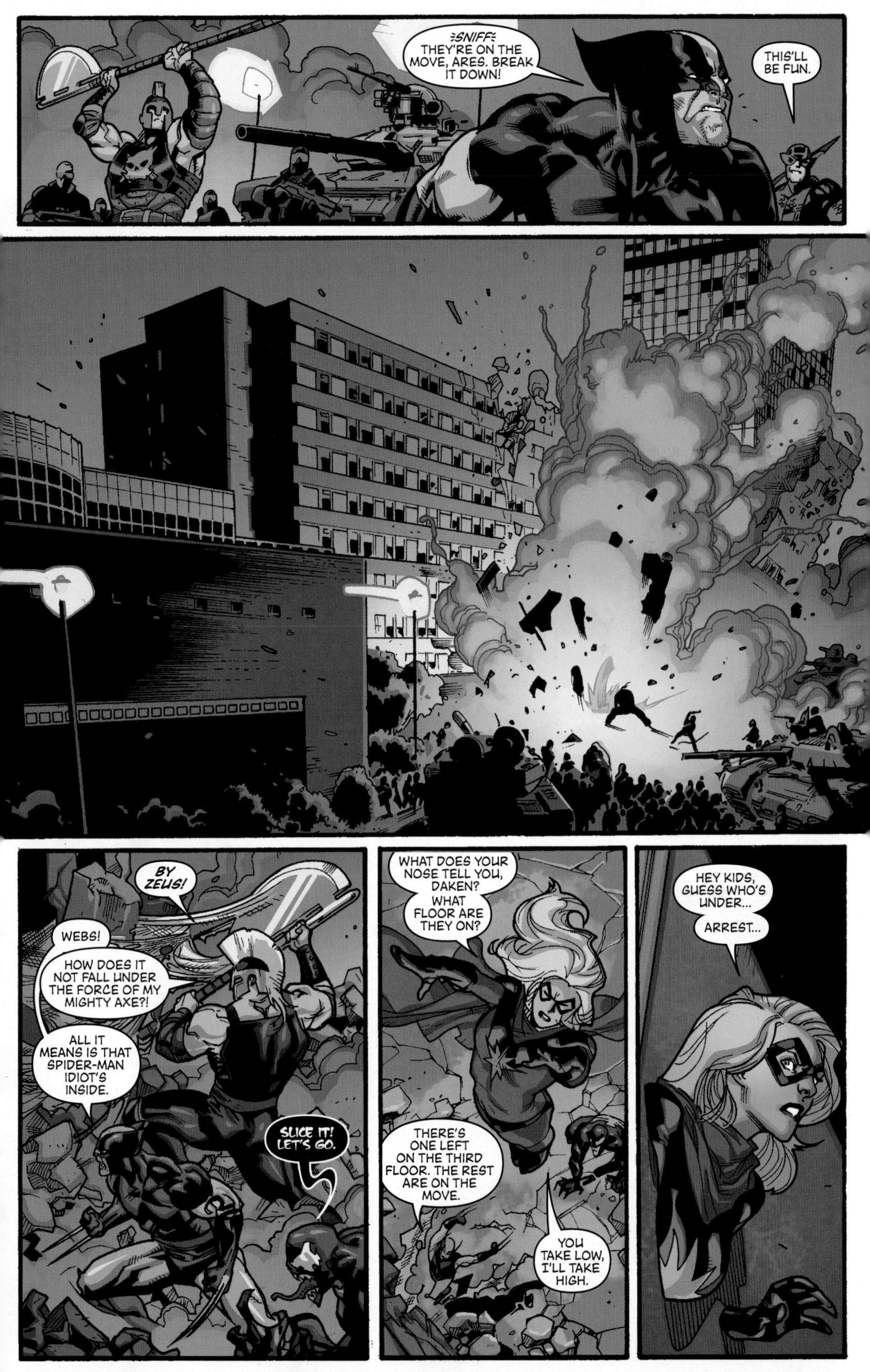

SNIFF
THEY'RE ON THE MOVE, ARES. BREAK IT DOWN!
THIS'LL BE FUN.
BY ZEUS!
WEBS!
HOW DOES IT NOT FALL UNDER THE FORCE OF MY MIGHTY AXE?!
ALL IT MEANS IS THAT SPIDER-MAN IDIOT'S INSIDE.
SLICE IT! LET'S GO.
WHAT DOES YOUR NOSE TELL YOU, DAKEN?
WHAT FLOOR ARE THEY ON?
THERE'S ONE LEFT ON THE THIRD FLOOR. THE REST ARE ON THE MOVE.
YOU TAKE LOW, I'LL TAKE HIGH.
HEY KIDS, GUESS WHO'S UNDER...
ARREST...

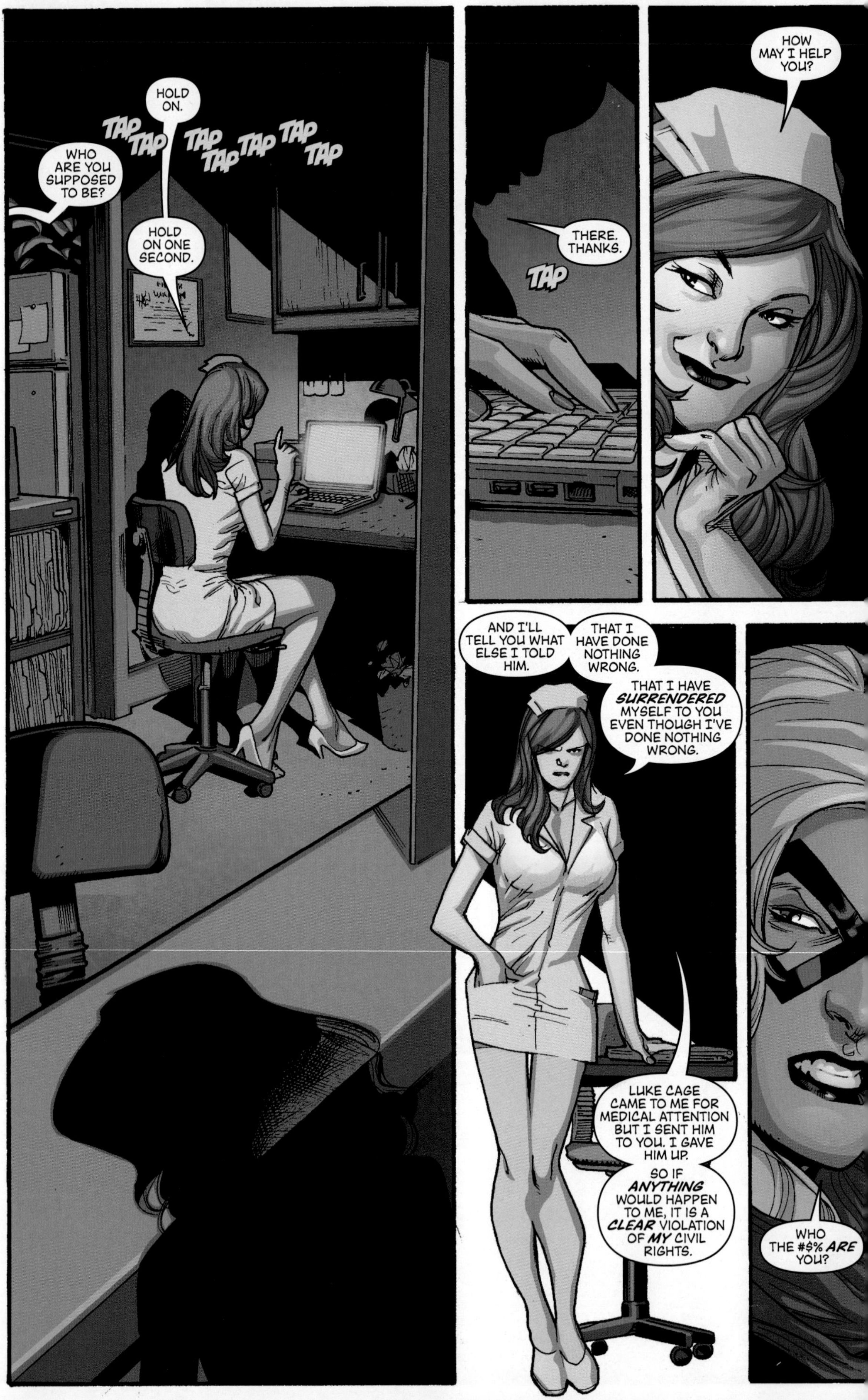
HOLD ON.
TAP TAP TAP TAP TAP TAP TAP
WHO ARE YOU SUPPOSED TO BE?
HOLD ON ONE SECOND.
THERE. THANKS.
TAP
HOW MAY I HELP YOU?
AND I'LL TELL YOU WHAT ELSE I TOLD HIM.
THAT I HAVE DONE NOTHING WRONG.
THAT I HAVE *SURRENDERED* MYSELF TO YOU EVEN THOUGH I'VE DONE NOTHING WRONG.
LUKE CAGE CAME TO ME FOR MEDICAL ATTENTION BUT I SENT HIM TO YOU. I GAVE HIM UP.
SO IF *ANYTHING* WOULD HAPPEN TO ME, IT IS A *CLEAR* VIOLATION OF *MY* CIVIL RIGHTS.
WHO THE #$% *ARE* YOU?

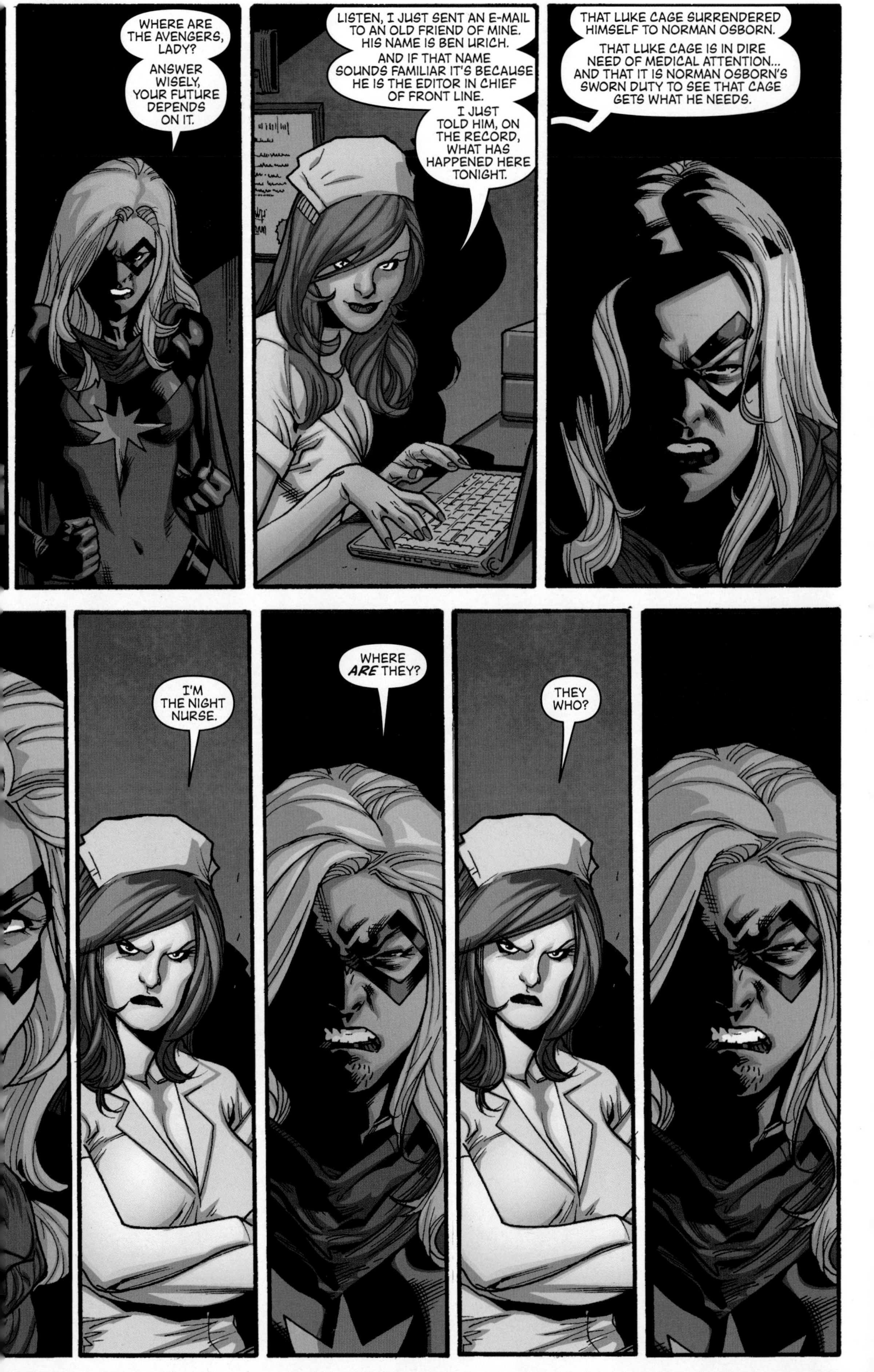

WHERE ARE THE AVENGERS, LADY?
ANSWER WISELY, YOUR FUTURE DEPENDS ON IT.
LISTEN, I JUST SENT AN E-MAIL TO AN OLD FRIEND OF MINE. HIS NAME IS BEN URICH.
AND IF THAT NAME SOUNDS FAMILIAR IT'S BECAUSE HE IS THE EDITOR IN CHIEF OF FRONT LINE.
I JUST TOLD HIM, ON THE RECORD, WHAT HAS HAPPENED HERE TONIGHT.
THAT LUKE CAGE SURRENDERED HIMSELF TO NORMAN OSBORN.
THAT LUKE CAGE IS IN DIRE NEED OF MEDICAL ATTENTION... AND THAT IT IS NORMAN OSBORN'S SWORN DUTY TO SEE THAT CAGE GETS WHAT HE NEEDS.
I'M THE NIGHT NURSE.
WHERE *ARE* THEY?
THEY WHO?

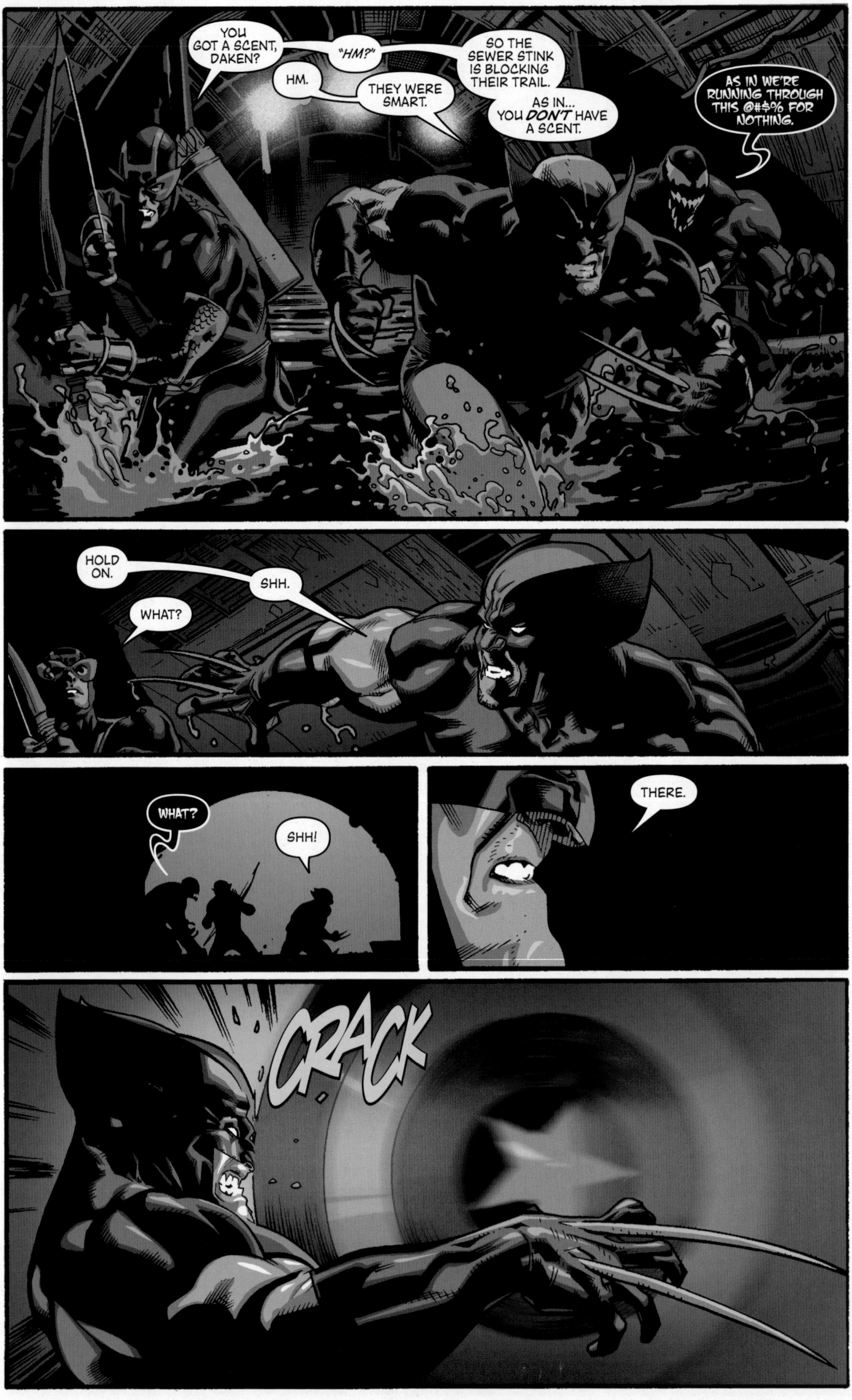
YOU GOT A SCENT, DAKEN?
"HM?"
HM.
THEY WERE SMART.
SO THE SEWER STINK IS BLOCKING THEIR TRAIL.
AS IN... YOU DON'T HAVE A SCENT.
AS IN WE'RE RUNNING THROUGH THIS @#$% FOR NOTHING.
HOLD ON.
SHH.
WHAT?
WHAT?
SHH!
THERE.
CRACK

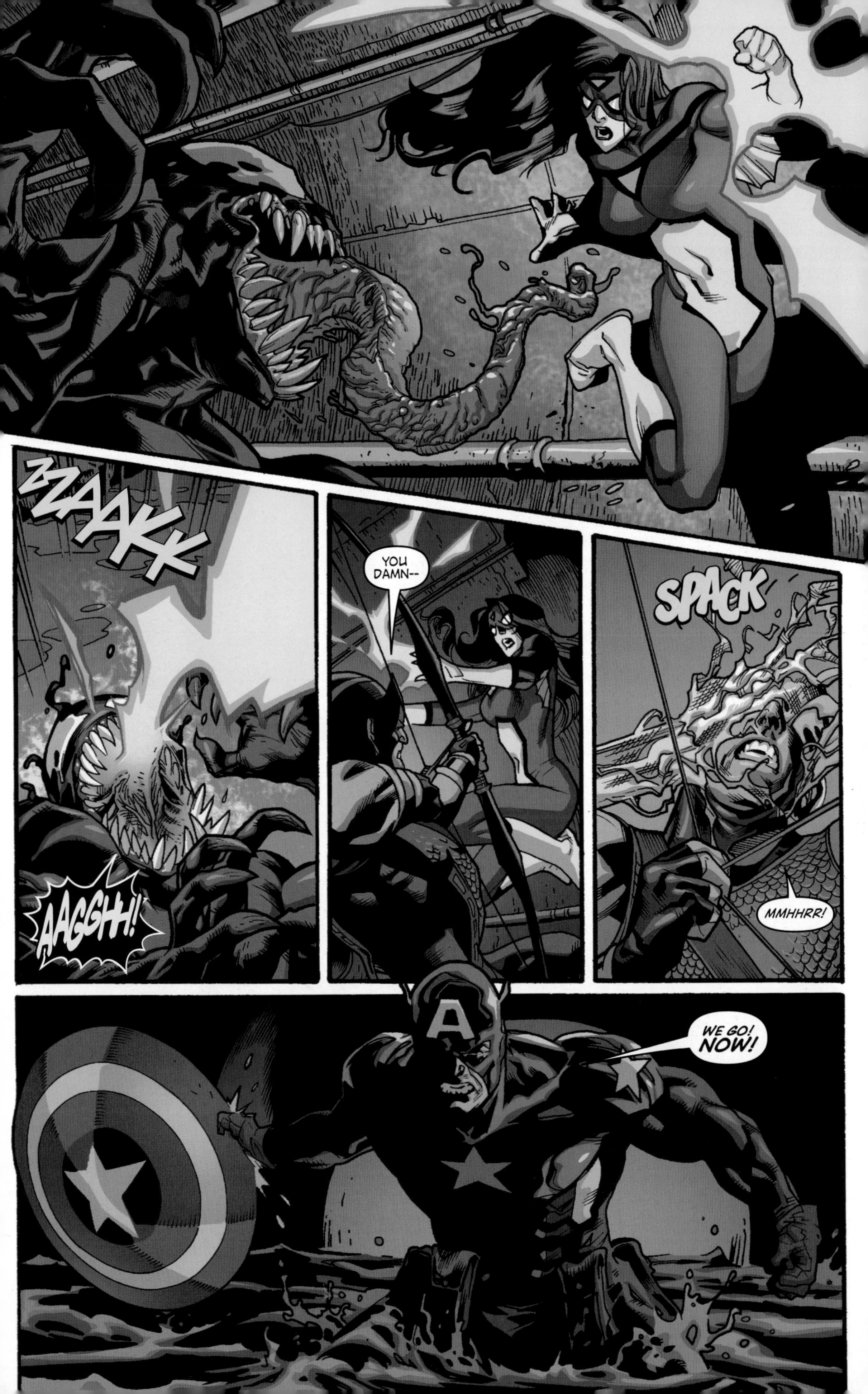
ZZAAKK
AAGGHH!
YOU DAMN--
SPACK
MMHHRR!
WE GO! NOW!

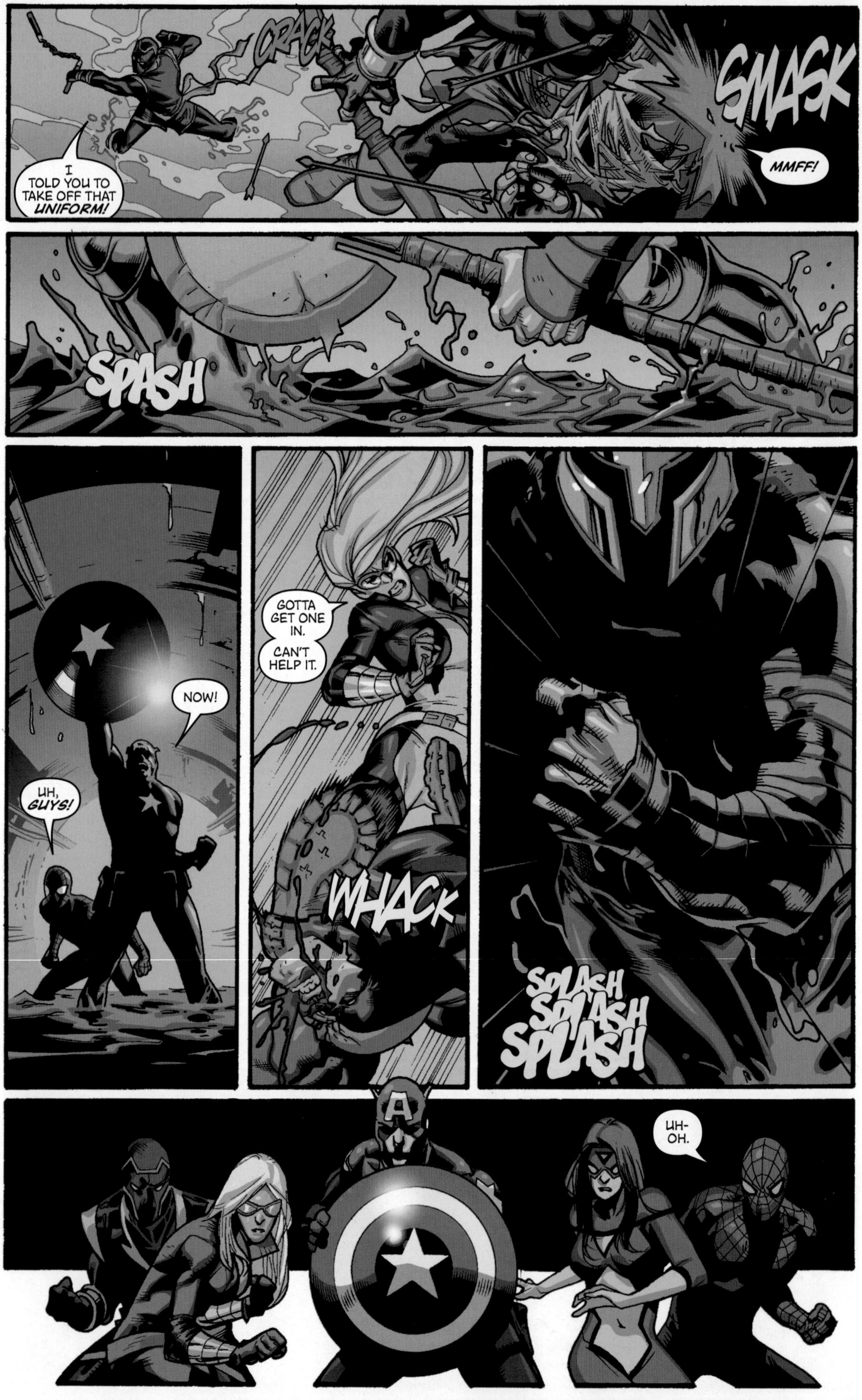
CRACK
SMASK
I TOLD YOU TO TAKE OFF THAT UNIFORM!
MMFF!
SPASH
NOW!
UH, GUYS!
GOTTA GET ONE IN.
CAN'T HELP IT.
WHACK
SPLASH SPLASH SPLASH
UH-OH.

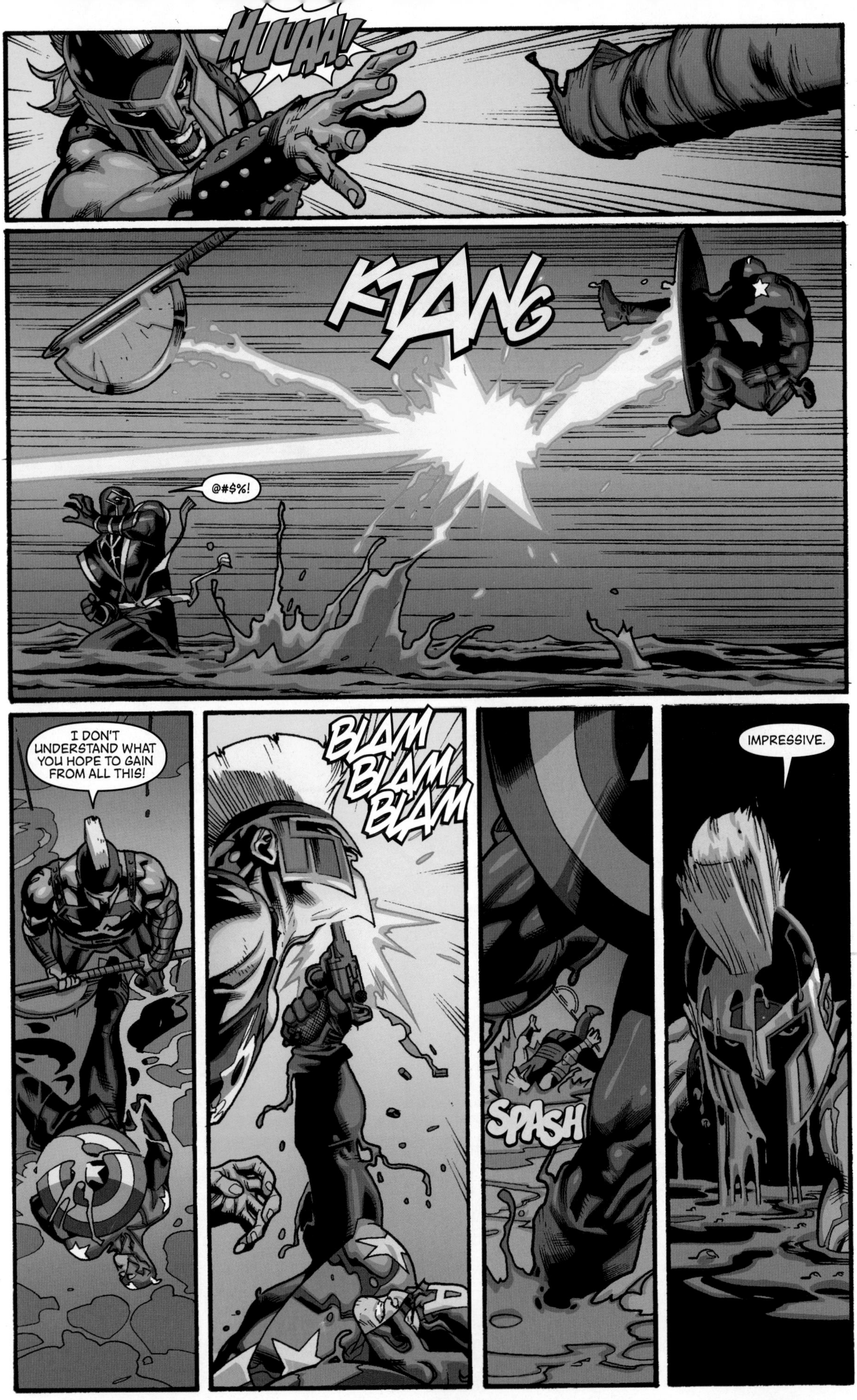
HUUAA!
KTANG
@#$%!
I DON'T UNDERSTAND WHAT YOU HOPE TO GAIN FROM ALL THIS!
BLAM BLAM BLAM
SPASH
IMPRESSIVE.

HOLY @#$%, PARKER? *PARKER?!*

WHERE YOU BEEN, MAN?

WHAT'S GOING ON, JOHN? WHERE IS EVERYBODY?

AS I PREDICTED, THE ENTIRETY OF YOUR MOTLEY CREW DEFECTED THE SECOND YOU TURNED YOUR BACK.

I TOLD YOU--

TELL ME EXACTLY WHAT HAPPENED.

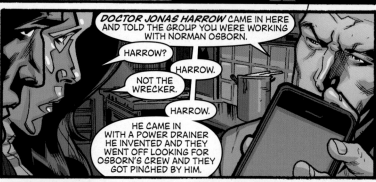

DOCTOR *JONAS HARROW* CAME IN HERE AND TOLD THE GROUP YOU WERE WORKING WITH NORMAN OSBORN.

HARROW?

HARROW.

NOT THE WRECKER.

HARROW.

HE CAME IN WITH A POWER DRAINER HE INVENTED AND THEY WENT OFF LOOKING FOR OSBORN'S CREW AND THEY GOT PINCHED BY HIM.

NORMAN OSBORN ARRESTED MY CREW?

IT'S ALL OVER THE NEWS, MAN. WHERE YOU BEEN?

OUT OF THE COUNTRY.

I THINK MAYBE WE ALL NEED TO GET OUT OF THE COUNTRY.

HARROW.

YOU KNOW, CUZ, YOU LOOK REALLY GOOD.

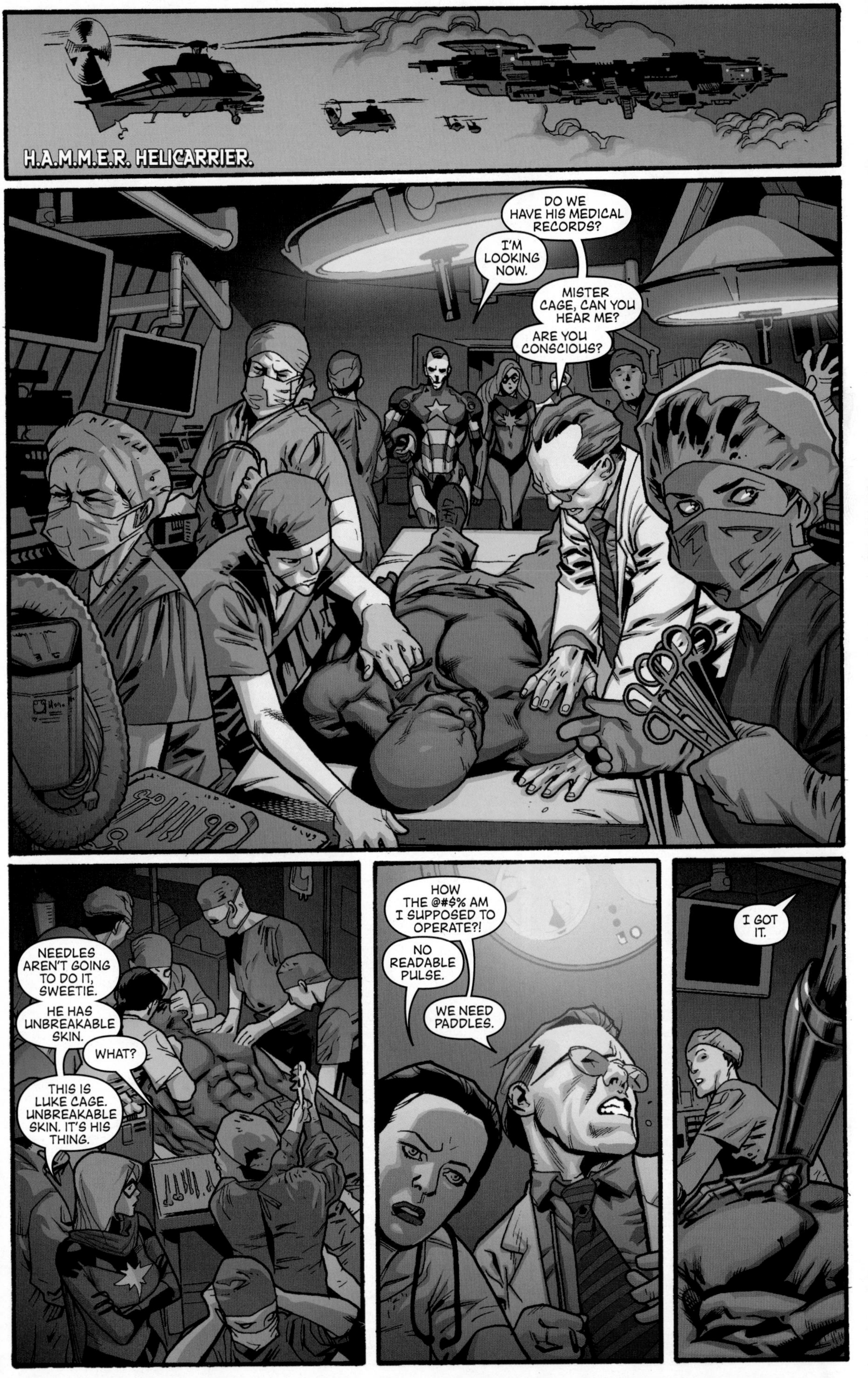
H.A.M.M.E.R. HELICARRIER.
DO WE HAVE HIS MEDICAL RECORDS?
I'M LOOKING NOW.
MISTER CAGE, CAN YOU HEAR ME?
ARE YOU CONSCIOUS?
NEEDLES AREN'T GOING TO DO IT, SWEETIE.
HE HAS UNBREAKABLE SKIN.
WHAT?
THIS IS LUKE CAGE. UNBREAKABLE SKIN. IT'S HIS THING.
HOW THE @#$% AM I SUPPOSED TO OPERATE?!
NO READABLE PULSE.
WE NEED PADDLES.
I GOT IT.

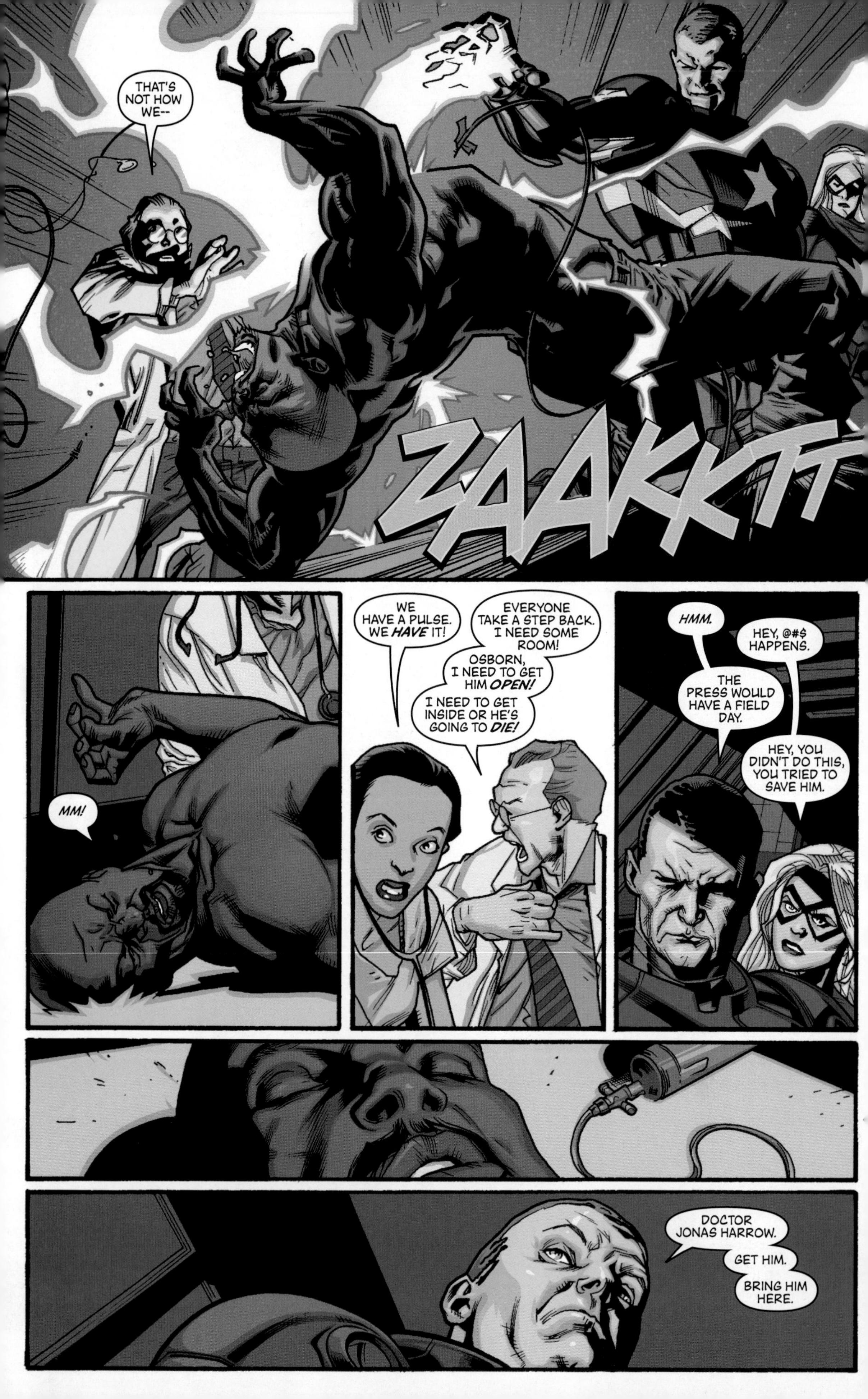
THAT'S NOT HOW WE--
ZAAKTT
MM!
WE HAVE A PULSE. WE *HAVE* IT!
EVERYONE TAKE A STEP BACK. I NEED SOME ROOM!
OSBORN, I NEED TO GET HIM *OPEN!*
I NEED TO GET INSIDE OR HE'S GOING TO *DIE!*
HMM.
HEY, @#$ HAPPENS.
THE PRESS WOULD HAVE A FIELD DAY.
HEY, YOU DIDN'T DO THIS, YOU TRIED TO SAVE HIM.
DOCTOR JONAS HARROW.
GET HIM.
BRING HIM HERE.

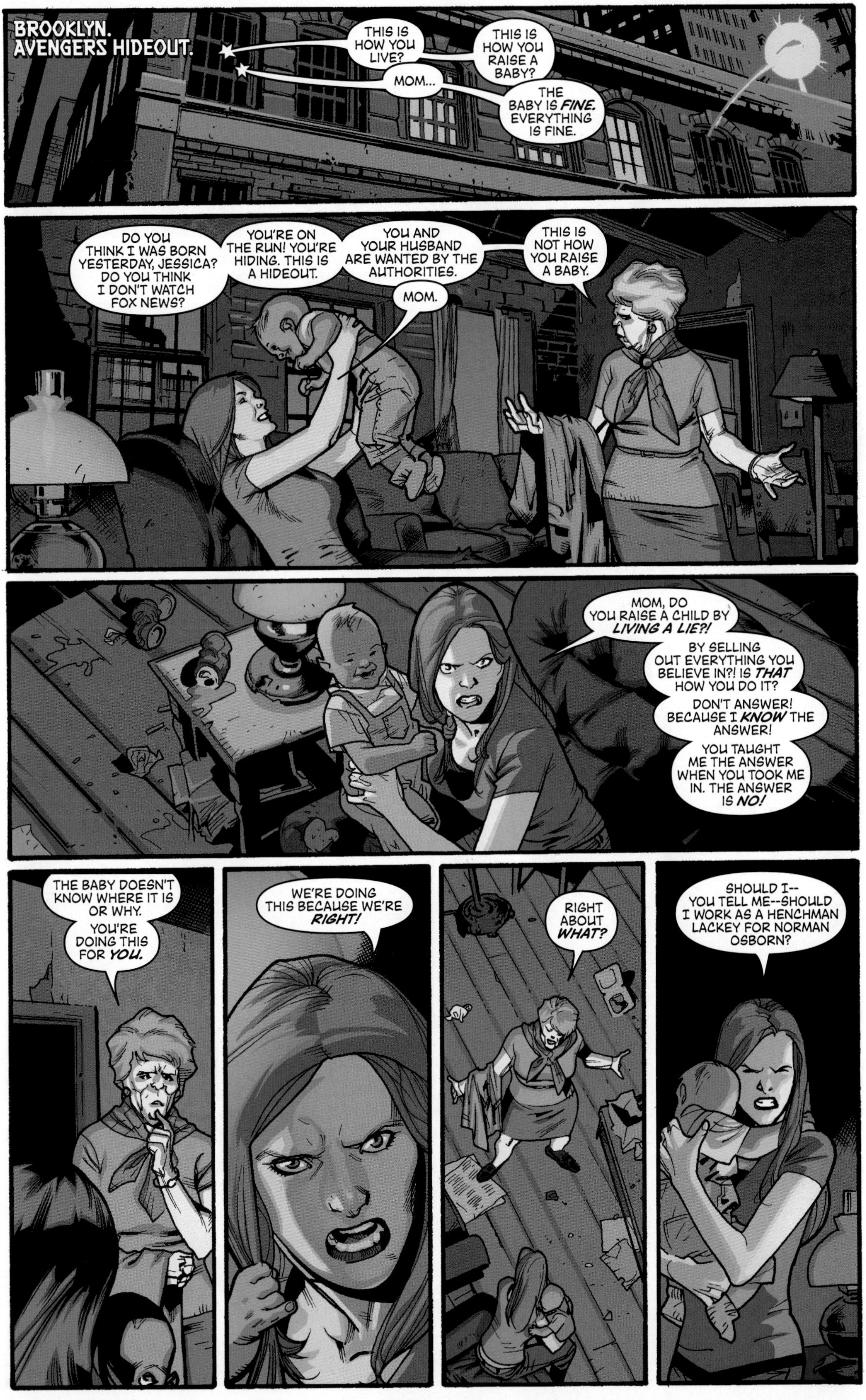
BROOKLYN. AVENGERS HIDEOUT.
THIS IS HOW YOU LIVE?
THIS IS HOW YOU RAISE A BABY?
MOM...
THE BABY IS FINE. EVERYTHING IS FINE.
DO YOU THINK I WAS BORN YESTERDAY, JESSICA? DO YOU THINK I DON'T WATCH FOX NEWS?
YOU'RE ON THE RUN! YOU'RE HIDING. THIS IS A HIDEOUT.
YOU AND YOUR HUSBAND ARE WANTED BY THE AUTHORITIES.
THIS IS NOT HOW YOU RAISE A BABY.
MOM.
MOM, DO YOU RAISE A CHILD BY LIVING A LIE?!
BY SELLING OUT EVERYTHING YOU BELIEVE IN?! IS THAT HOW YOU DO IT?
DON'T ANSWER! BECAUSE I KNOW THE ANSWER!
YOU TAUGHT ME THE ANSWER WHEN YOU TOOK ME IN. THE ANSWER IS NO!
THE BABY DOESN'T KNOW WHERE IT IS OR WHY.
YOU'RE DOING THIS FOR YOU.
WE'RE DOING THIS BECAUSE WE'RE RIGHT!
RIGHT ABOUT WHAT?
SHOULD I-- YOU TELL ME--SHOULD I WORK AS A HENCHMAN LACKEY FOR NORMAN OSBORN?

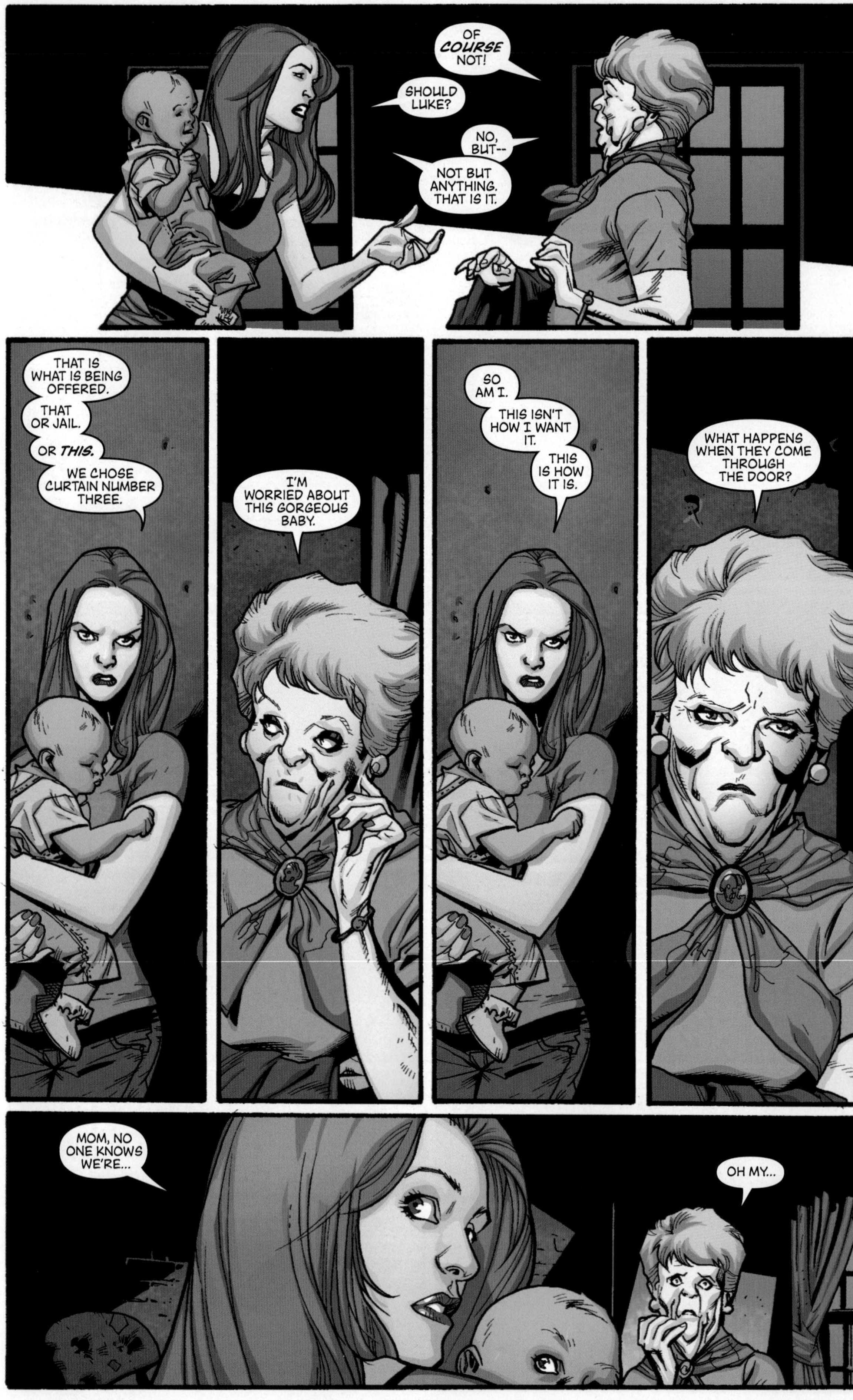
OF *COURSE* NOT!
SHOULD LUKE?
NO, BUT--
NOT BUT ANYTHING. THAT IS IT.
THAT IS WHAT IS BEING OFFERED.
THAT OR JAIL.
OR *THIS.*
WE CHOSE CURTAIN NUMBER THREE.
I'M WORRIED ABOUT THIS GORGEOUS BABY.
SO AM I.
THIS ISN'T HOW I WANT IT.
THIS IS HOW IT IS.
WHAT HAPPENS WHEN THEY COME THROUGH THE DOOR?
MOM, NO ONE KNOWS WE'RE...
OH MY...

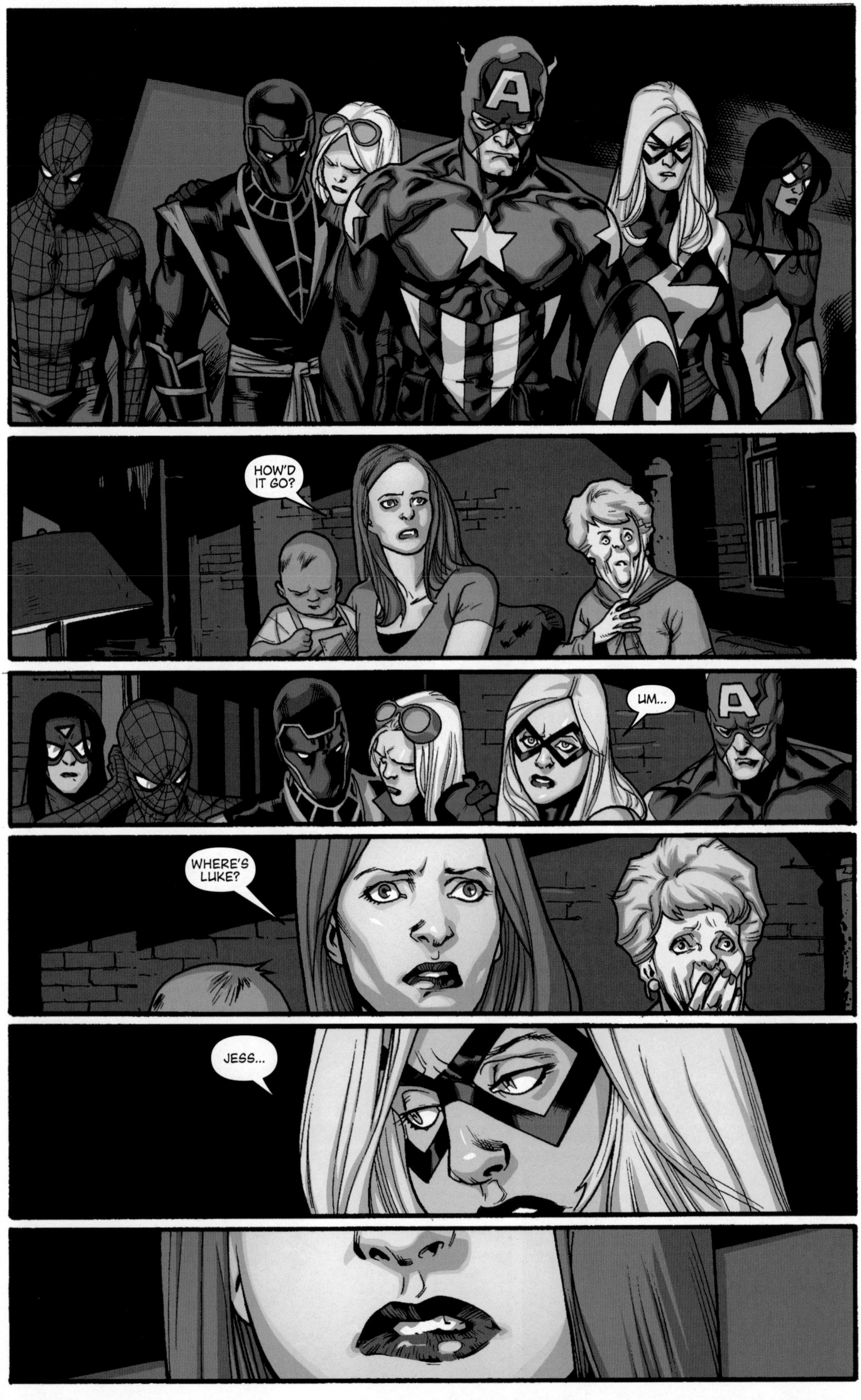
HOW'D IT GO?
UM...
WHERE'S LUKE?
JESS...

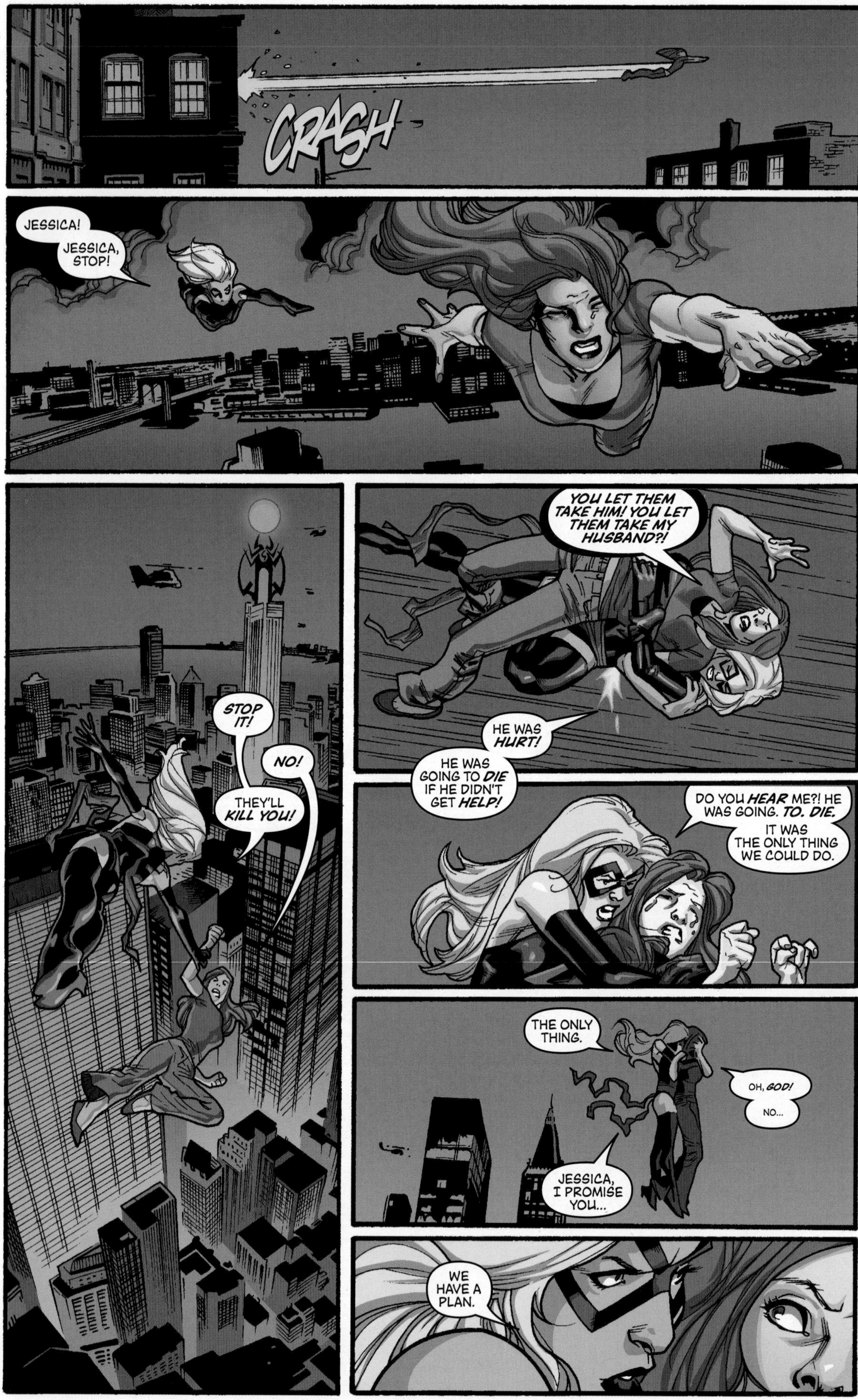

CRASH
JESSICA!
JESSICA, STOP!
STOP IT!
NO!
THEY'LL KILL YOU!
YOU LET THEM TAKE HIM! YOU LET THEM TAKE MY HUSBAND?!
HE WAS HURT!
HE WAS GOING TO DIE IF HE DIDN'T GET HELP!
DO YOU HEAR ME?! HE WAS GOING. TO. DIE.
IT WAS THE ONLY THING WE COULD DO.
THE ONLY THING.
OH, GOD!
NO...
JESSICA, I PROMISE YOU...
WE HAVE A PLAN.

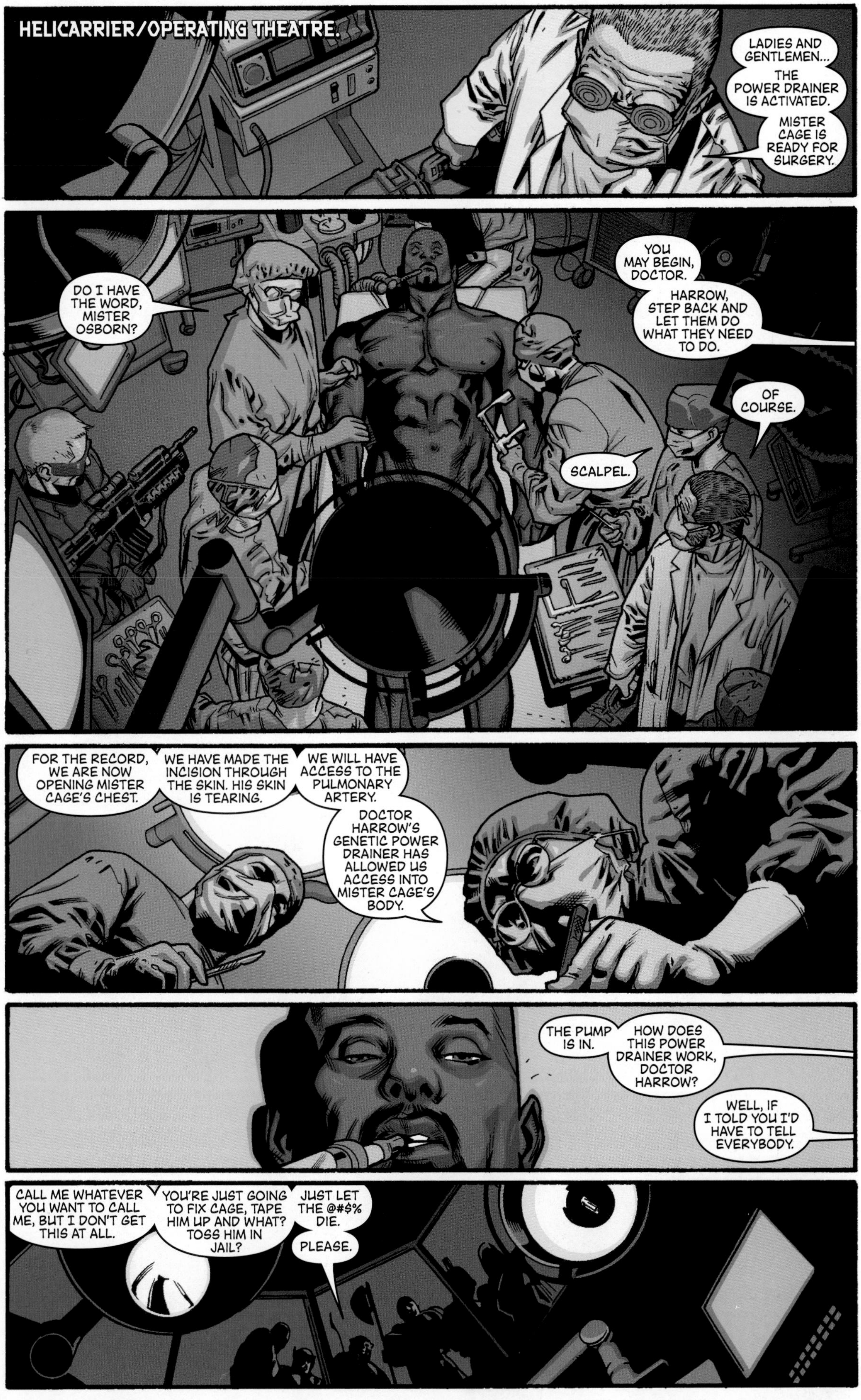
HELICARRIER/OPERATING THEATRE.
LADIES AND GENTLEMEN...
THE POWER DRAINER IS ACTIVATED.
MISTER CAGE IS READY FOR SURGERY.
DO I HAVE THE WORD, MISTER OSBORN?
YOU MAY BEGIN, DOCTOR.
HARROW, STEP BACK AND LET THEM DO WHAT THEY NEED TO DO.
OF COURSE.
SCALPEL.
FOR THE RECORD, WE ARE NOW OPENING MISTER CAGE'S CHEST.
WE HAVE MADE THE INCISION THROUGH THE SKIN. HIS SKIN IS TEARING.
WE WILL HAVE ACCESS TO THE PULMONARY ARTERY.
DOCTOR HARROW'S GENETIC POWER DRAINER HAS ALLOWED US ACCESS INTO MISTER CAGE'S BODY.
THE PUMP IS IN.
HOW DOES THIS POWER DRAINER WORK, DOCTOR HARROW?
WELL, IF I TOLD YOU I'D HAVE TO TELL EVERYBODY.
CALL ME WHATEVER YOU WANT TO CALL ME, BUT I DON'T GET THIS AT ALL.
YOU'RE JUST GOING TO FIX CAGE, TAPE HIM UP AND WHAT? TOSS HIM IN JAIL?
JUST LET THE @#$% DIE.
PLEASE.

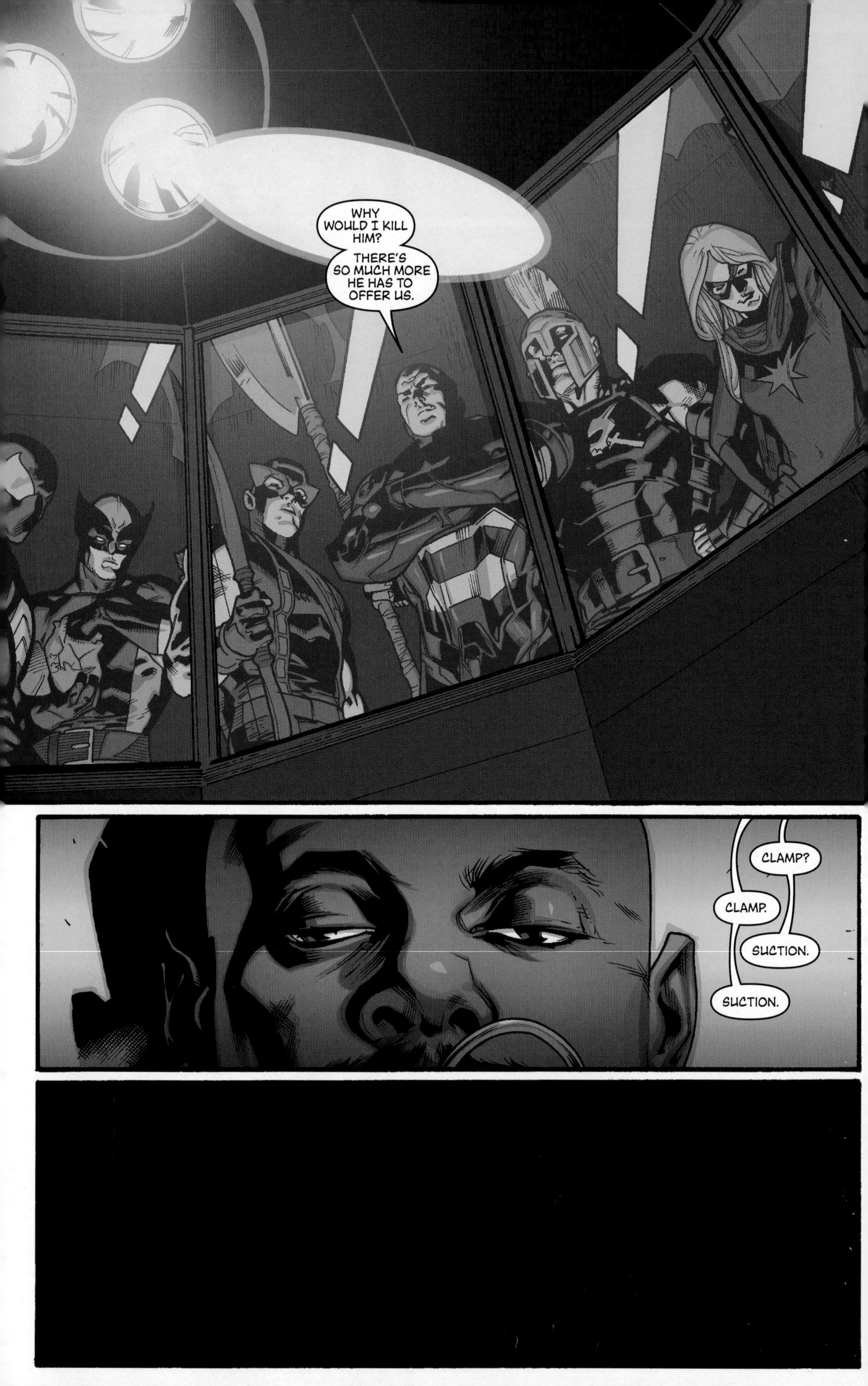
WHY WOULD I KILL HIM?
THERE'S SO MUCH MORE HE HAS TO OFFER US.
CLAMP?
CLAMP.
SUCTION.
SUCTION.

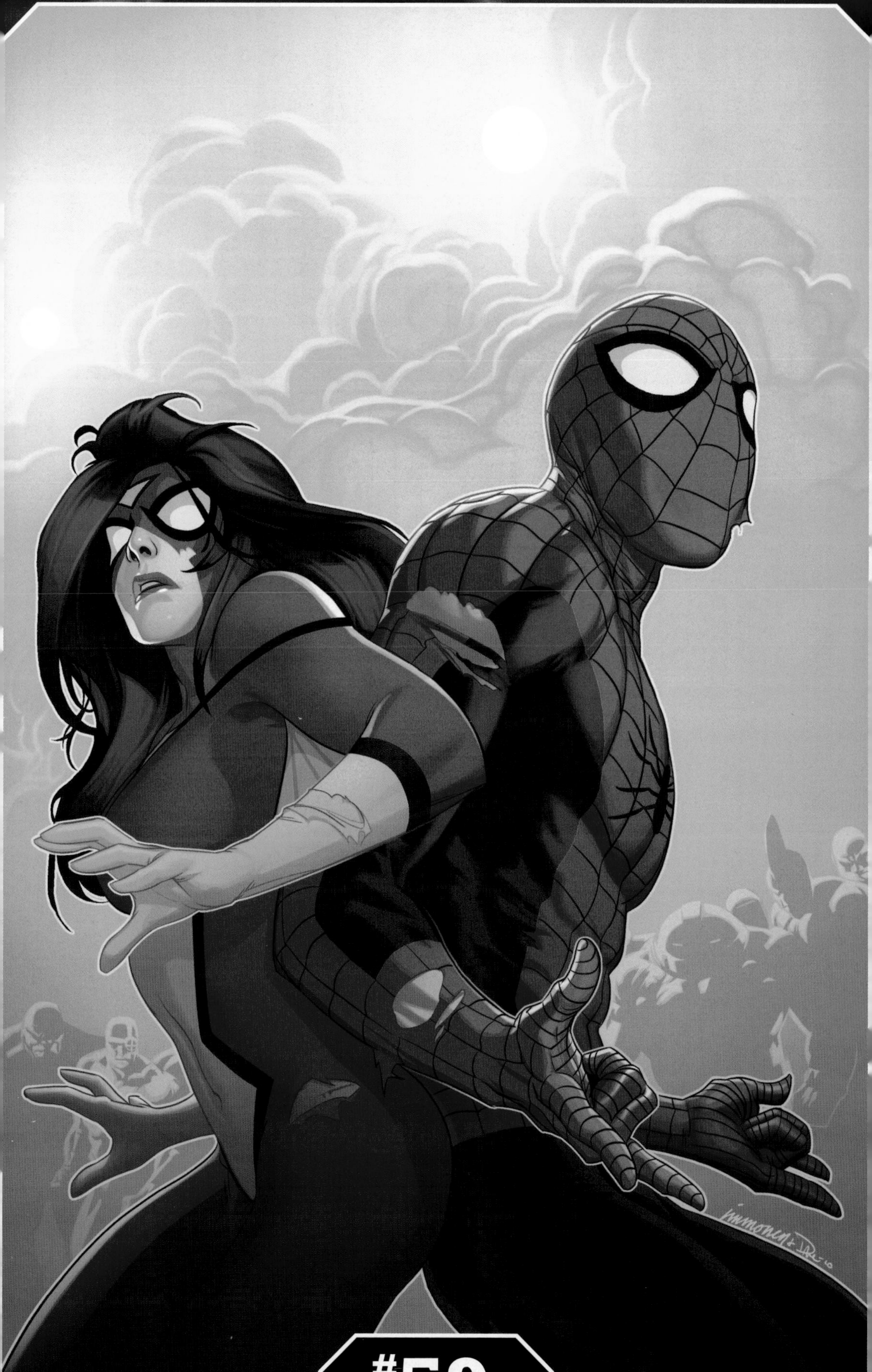

#59

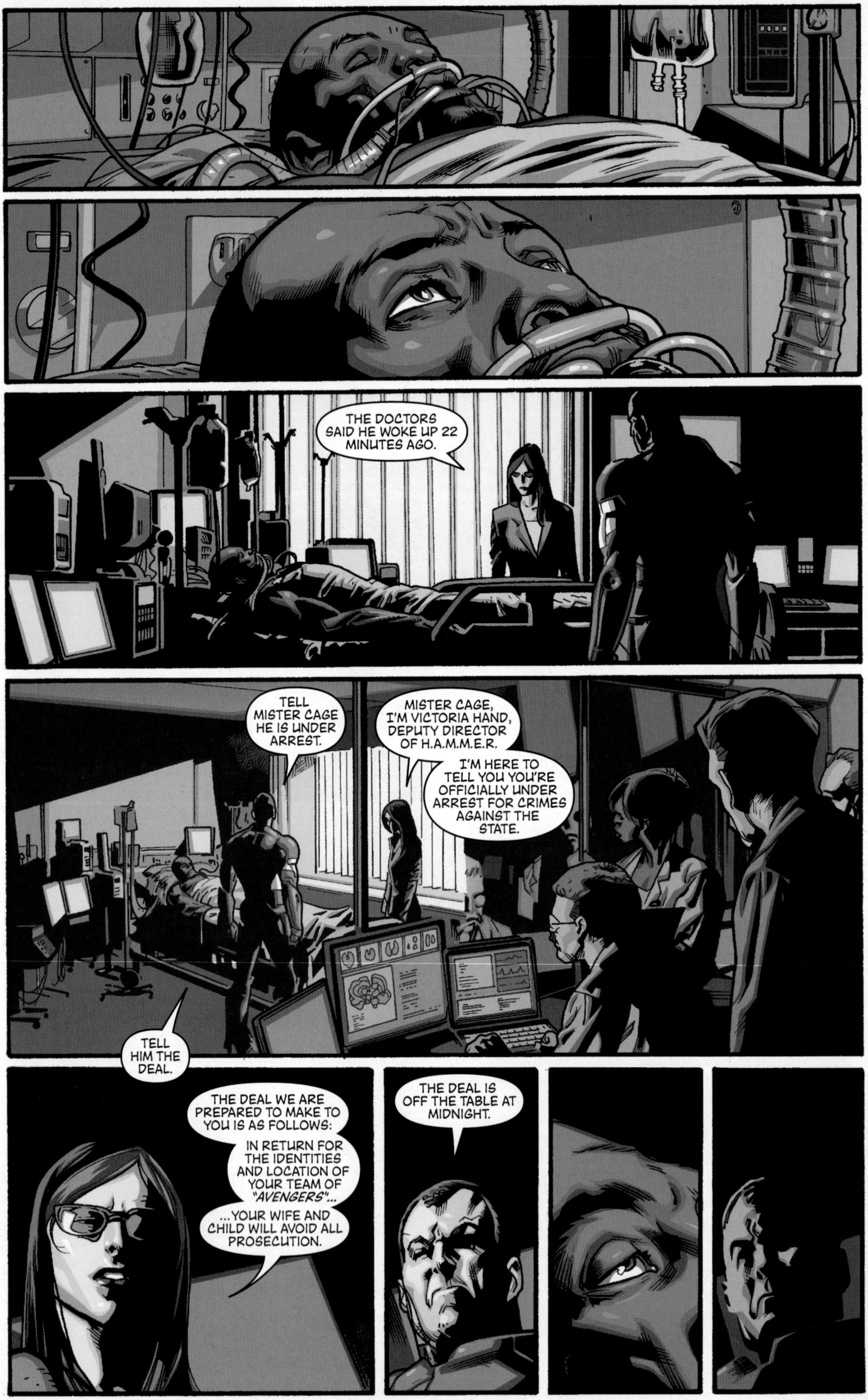
THE DOCTORS SAID HE WOKE UP 22 MINUTES AGO.
TELL MISTER CAGE HE IS UNDER ARREST.
MISTER CAGE, I'M VICTORIA HAND, DEPUTY DIRECTOR OF H.A.M.M.E.R.
I'M HERE TO TELL YOU YOU'RE OFFICIALLY UNDER ARREST FOR CRIMES AGAINST THE STATE.
TELL HIM THE DEAL.
THE DEAL WE ARE PREPARED TO MAKE TO YOU IS AS FOLLOWS:
IN RETURN FOR THE IDENTITIES AND LOCATION OF YOUR TEAM OF *"AVENGERS"*...
...YOUR WIFE AND CHILD WILL AVOID ALL PROSECUTION.
THE DEAL IS OFF THE TABLE AT MIDNIGHT.

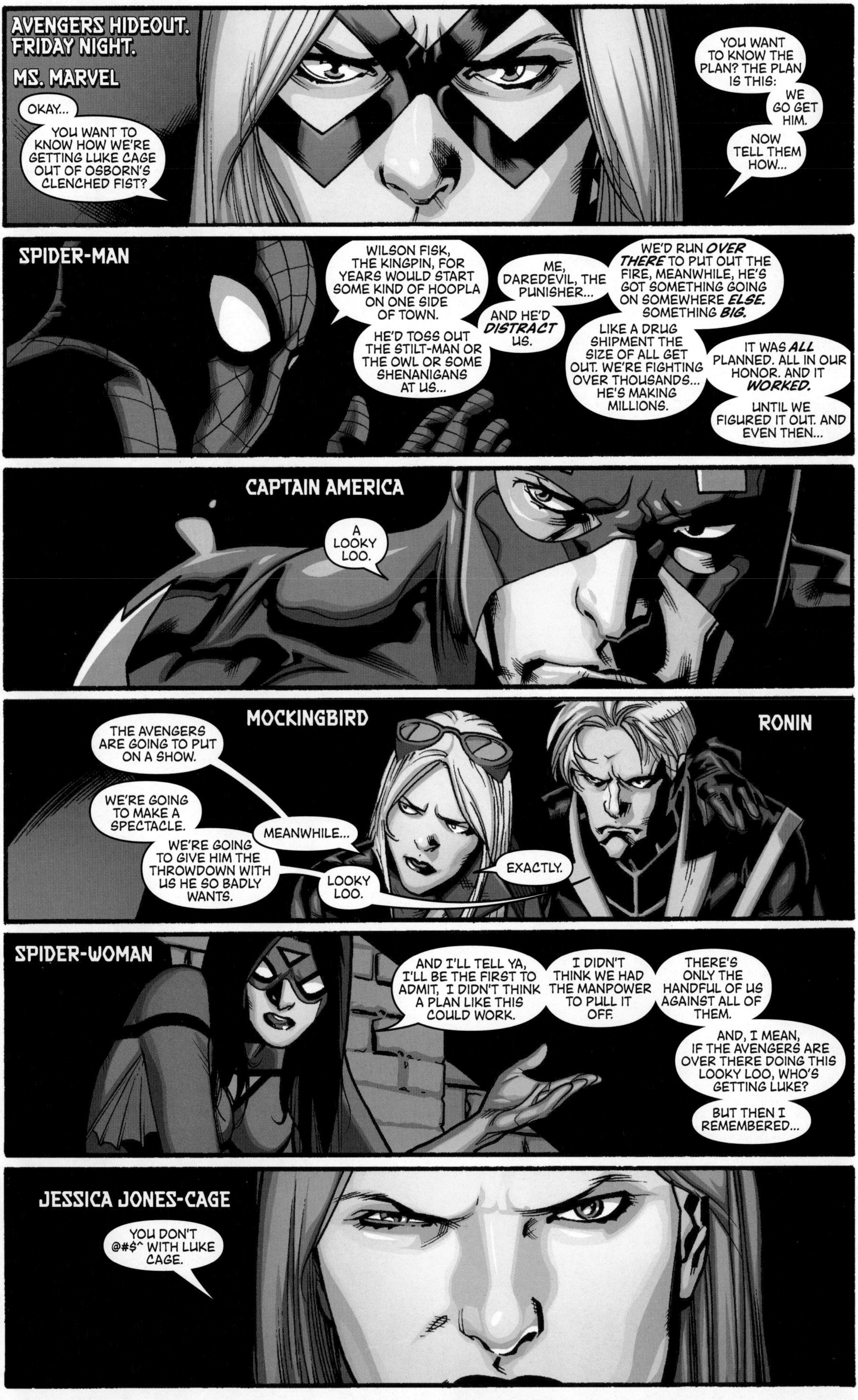

AVENGERS HIDEOUT. FRIDAY NIGHT.
MS. MARVEL
OKAY...
YOU WANT TO KNOW HOW WE'RE GETTING LUKE CAGE OUT OF OSBORN'S CLENCHED FIST?
YOU WANT TO KNOW THE PLAN? THE PLAN IS THIS:
WE GO GET HIM.
NOW TELL THEM HOW...
SPIDER-MAN
WILSON FISK, THE KINGPIN, FOR YEARS WOULD START SOME KIND OF HOOPLA ON ONE SIDE OF TOWN.
HE'D TOSS OUT THE STILT-MAN OR THE OWL OR SOME SHENANIGANS AT US...
ME, DAREDEVIL, THE PUNISHER...
AND HE'D DISTRACT US.
WE'D RUN OVER THERE TO PUT OUT THE FIRE, MEANWHILE, HE'S GOT SOMETHING GOING ON SOMEWHERE ELSE. SOMETHING BIG.
LIKE A DRUG SHIPMENT THE SIZE OF ALL GET OUT. WE'RE FIGHTING OVER THOUSANDS... HE'S MAKING MILLIONS.
IT WAS ALL PLANNED. ALL IN OUR HONOR. AND IT WORKED.
UNTIL WE FIGURED IT OUT. AND EVEN THEN...
CAPTAIN AMERICA
A LOOKY LOO.
MOCKINGBIRD
RONIN
THE AVENGERS ARE GOING TO PUT ON A SHOW.
WE'RE GOING TO MAKE A SPECTACLE.
WE'RE GOING TO GIVE HIM THE THROWDOWN WITH US HE SO BADLY WANTS.
MEANWHILE...
LOOKY LOO.
EXACTLY.
SPIDER-WOMAN
AND I'LL TELL YA, I'LL BE THE FIRST TO ADMIT, I DIDN'T THINK A PLAN LIKE THIS COULD WORK.
I DIDN'T THINK WE HAD THE MANPOWER TO PULL IT OFF.
THERE'S ONLY THE HANDFUL OF US AGAINST ALL OF THEM.
AND, I MEAN, IF THE AVENGERS ARE OVER THERE DOING THIS LOOKY LOO, WHO'S GETTING LUKE?
BUT THEN I REMEMBERED...
JESSICA JONES-CAGE
YOU DON'T @#$^ WITH LUKE CAGE.

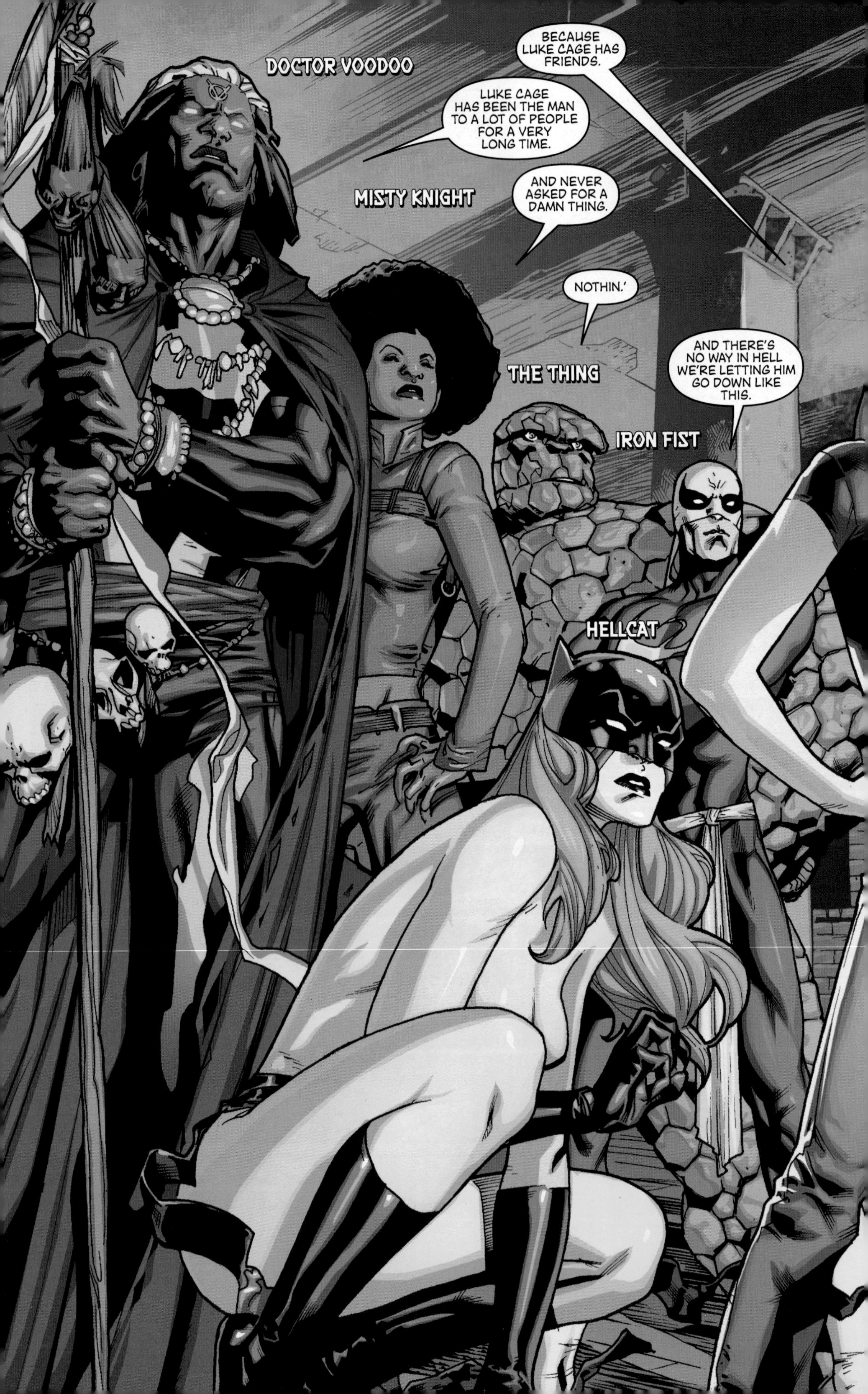

DOCTOR VOODOO
LUKE CAGE HAS BEEN THE MAN TO A LOT OF PEOPLE FOR A VERY LONG TIME.
BECAUSE LUKE CAGE HAS FRIENDS.
MISTY KNIGHT
AND NEVER ASKED FOR A DAMN THING.
NOTHIN.'
THE THING
AND THERE'S NO WAY IN HELL WE'RE LETTING HIM GO DOWN LIKE THIS.
IRON FIST
HELLCAT

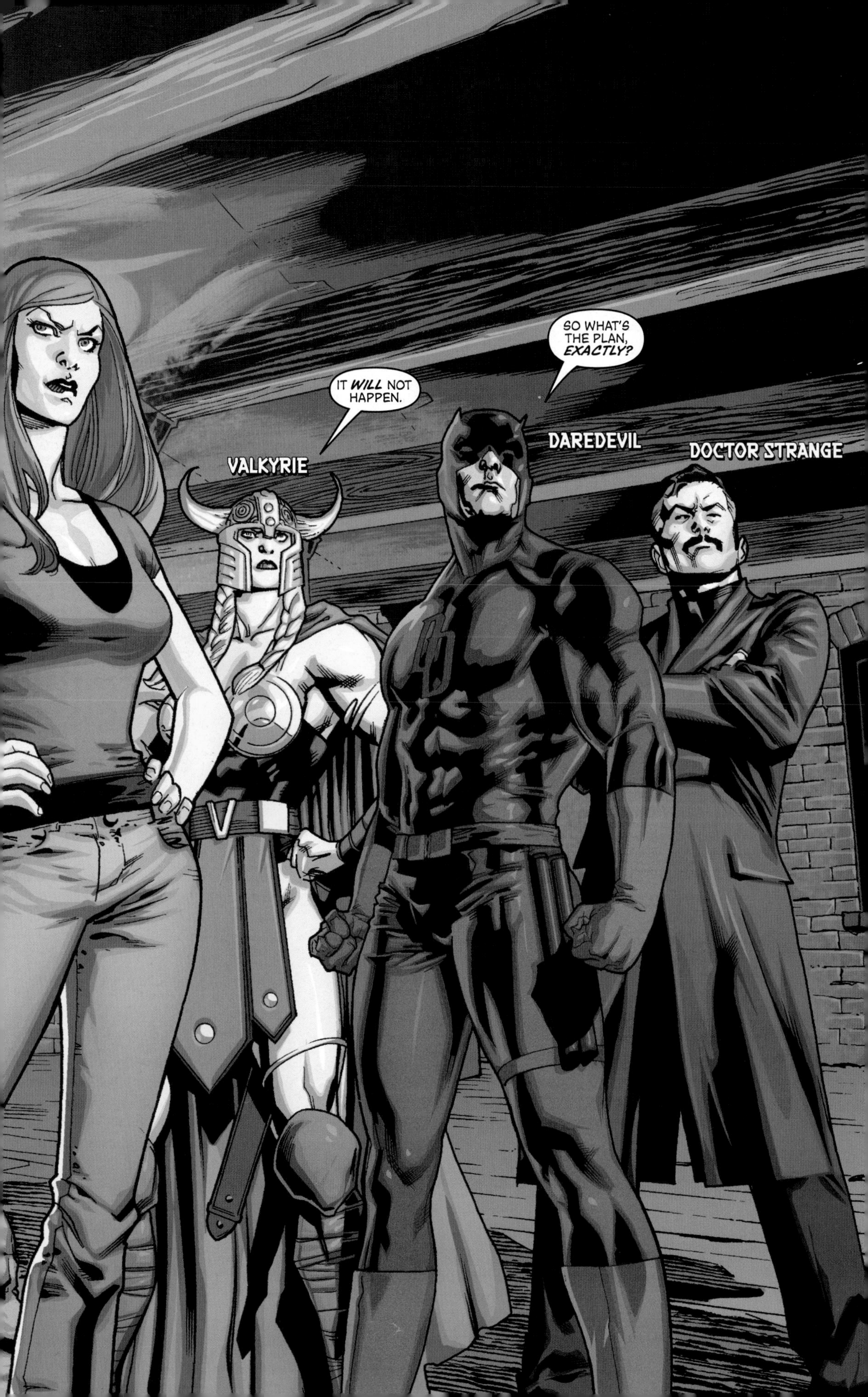
SO WHAT'S THE PLAN, *EXACTLY?*
IT *WILL* NOT HAPPEN.
VALKYRIE
DAREDEVIL
DOCTOR STRANGE

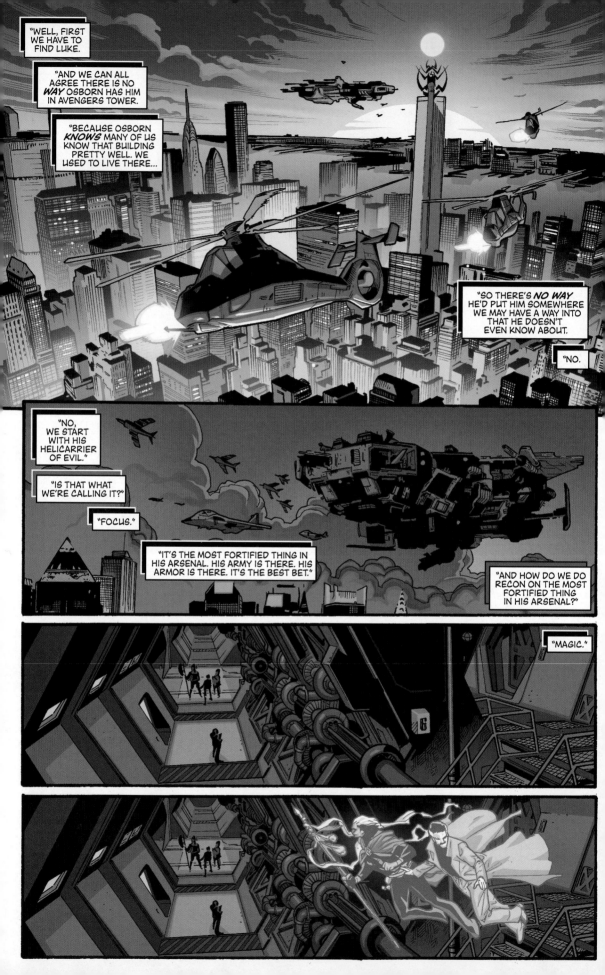

"WELL, FIRST WE HAVE TO FIND LUKE.

"AND WE CAN ALL AGREE THERE IS NO *WAY* OSBORN HAS HIM IN AVENGERS TOWER.

"BECAUSE OSBORN *KNOWS* MANY OF US KNOW THAT BUILDING PRETTY WELL. WE USED TO LIVE THERE...

"SO THERE'S *NO WAY* HE'D PUT HIM SOMEWHERE WE MAY HAVE A WAY INTO THAT HE DOESN'T EVEN KNOW ABOUT.

"NO.

"NO, WE START WITH HIS HELICARRIER OF EVIL."

"IS THAT WHAT WE'RE CALLING IT?"

"FOCUS."

"IT'S THE MOST FORTIFIED THING IN HIS ARSENAL. HIS ARMY IS THERE. HIS ARMOR IS THERE. IT'S THE BEST BET."

"AND HOW DO WE DO RECON ON THE MOST FORTIFIED THING IN HIS ARSENAL?"

"MAGIC."

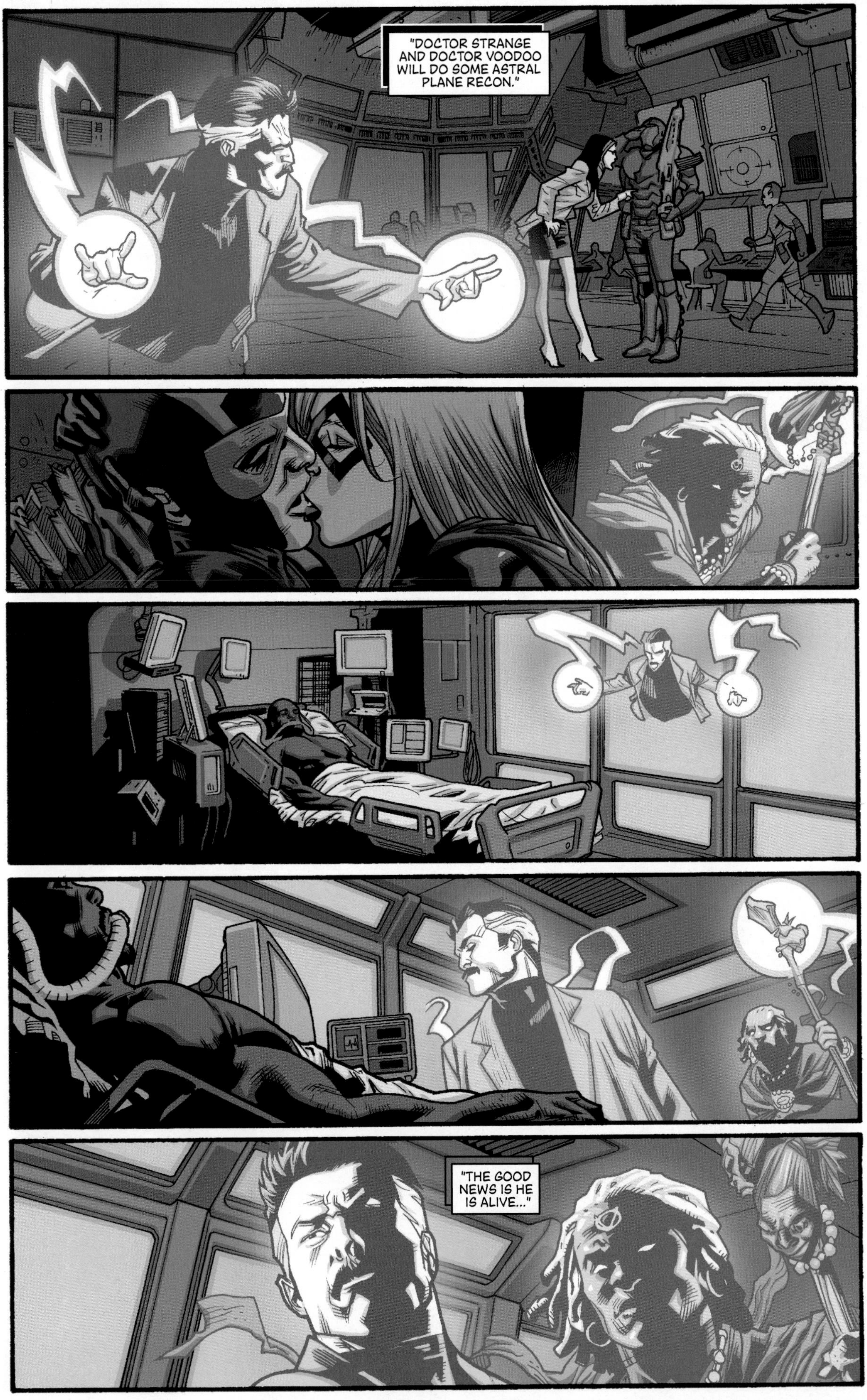
"DOCTOR STRANGE AND DOCTOR VOODOO WILL DO SOME ASTRAL PLANE RECON."
"THE GOOD NEWS IS HE IS ALIVE..."

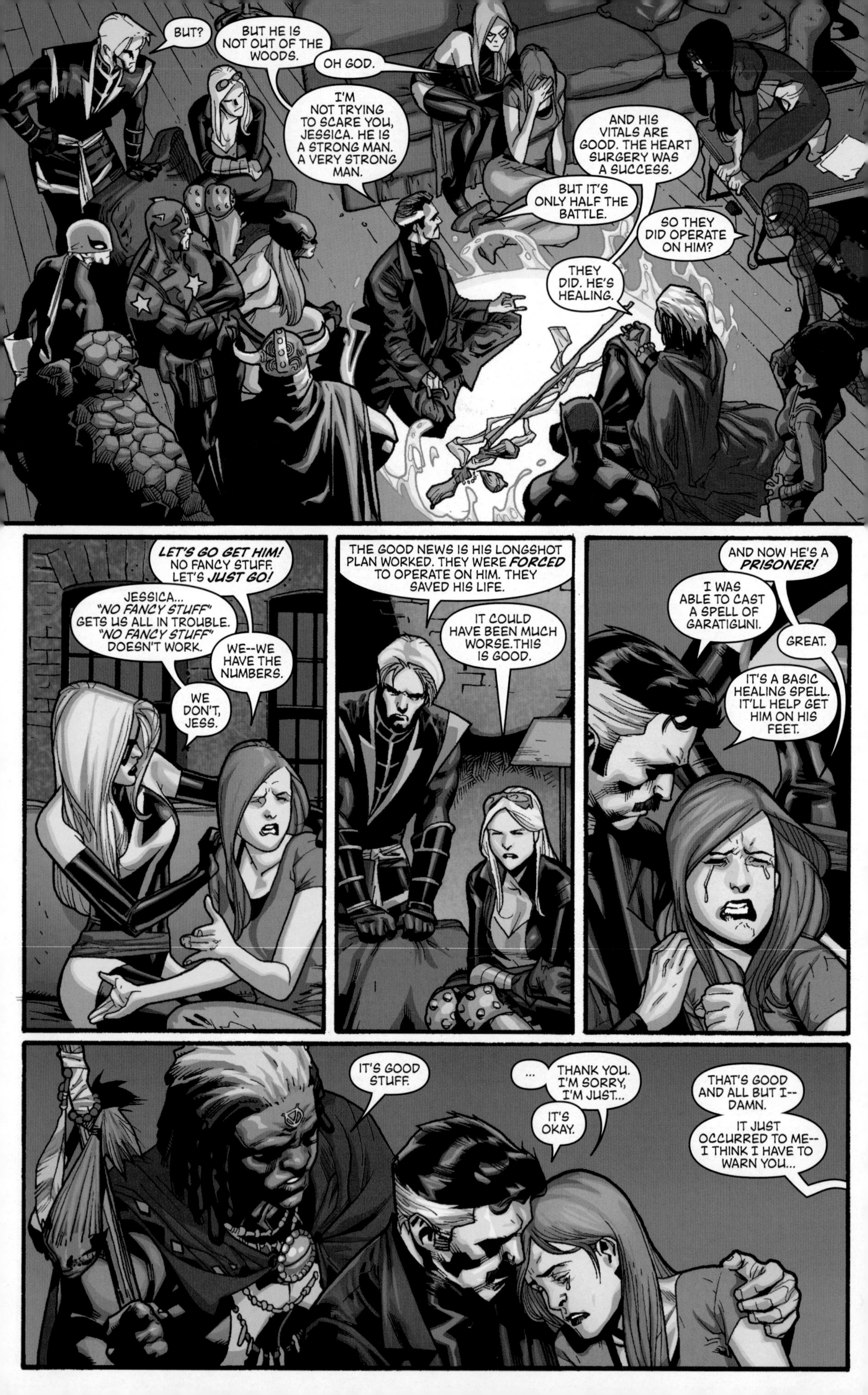

BUT?
BUT HE IS NOT OUT OF THE WOODS.
OH GOD.
I'M NOT TRYING TO SCARE YOU, JESSICA. HE IS A STRONG MAN. A VERY STRONG MAN.
AND HIS VITALS ARE GOOD. THE HEART SURGERY WAS A SUCCESS.
BUT IT'S ONLY HALF THE BATTLE.
SO THEY DID OPERATE ON HIM?
THEY DID. HE'S HEALING.
LET'S GO GET HIM! NO FANCY STUFF. LET'S JUST GO!
JESSICA... "NO FANCY STUFF" GETS US ALL IN TROUBLE. "NO FANCY STUFF" DOESN'T WORK.
WE--WE HAVE THE NUMBERS.
WE DON'T, JESS.
THE GOOD NEWS IS HIS LONGSHOT PLAN WORKED. THEY WERE FORCED TO OPERATE ON HIM. THEY SAVED HIS LIFE.
IT COULD HAVE BEEN MUCH WORSE.THIS IS GOOD.
AND NOW HE'S A PRISONER!
I WAS ABLE TO CAST A SPELL OF GARATIGUNI.
GREAT.
IT'S A BASIC HEALING SPELL. IT'LL HELP GET HIM ON HIS FEET.
IT'S GOOD STUFF.
...
THANK YOU. I'M SORRY, I'M JUST...
IT'S OKAY.
THAT'S GOOD AND ALL BUT I-- DAMN.
IT JUST OCCURRED TO ME-- I THINK I HAVE TO WARN YOU...

THERE'S A VERY GOOD CHANCE OSBORN WILL KNOW YOU WERE THERE.

HOW WOULD SOMEONE LIKE NORMAN OSBORN EVEN KNOW THE ASTRAL PLANE EXISTS?

LAST YEAR, MY COMPANY WAS ASKED TO BID ON SOME SECURITY TECH THAT WOULD ENABLE SOMEONE LIKE ME TO KNOW IF SOMEONE LIKE YOU WAS SNEAKING AROUND.

AND IF I KNEW ABOUT IT, THAT MEANS TONY STARK KNEW ABOUT IT.

AND IF TONY STARK KNEW ABOUT IT, HE BOUGHT IT OR HE PROBABLY WENT BACK TO HIS LAB AND FIGURED OUT HOW TO DO IT ALL BY HIMSELF.

THAT'S BEEN MY EXPERIENCE.

MAN.

REALLY?

THAT--THAT IS DISCONCERTING.

AND WHAT WAS TONY STARK'S IS NOW NORMAN OSBORN'S.

EXACTLY.

SO WHAT? HE *KNOWS* WE'RE GOING TO GO AFTER LUKE. HE KNOWS SOMEONE--

EXACTLY, SO...

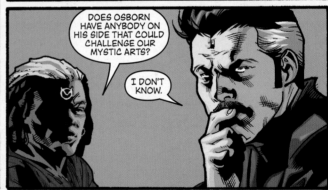

DOES OSBORN HAVE ANYBODY ON HIS SIDE THAT COULD CHALLENGE OUR MYSTIC ARTS?

I DON'T KNOW.

ASSUME YES.

EXACTLY.

FINE, FINE! *NOW* WHAT?

SUIT UP.

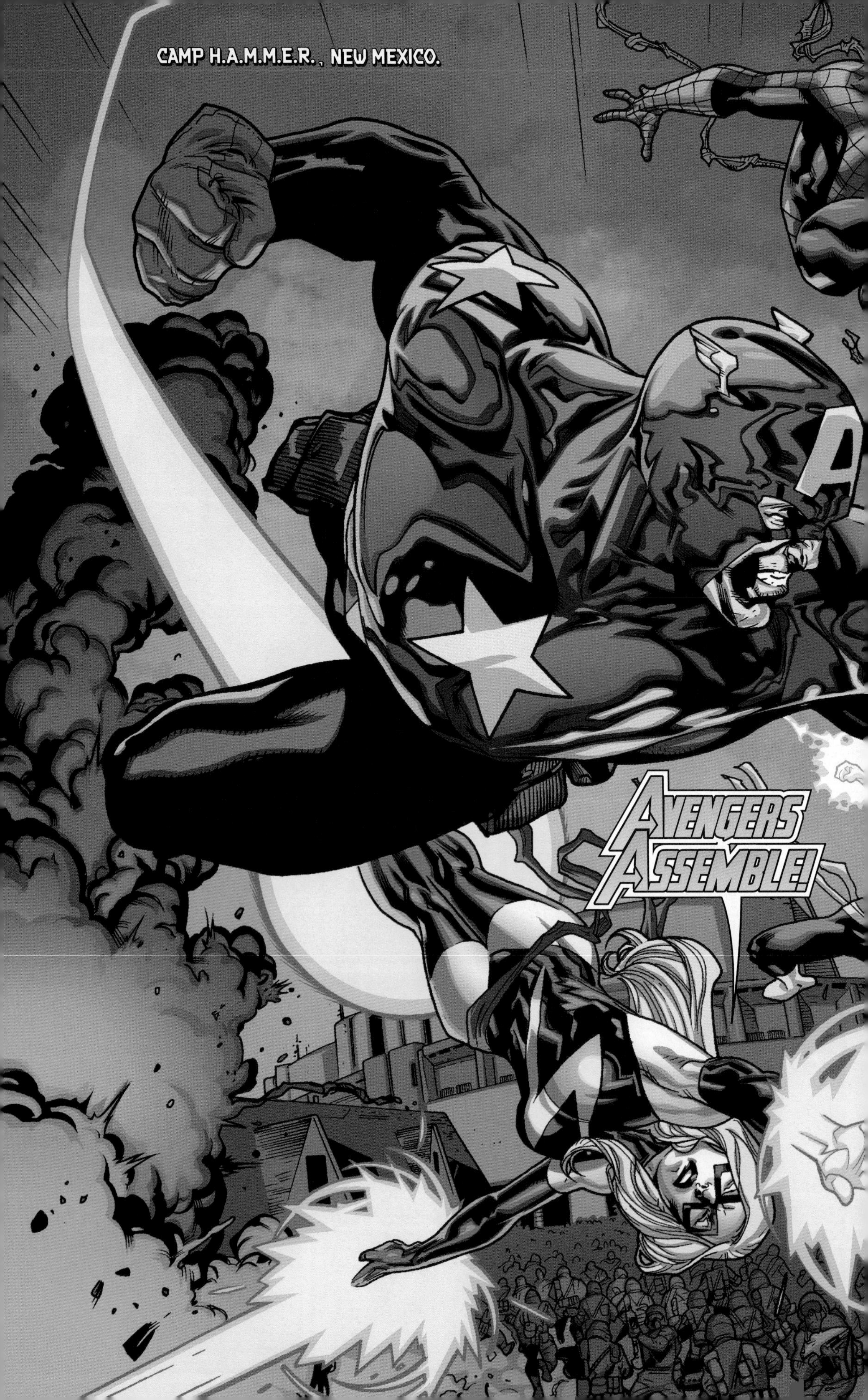
CAMP H.A.M.M.E.R., NEW MEXICO.
AVENGERS ASSEMBLE!

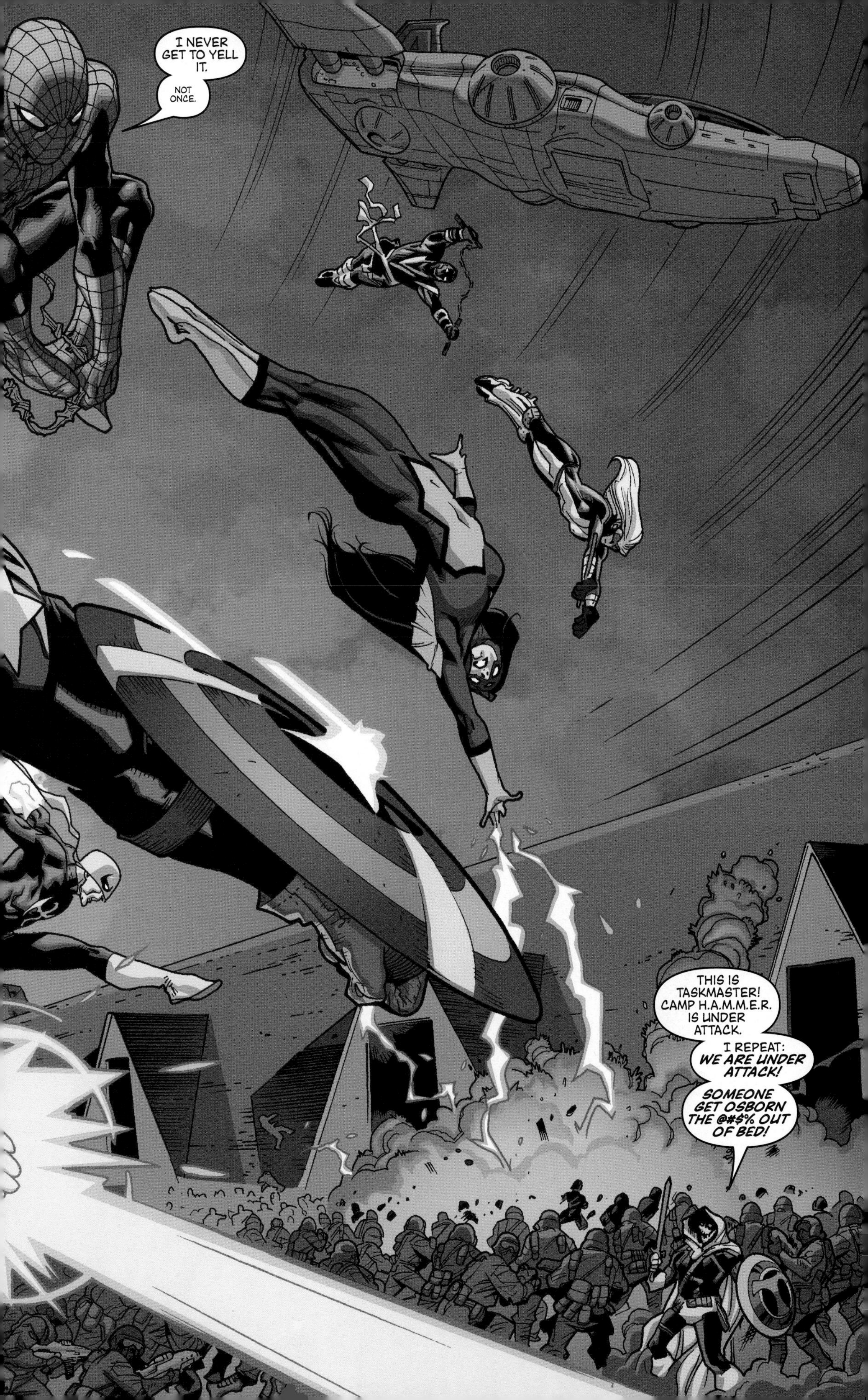
I NEVER GET TO YELL IT.
NOT ONCE.
THIS IS TASKMASTER! CAMP H.A.M.M.E.R. IS UNDER ATTACK.
I REPEAT: WE ARE UNDER ATTACK!
SOMEONE GET OSBORN THE @#$% OUT OF BED!

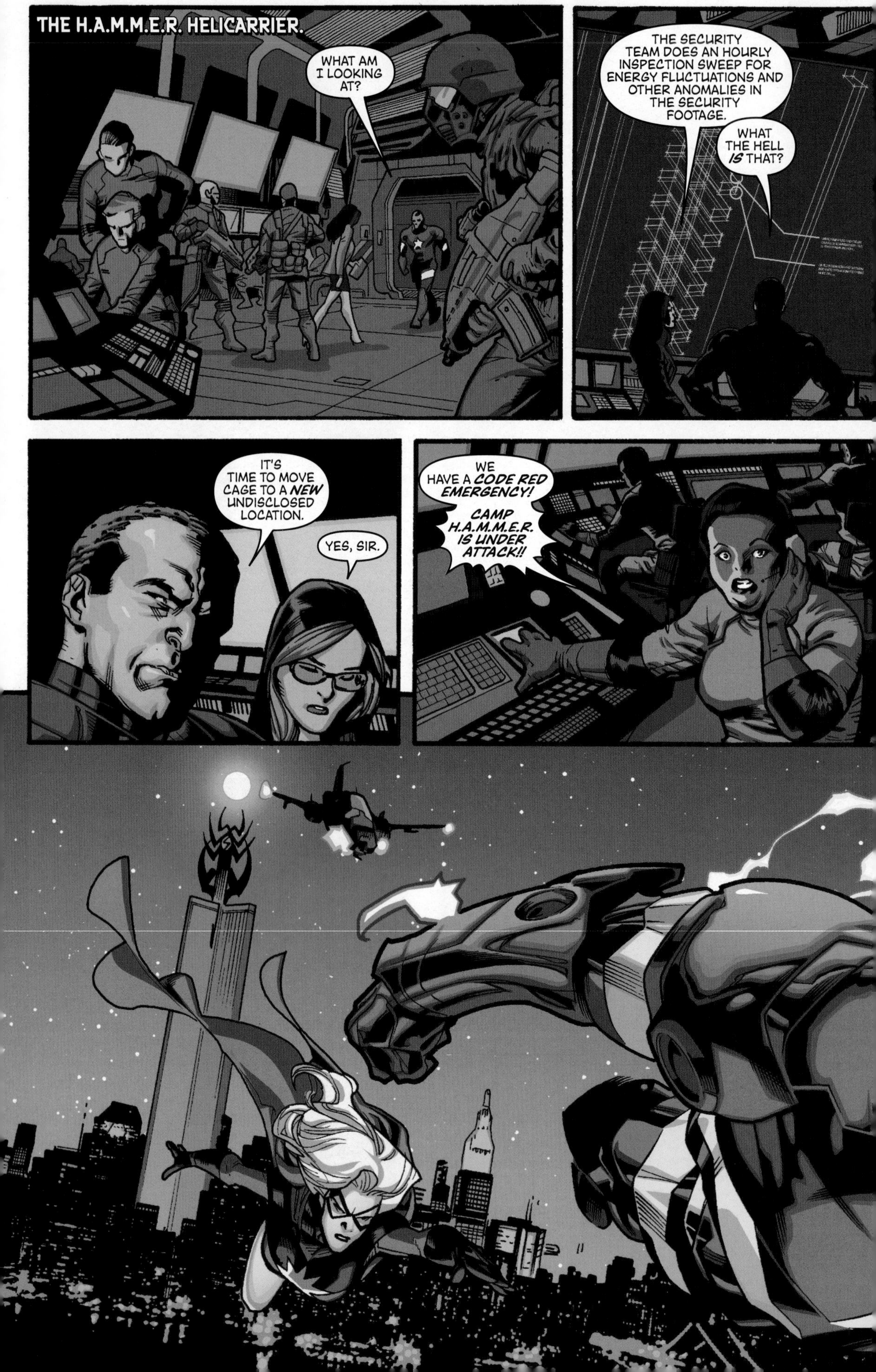
THE H.A.M.M.E.R. HELICARRIER.
WHAT AM I LOOKING AT?
THE SECURITY TEAM DOES AN HOURLY INSPECTION SWEEP FOR ENERGY FLUCTUATIONS AND OTHER ANOMALIES IN THE SECURITY FOOTAGE.
WHAT THE HELL *IS* THAT?
IT'S TIME TO MOVE CAGE TO A *NEW* UNDISCLOSED LOCATION.
YES, SIR.
WE HAVE A *CODE RED EMERGENCY!*
CAMP H.A.M.M.E.R. IS UNDER ATTACK!!

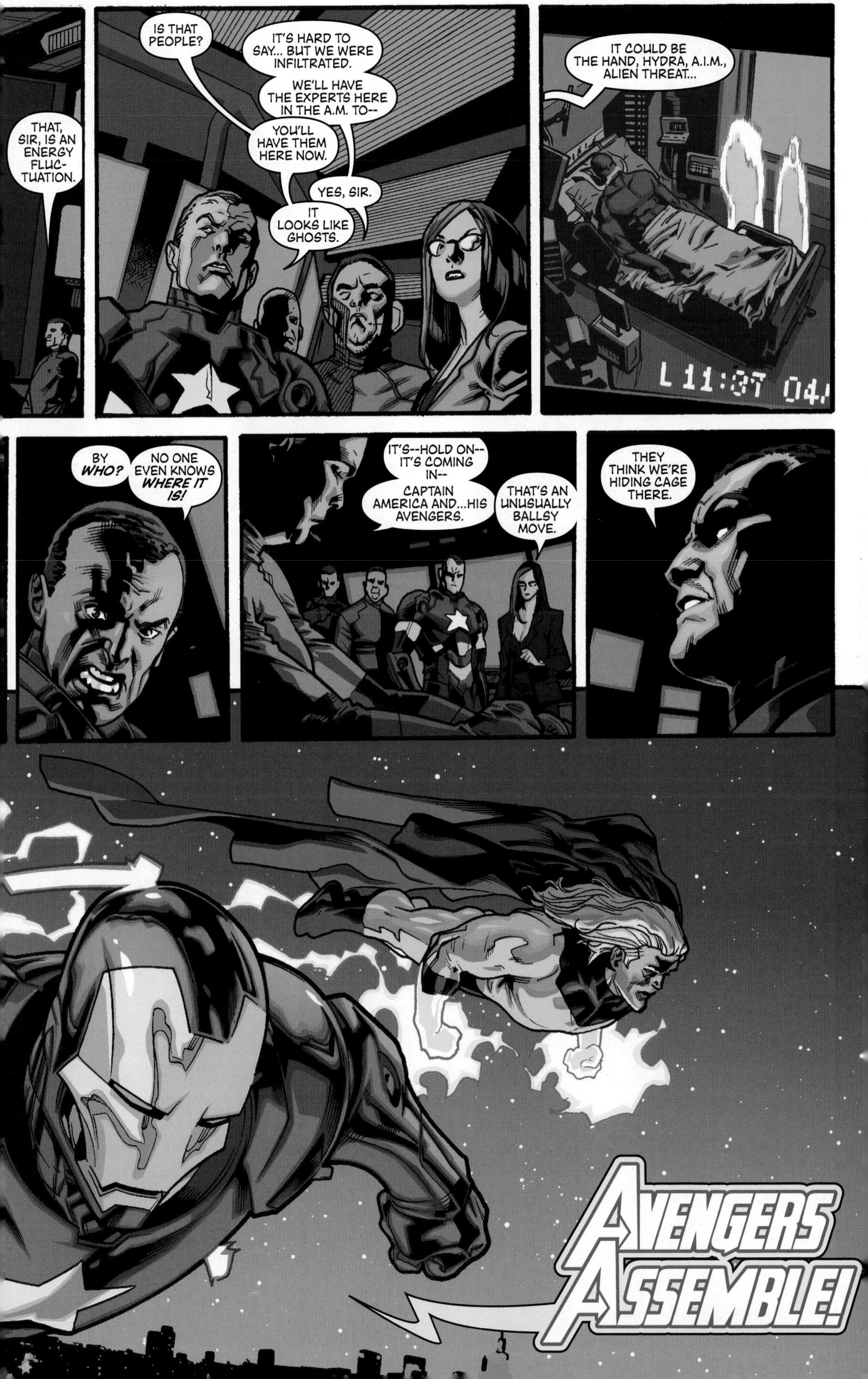
THAT, SIR, IS AN ENERGY FLUC-TUATION.
IS THAT PEOPLE?
IT'S HARD TO SAY... BUT WE WERE INFILTRATED.
WE'LL HAVE THE EXPERTS HERE IN THE A.M. TO--
YOU'LL HAVE THEM HERE NOW.
YES, SIR.
IT LOOKS LIKE GHOSTS.
IT COULD BE THE HAND, HYDRA, A.I.M., ALIEN THREAT...
L 11:07 04/
BY WHO?
NO ONE EVEN KNOWS WHERE IT IS!
IT'S--HOLD ON-- IT'S COMING IN--
CAPTAIN AMERICA AND...HIS AVENGERS.
THAT'S AN UNUSUALLY BALLSY MOVE.
THEY THINK WE'RE HIDING CAGE THERE.
AVENGERS ASSEMBLE!

I WANT ALL HANDS ON DECK!

ALL BATTLE-STATIONS REPORTING IN SEQUENCE AND IN ORDER!

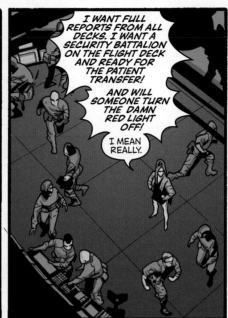

I WANT FULL REPORTS FROM ALL DECKS. I WANT A SECURITY BATTALION ON THE FLIGHT DECK AND READY FOR THE PATIENT TRANSFER!

AND WILL SOMEONE TURN THE DAMN RED LIGHT OFF!

I MEAN REALLY.

THANK YOU.

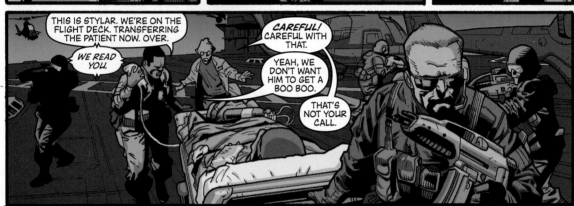

THIS IS STYLAR. WE'RE ON THE FLIGHT DECK. TRANSFERRING THE PATIENT NOW. OVER.

WE READ YOU.

CAREFUL! CAREFUL WITH THAT.

YEAH, WE DON'T WANT HIM TO GET A BOO BOO.

THAT'S NOT YOUR CALL.

TRANSPORT COPTER NINE IS JUICED AND READY FOR TAKEOFF, OVER.

EASY!

THE FLIGHT CREW IS UP AND READY.

YOU GUYS WANT TO GIVE US A HAND WITH THE--

OH MY GOD.

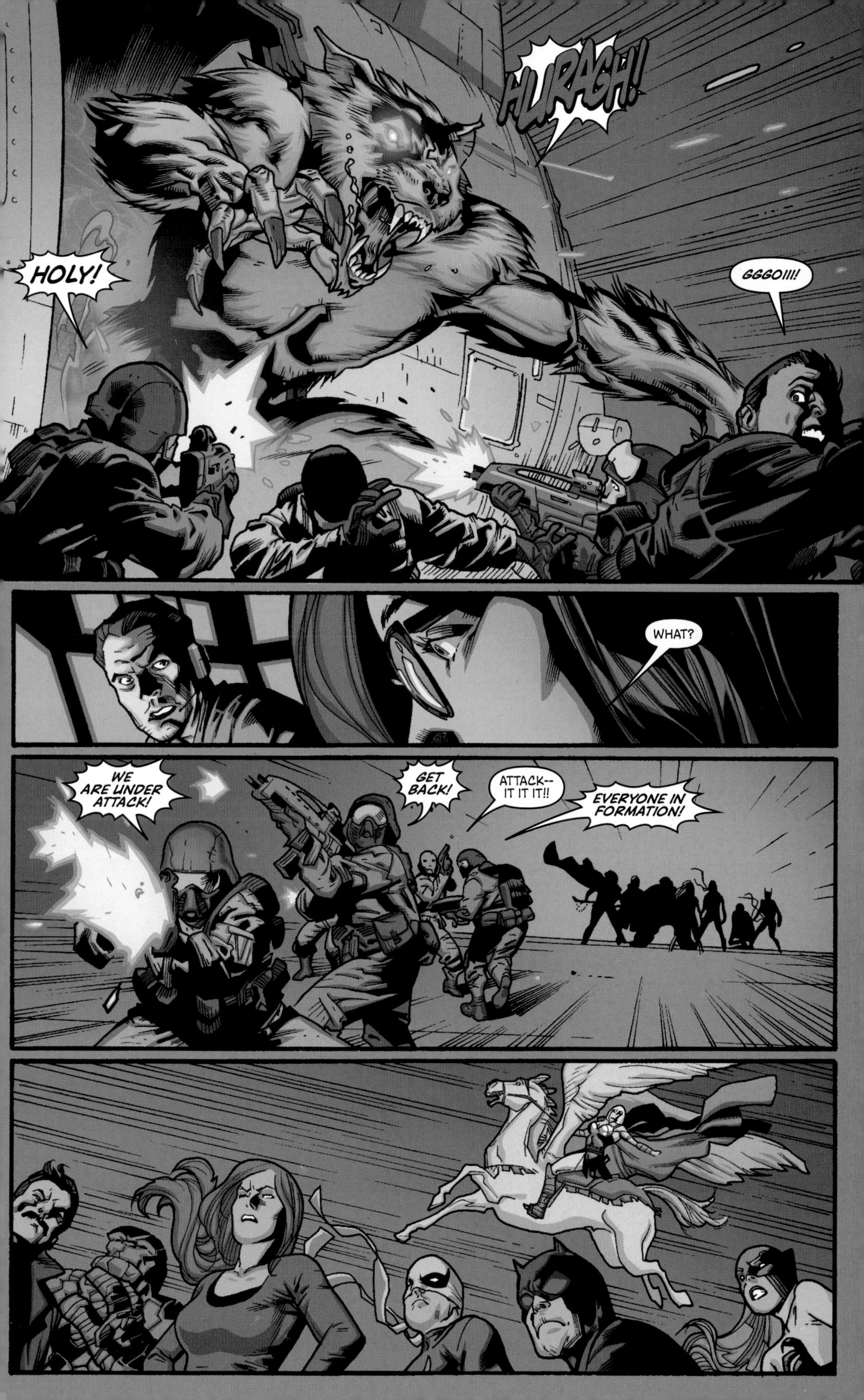
HURAGH!
HOLY!
GGGOIII!
WHAT?
WE ARE UNDER ATTACK!
GET BACK!
ATTACK-- IT IT IT!!
EVERYONE IN FORMATION!

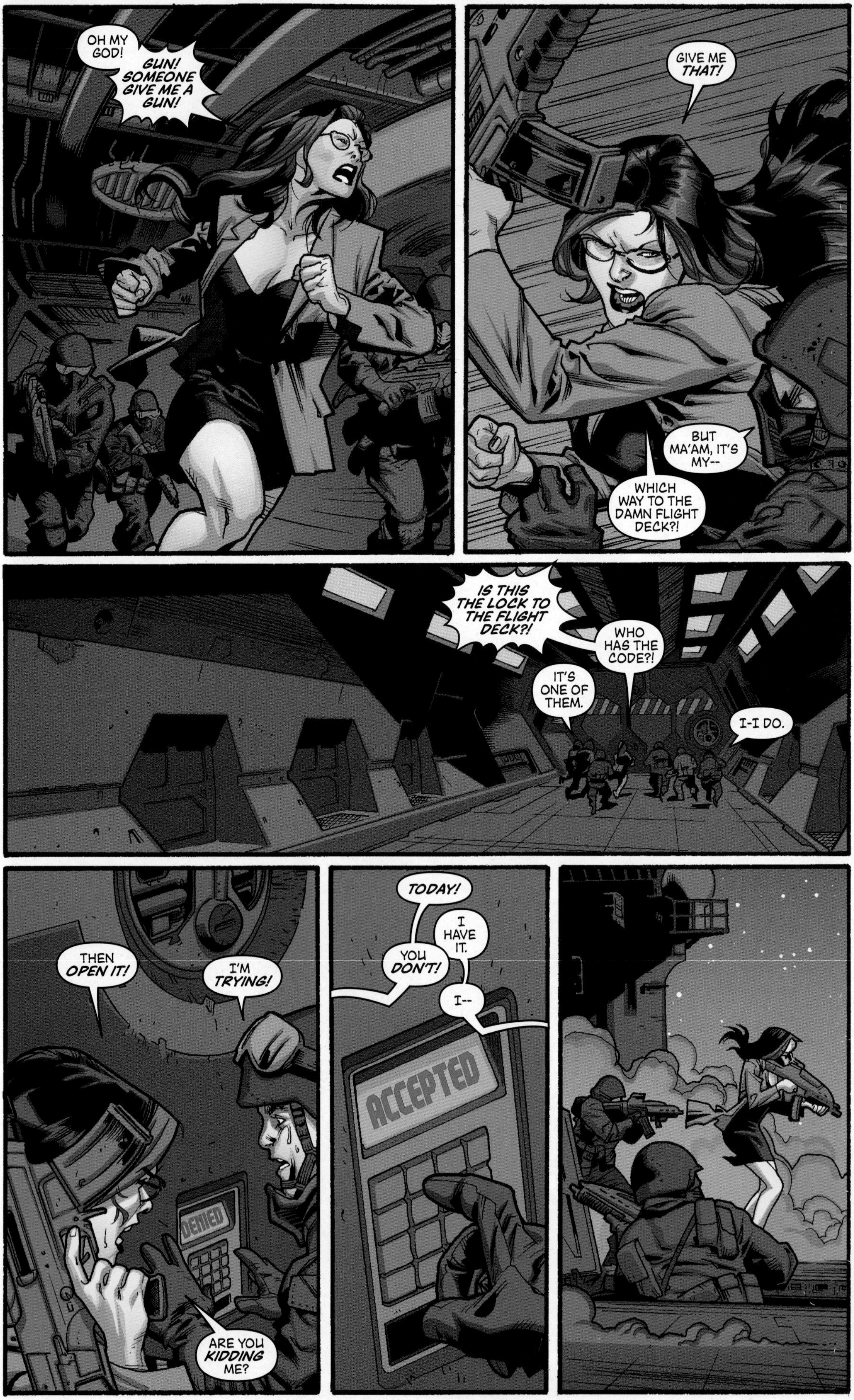
OH MY GOD!
GUN! SOMEONE GIVE ME A GUN!
GIVE ME THAT!
BUT MA'AM, IT'S MY--
WHICH WAY TO THE DAMN FLIGHT DECK?!
IS THIS THE LOCK TO THE FLIGHT DECK?!
WHO HAS THE CODE?!
IT'S ONE OF THEM.
I-I DO.
THEN OPEN IT!
I'M TRYING!
DENIED
ARE YOU KIDDING ME?
TODAY!
YOU DON'T!
I HAVE IT.
I--
ACCEPTED

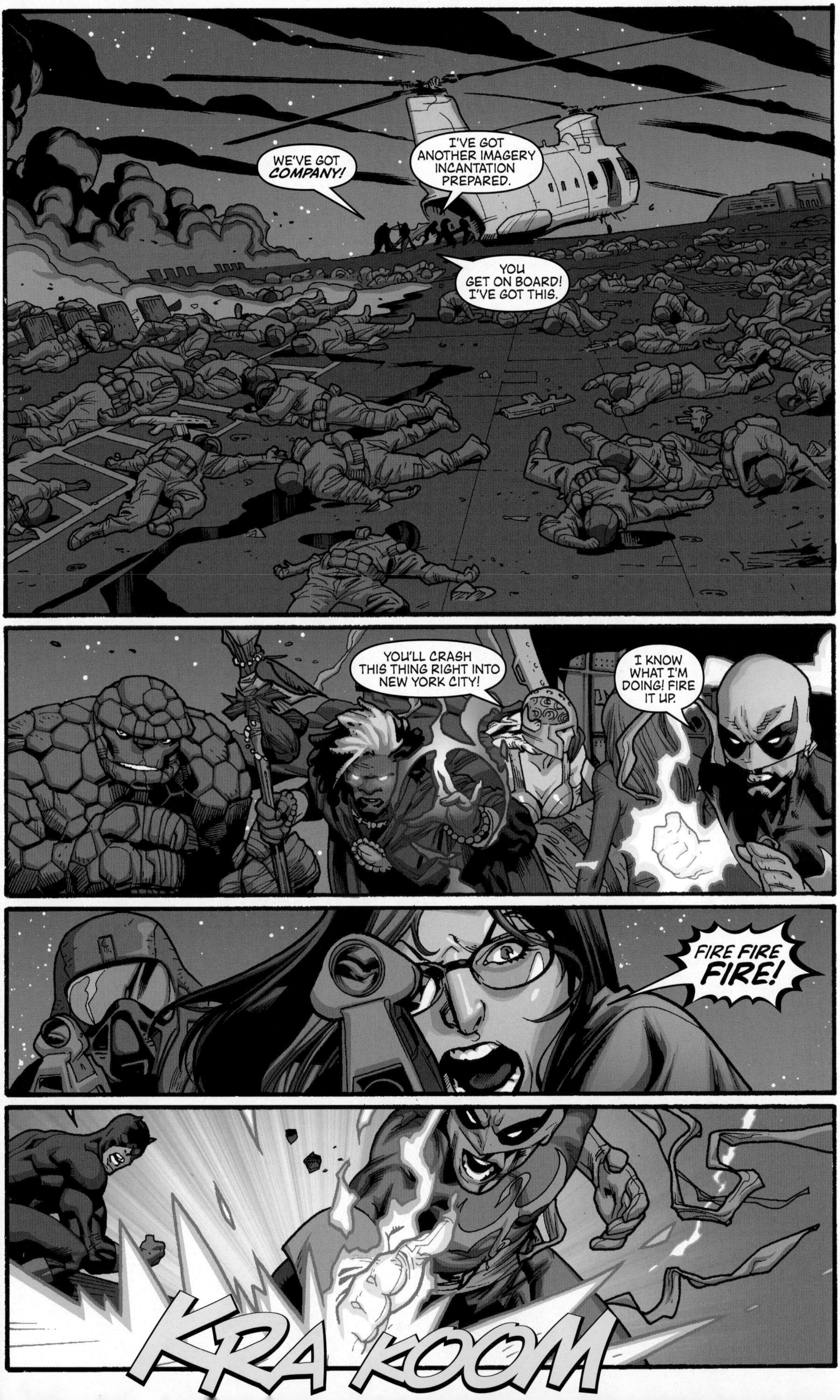
WE'VE GOT COMPANY!
I'VE GOT ANOTHER IMAGERY INCANTATION PREPARED.
YOU GET ON BOARD! I'VE GOT THIS.
YOU'LL CRASH THIS THING RIGHT INTO NEW YORK CITY!
I KNOW WHAT I'M DOING! FIRE IT UP.
FIRE FIRE FIRE!
KRA KOOM

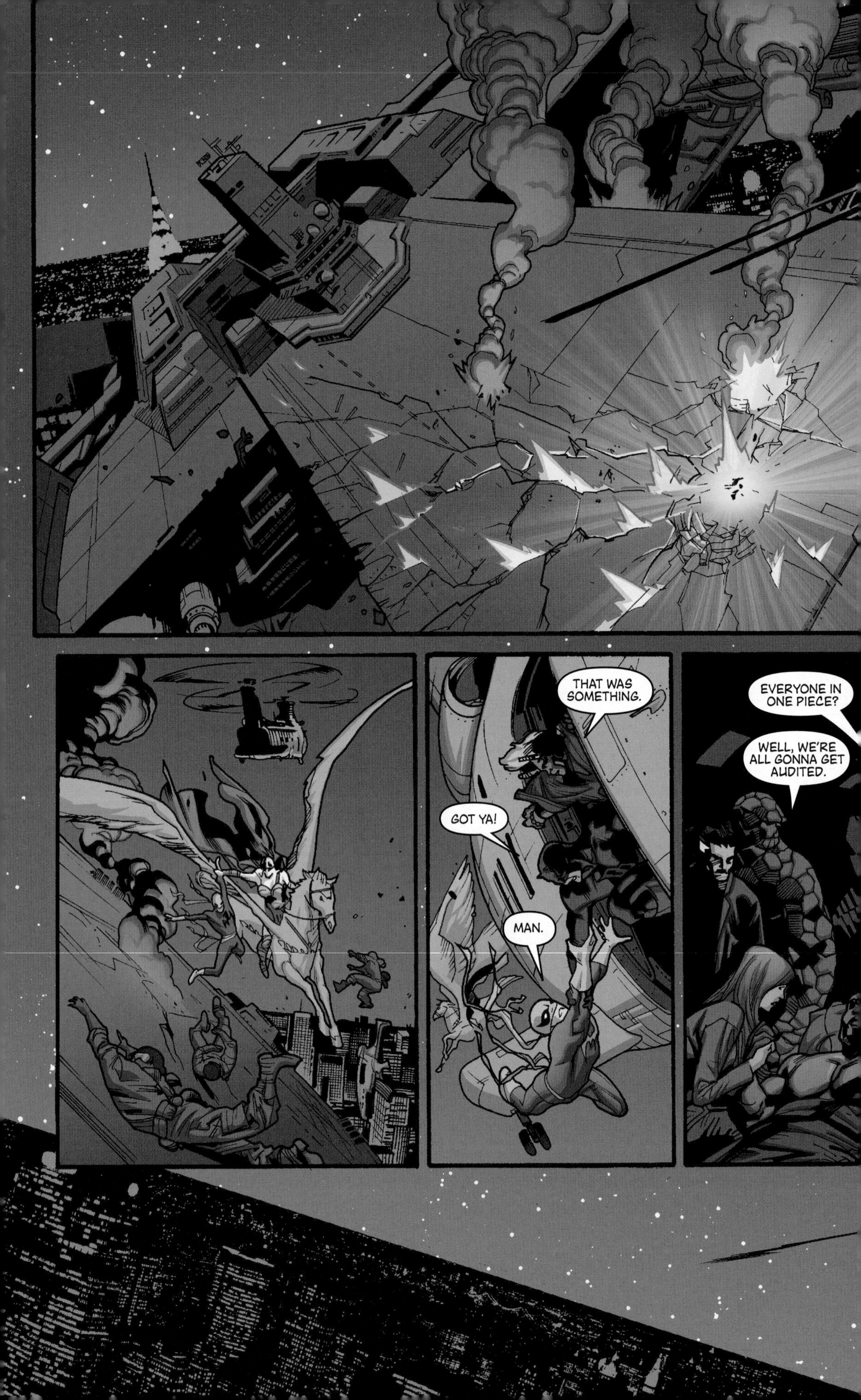
GOT YA!
THAT WAS SOMETHING.
MAN.
EVERYONE IN ONE PIECE?
WELL, WE'RE ALL GONNA GET AUDITED.

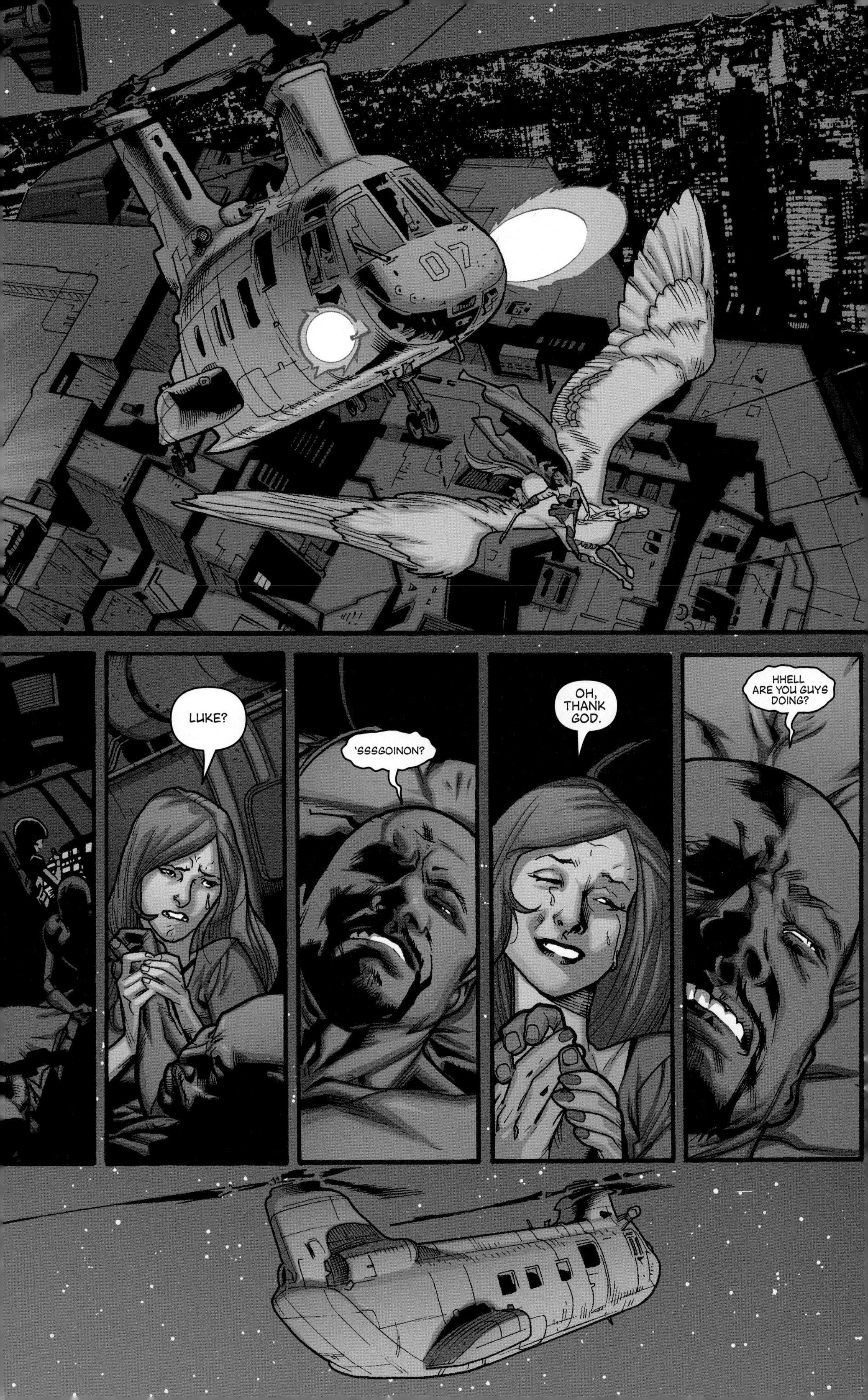
LUKE?
'SSSGOINON?
OH, THANK GOD.
HHELL ARE YOU GUYS DOING?

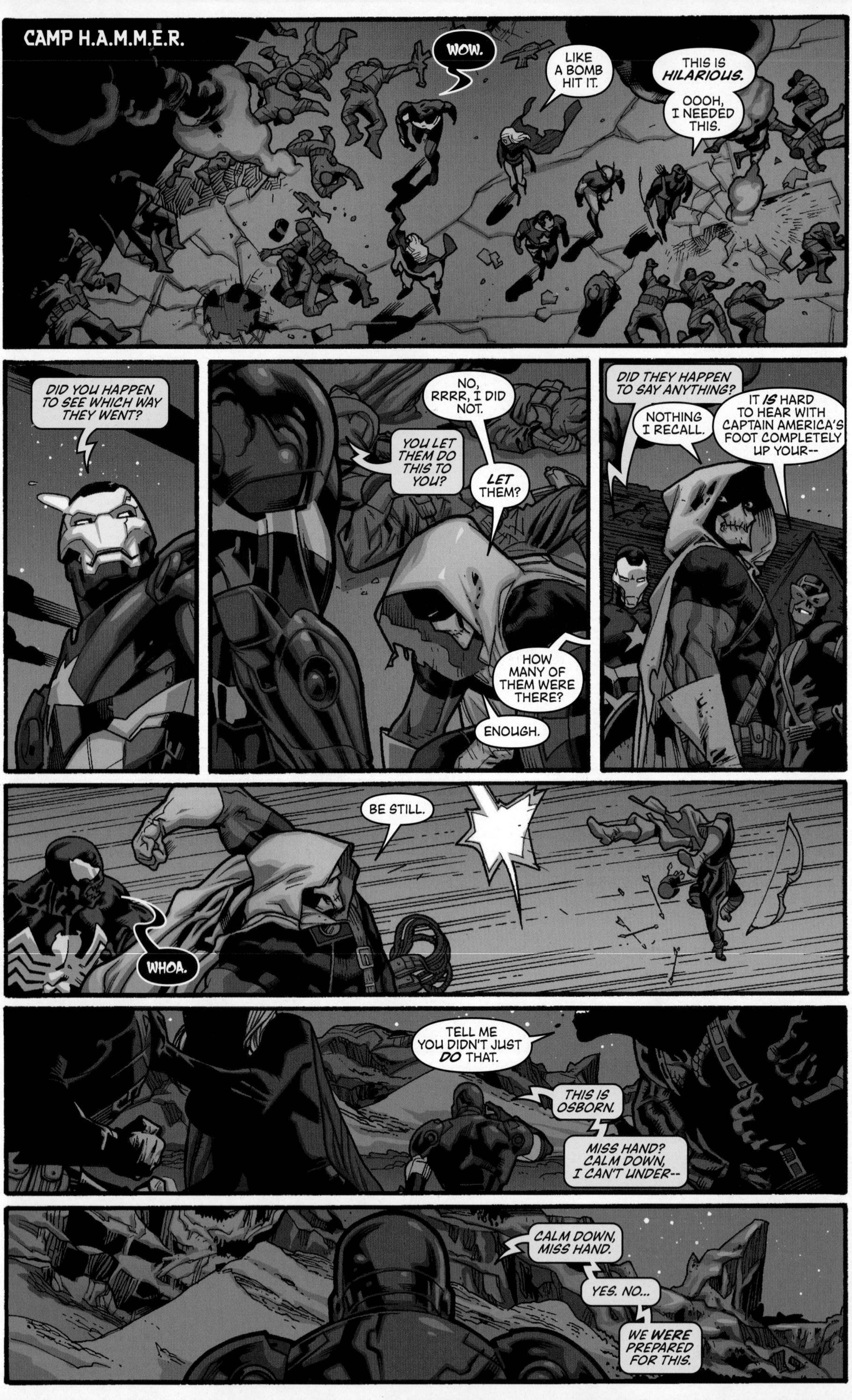
CAMP H.A.M.M.E.R.
WOW.
LIKE A BOMB HIT IT.
THIS IS HILARIOUS.
OOOH, I NEEDED THIS.
DID YOU HAPPEN TO SEE WHICH WAY THEY WENT?
NO, RRRR, I DID NOT.
YOU LET THEM DO THIS TO YOU?
LET THEM?
HOW MANY OF THEM WERE THERE?
ENOUGH.
DID THEY HAPPEN TO SAY ANYTHING?
NOTHING I RECALL.
IT IS HARD TO HEAR WITH CAPTAIN AMERICA'S FOOT COMPLETELY UP YOUR--
BE STILL.
WHOA.
TELL ME YOU DIDN'T JUST DO THAT.
THIS IS OSBORN.
MISS HAND? CALM DOWN, I CAN'T UNDER--
CALM DOWN, MISS HAND.
YES. NO...
WE WERE PREPARED FOR THIS.

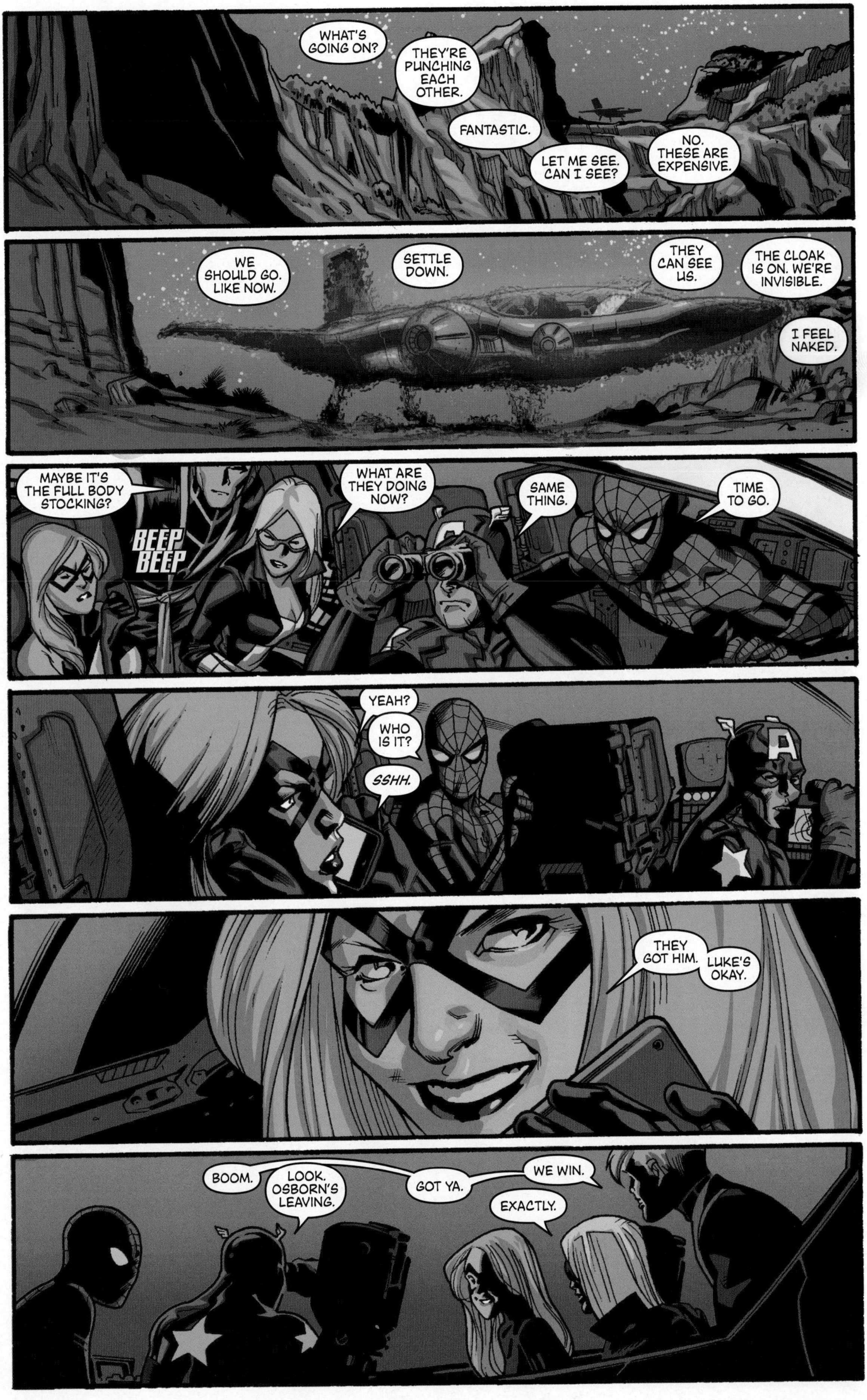
WHAT'S GOING ON?
THEY'RE PUNCHING EACH OTHER.
FANTASTIC.
LET ME SEE. CAN I SEE?
NO. THESE ARE EXPENSIVE.
WE SHOULD GO. LIKE NOW.
SETTLE DOWN.
THEY CAN SEE US.
THE CLOAK IS ON. WE'RE INVISIBLE.
I FEEL NAKED.
MAYBE IT'S THE FULL BODY STOCKING?
WHAT ARE THEY DOING NOW?
SAME THING.
TIME TO GO.
BEEP BEEP
YEAH?
WHO IS IT?
SSHH.
THEY GOT HIM.
LUKE'S OKAY.
BOOM.
LOOK. OSBORN'S LEAVING.
GOT YA.
WE WIN.
EXACTLY.

YOU DID WHAT?

HEY, IT WASN'T *MY* PLAN. IT WAS YOURS.

FEH BUMP FEH BUMP FEH BUMP

YOU NEVER KNOW.

IT'LL BE A WEIRD DAY IN MY LIFE WHEN TECHNOLOGY CATCHES UP TO THE MYSTIC ARTS.

WELL, I'M TELLING YOU, THAT ALREADY HAPPENED.

DOESN'T MATTER. LUKE'S BACK. AND HE'S SAFE.

FEH BUMP FEH BUMP

THANK YOU ALL.

THANK YOU.

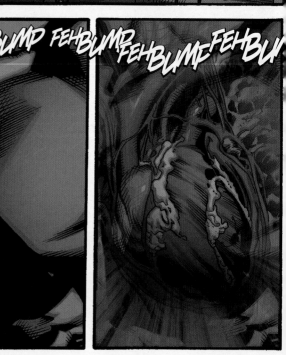

FEH BUMP FEH BUMP FEH BU

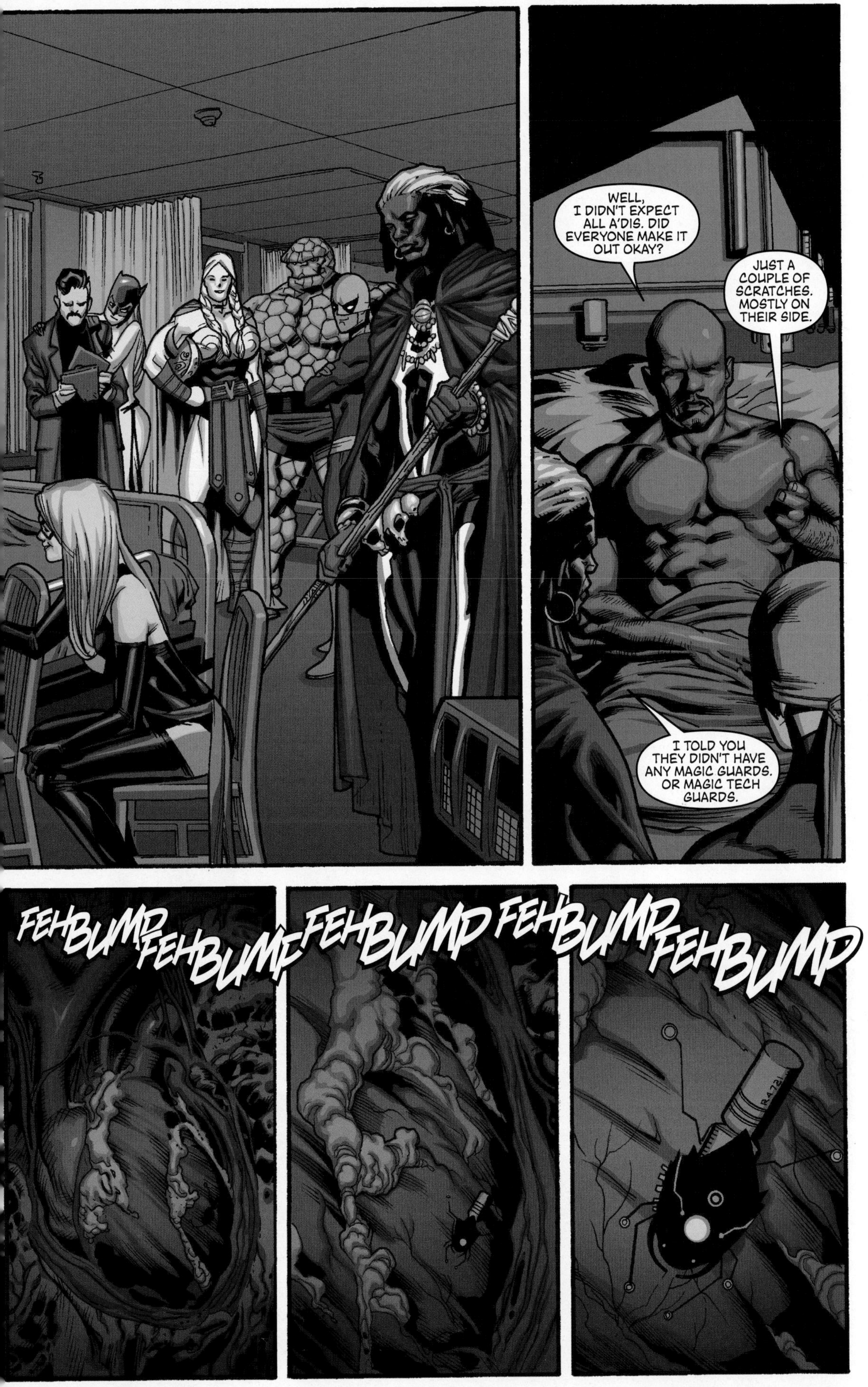

WELL, I DIDN'T EXPECT ALL A'DIS. DID EVERYONE MAKE IT OUT OKAY?
JUST A COUPLE OF SCRATCHES. MOSTLY ON THEIR SIDE.
I TOLD YOU THEY DIDN'T HAVE ANY MAGIC GUARDS. OR MAGIC TECH GUARDS.
FEHBUMP FEHBUMP
FEHBUMP
FEHBUMP FEHBUMP

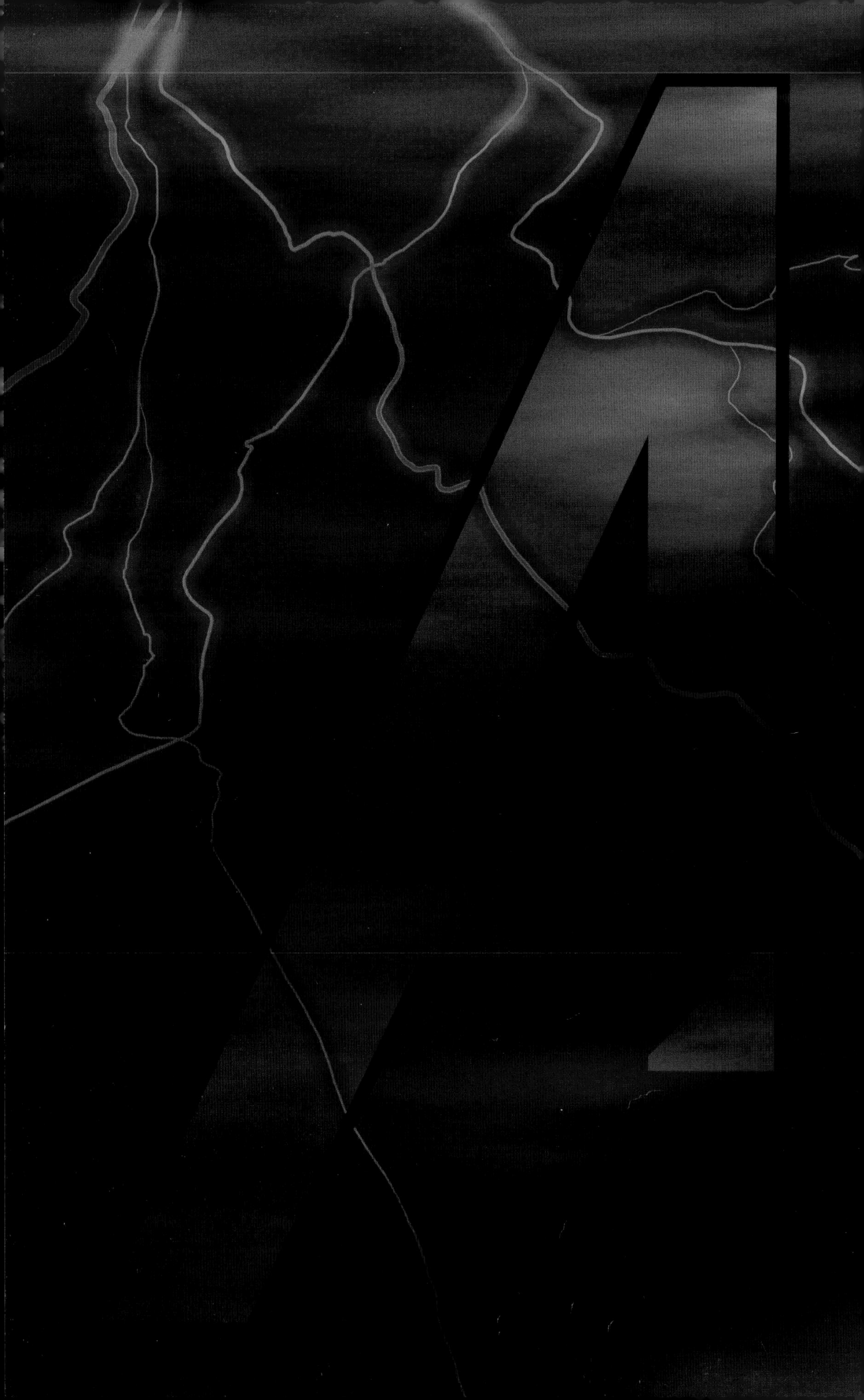
4

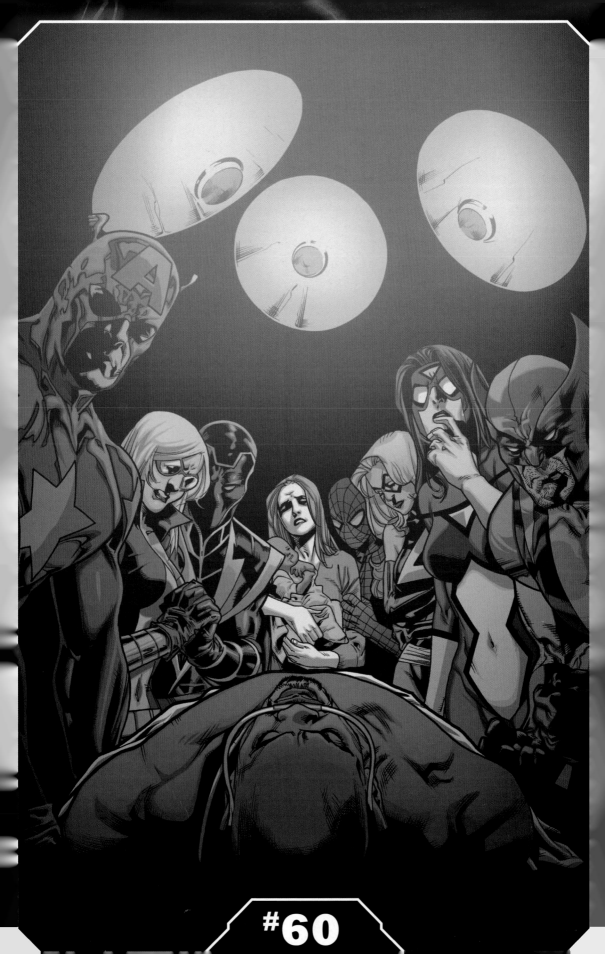

#60

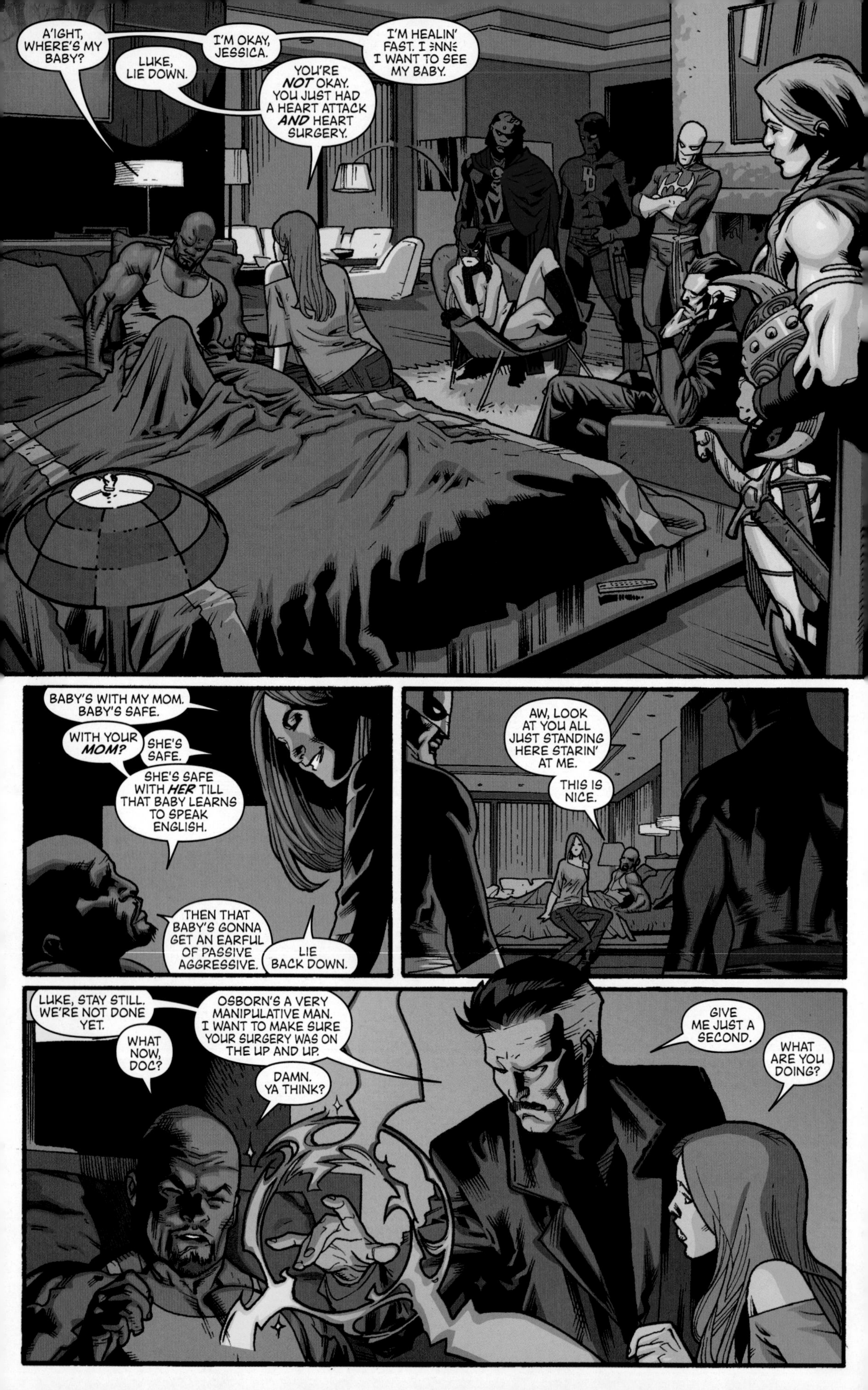
A'IGHT, WHERE'S MY BABY?
I'M OKAY, JESSICA.
I'M HEALIN' FAST. I
I WANT TO SEE MY BABY.
LUKE, LIE DOWN.
YOU'RE NOT OKAY. YOU JUST HAD A HEART ATTACK AND HEART SURGERY.
BABY'S WITH MY MOM. BABY'S SAFE.
WITH YOUR MOM?
SHE'S SAFE.
SHE'S SAFE WITH HER TILL THAT BABY LEARNS TO SPEAK ENGLISH.
THEN THAT BABY'S GONNA GET AN EARFUL OF PASSIVE AGGRESSIVE.
LIE BACK DOWN.
AW, LOOK AT YOU ALL JUST STANDING HERE STARIN' AT ME.
THIS IS NICE.
LUKE, STAY STILL. WE'RE NOT DONE YET.
WHAT NOW, DOC?
OSBORN'S A VERY MANIPULATIVE MAN. I WANT TO MAKE SURE YOUR SURGERY WAS ON THE UP AND UP.
DAMN. YA THINK?
GIVE ME JUST A SECOND.
WHAT ARE YOU DOING?

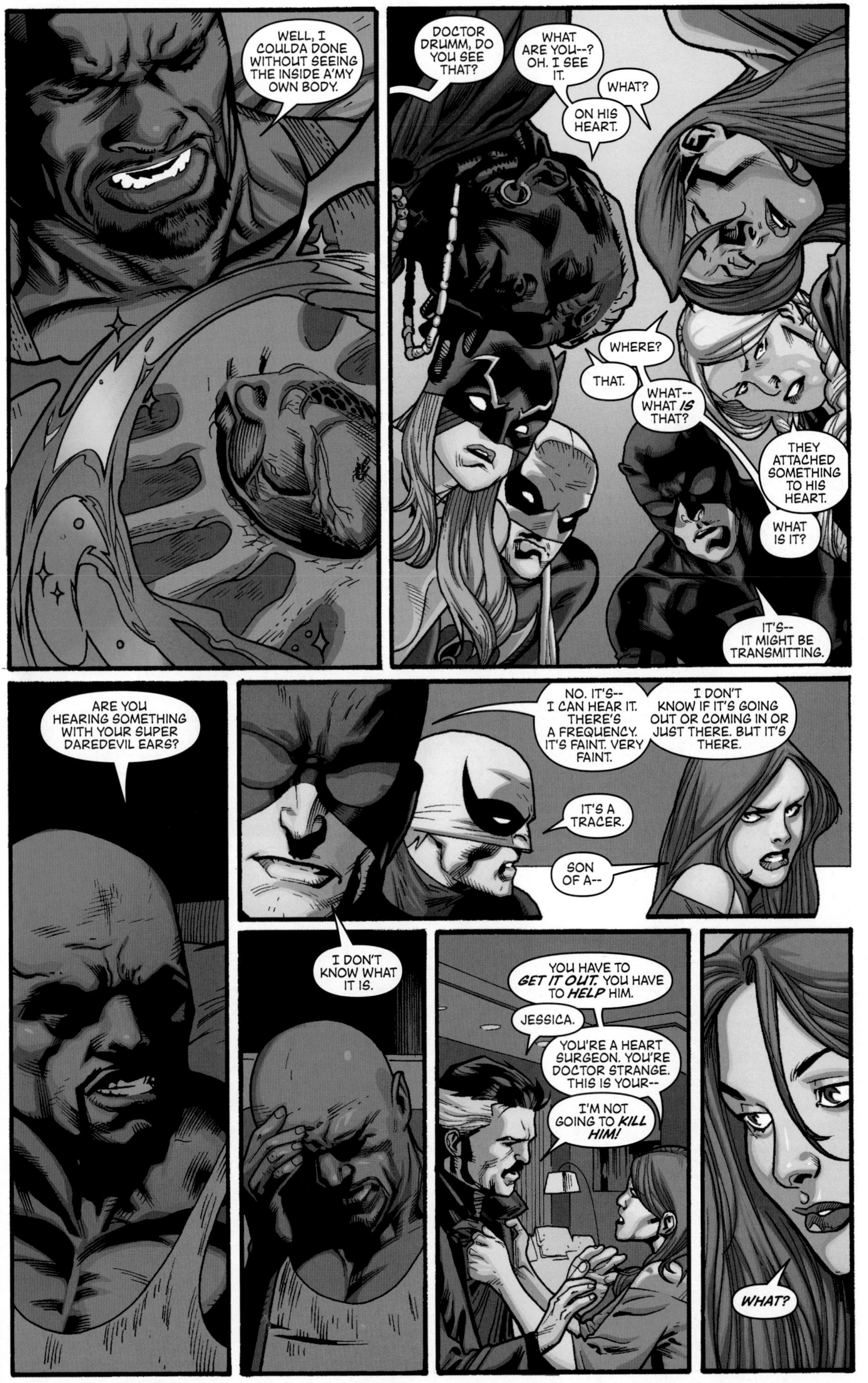
WELL, I COULDA DONE WITHOUT SEEING THE INSIDE A'MY OWN BODY.
DOCTOR DRUMM, DO YOU SEE THAT?
WHAT ARE YOU--? OH. I SEE IT.
WHAT?
ON HIS HEART.
WHERE?
THAT.
WHAT-- WHAT *IS* THAT?
THEY ATTACHED SOMETHING TO HIS HEART.
WHAT IS IT?
IT'S-- IT MIGHT BE TRANSMITTING.
ARE YOU HEARING SOMETHING WITH YOUR SUPER DAREDEVIL EARS?
NO. IT'S-- I CAN HEAR IT. THERE'S A FREQUENCY. IT'S FAINT. VERY FAINT.
I DON'T KNOW IF IT'S GOING OUT OR COMING IN OR JUST THERE. BUT IT'S THERE.
IT'S A TRACER.
SON OF A--
I DON'T KNOW WHAT IT IS.
YOU HAVE TO ***GET IT OUT.*** YOU HAVE TO ***HELP*** HIM.
JESSICA.
YOU'RE A HEART SURGEON. YOU'RE DOCTOR STRANGE. THIS IS YOUR--
I'M NOT GOING TO ***KILL HIM!***
WHAT?

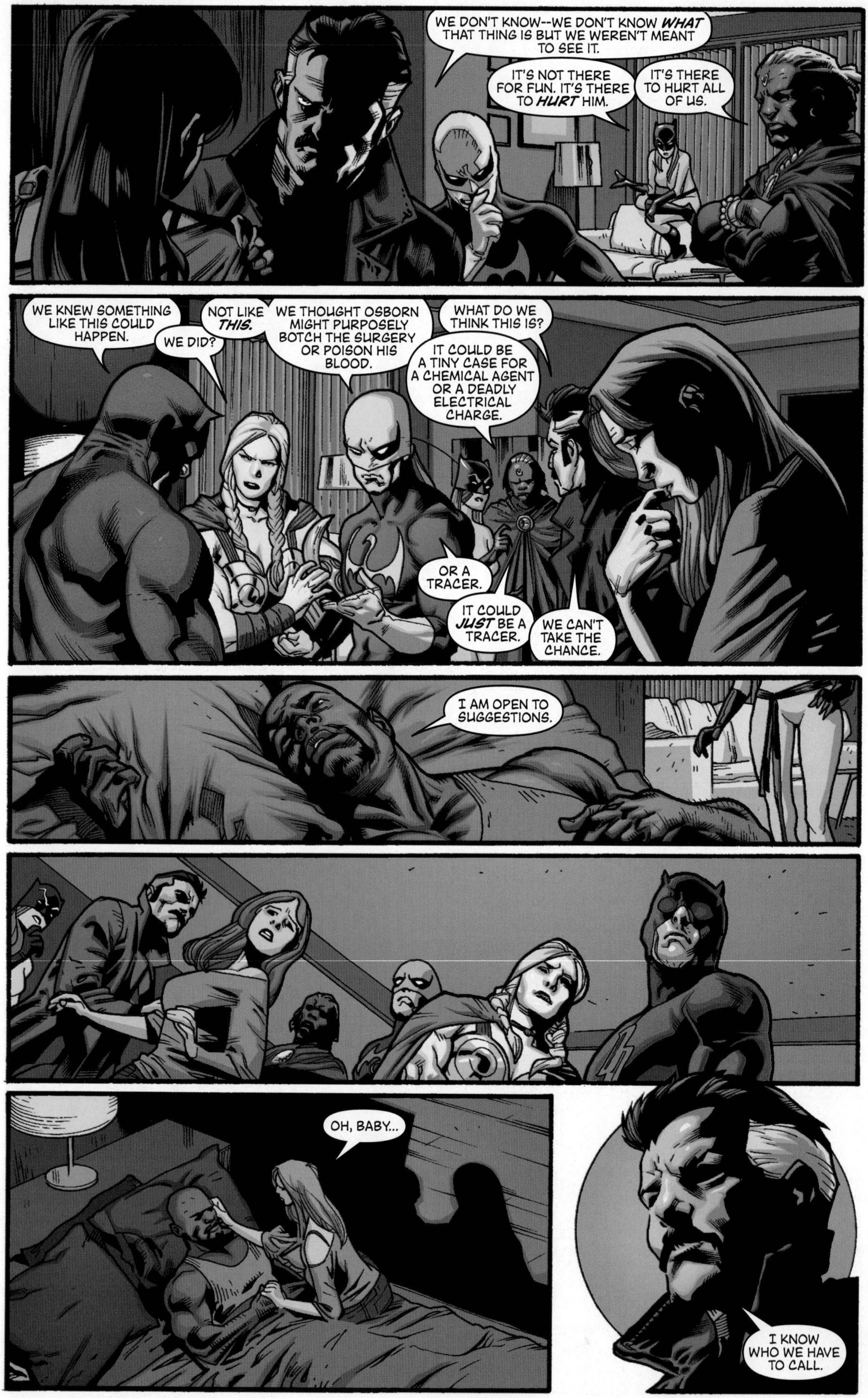
WE DON'T KNOW--WE DON'T KNOW WHAT THAT THING IS BUT WE WEREN'T MEANT TO SEE IT.
IT'S NOT THERE FOR FUN. IT'S THERE TO HURT HIM.
IT'S THERE TO HURT ALL OF US.
WE KNEW SOMETHING LIKE THIS COULD HAPPEN.
WE DID?
NOT LIKE THIS.
WE THOUGHT OSBORN MIGHT PURPOSELY BOTCH THE SURGERY OR POISON HIS BLOOD.
WHAT DO WE THINK THIS IS?
IT COULD BE A TINY CASE FOR A CHEMICAL AGENT OR A DEADLY ELECTRICAL CHARGE.
OR A TRACER.
IT COULD JUST BE A TRACER.
WE CAN'T TAKE THE CHANCE.
I AM OPEN TO SUGGESTIONS.
OH, BABY...
I KNOW WHO WE HAVE TO CALL.

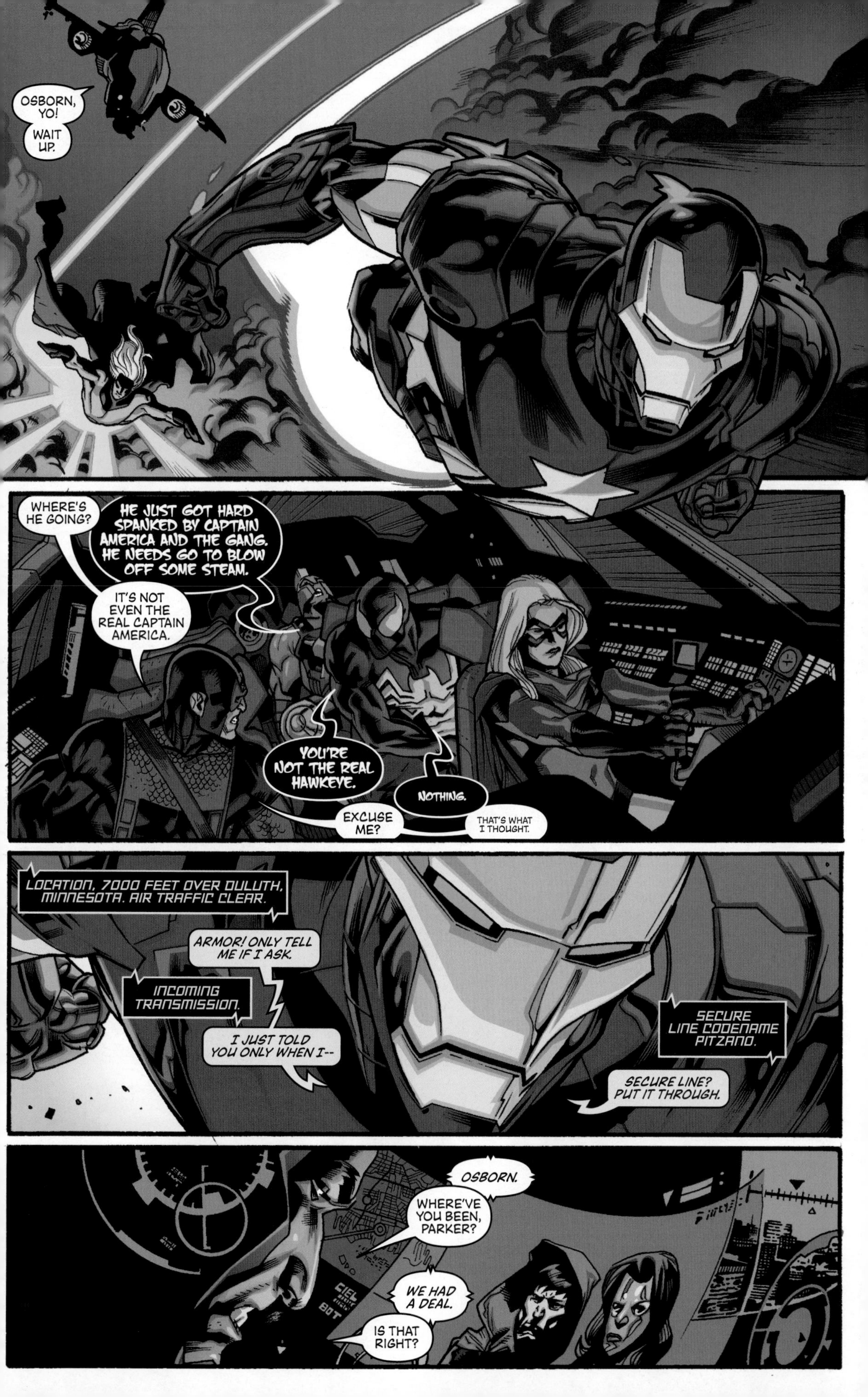
OSBORN, YO!
WAIT UP.
WHERE'S HE GOING?
HE JUST GOT HARD SPANKED BY CAPTAIN AMERICA AND THE GANG. HE NEEDS GO TO BLOW OFF SOME STEAM.
IT'S NOT EVEN THE REAL CAPTAIN AMERICA.
YOU'RE NOT THE REAL HAWKEYE.
EXCUSE ME?
NOTHING.
THAT'S WHAT I THOUGHT.
LOCATION, 7000 FEET OVER DULUTH, MINNESOTA. AIR TRAFFIC CLEAR.
ARMOR! ONLY TELL ME IF I ASK.
INCOMING TRANSMISSION.
I JUST TOLD YOU ONLY WHEN I--
SECURE LINE CODENAME PITZANO.
SECURE LINE? PUT IT THROUGH.
OSBORN.
WHERE'VE YOU BEEN, PARKER?
WE HAD A DEAL.
IS THAT RIGHT?

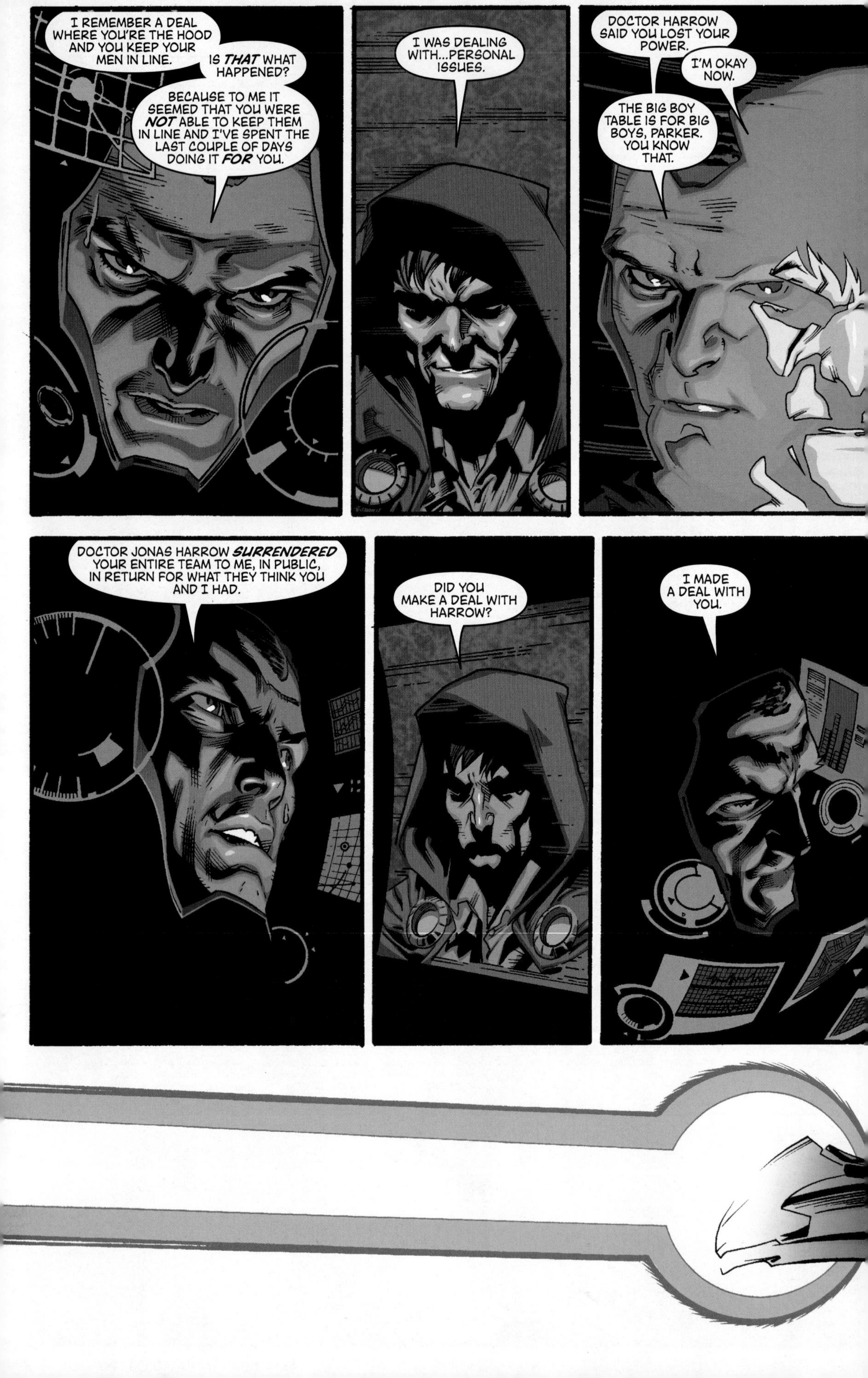
I REMEMBER A DEAL WHERE YOU'RE THE HOOD AND YOU KEEP YOUR MEN IN LINE.
IS *THAT* WHAT HAPPENED?
BECAUSE TO ME IT SEEMED THAT YOU WERE *NOT* ABLE TO KEEP THEM IN LINE AND I'VE SPENT THE LAST COUPLE OF DAYS DOING IT *FOR* YOU.
I WAS DEALING WITH...PERSONAL ISSUES.
DOCTOR HARROW SAID YOU LOST YOUR POWER.
I'M OKAY NOW.
THE BIG BOY TABLE IS FOR BIG BOYS, PARKER. YOU KNOW THAT.
DOCTOR JONAS HARROW *SURRENDERED* YOUR ENTIRE TEAM TO ME, IN PUBLIC, IN RETURN FOR WHAT THEY THINK YOU AND I HAD.
DID YOU MAKE A DEAL WITH HARROW?
I MADE A DEAL WITH YOU.

I'M GOOD. LOKI HELPED ME.

LOKI?

WHY WOULD LOKI HELP YOU GET YOUR POWERS BACK?

YOU'LL HAVE TO ASK HER/HIM.

BUT I'M BACK AND I'M BETTER THAN EVER.

AND HARROW.

WELL...

WHAT ARE WE GOING TO DO ABOUT THAT?

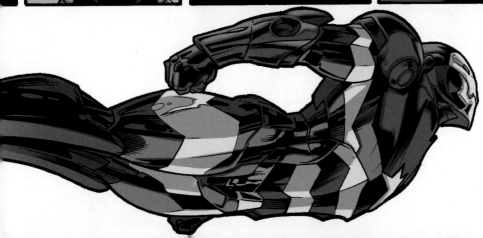

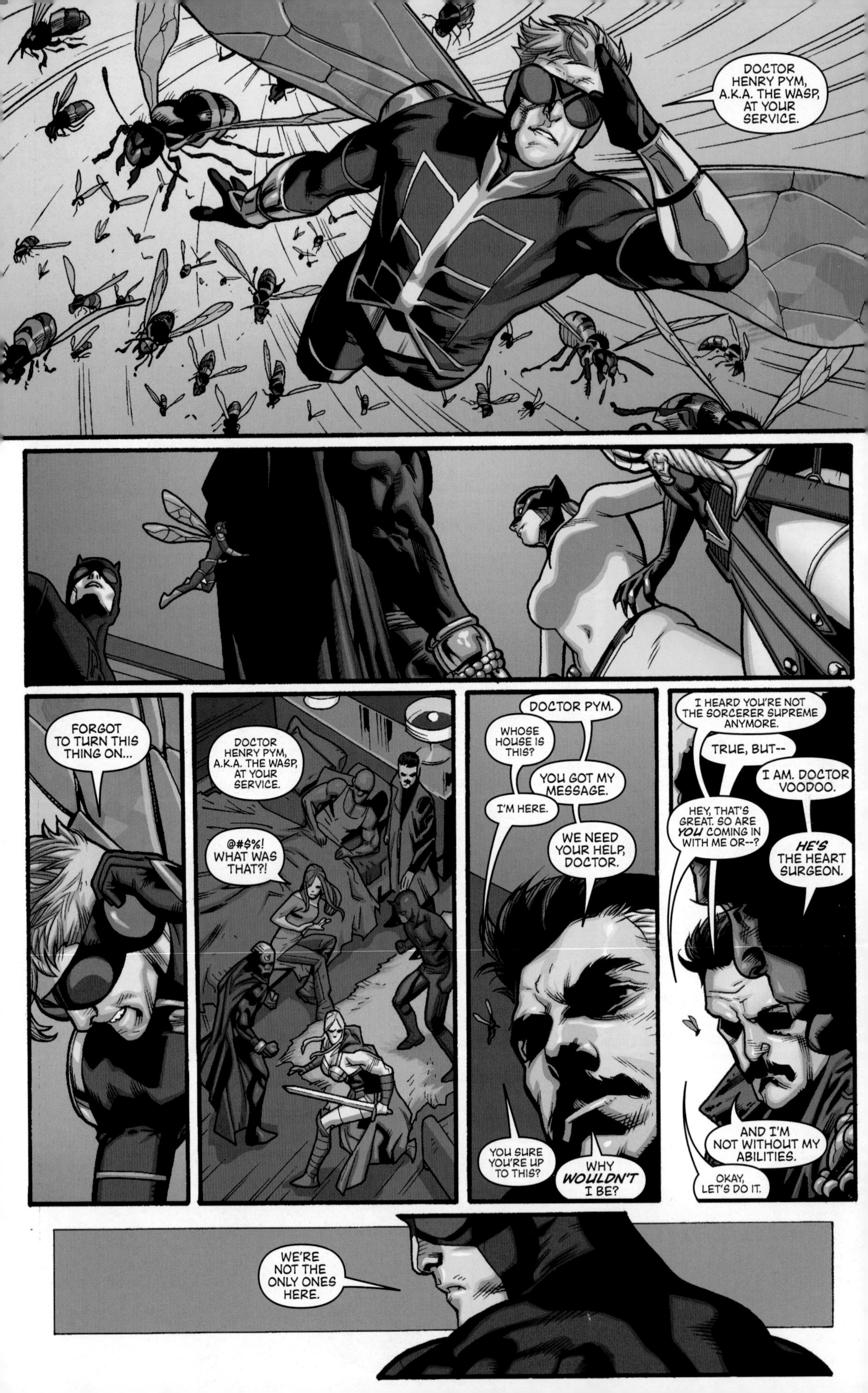
DOCTOR HENRY PYM, A.K.A. THE WASP, AT YOUR SERVICE.
FORGOT TO TURN THIS THING ON...
DOCTOR HENRY PYM, A.K.A. THE WASP, AT YOUR SERVICE.
@#$%! WHAT WAS THAT?!
DOCTOR PYM.
WHOSE HOUSE IS THIS?
YOU GOT MY MESSAGE.
I'M HERE.
WE NEED YOUR HELP, DOCTOR.
YOU SURE YOU'RE UP TO THIS?
WHY WOULDN'T I BE?
I HEARD YOU'RE NOT THE SORCERER SUPREME ANYMORE.
TRUE, BUT--
I AM. DOCTOR VOODOO.
HEY, THAT'S GREAT. SO ARE YOU COMING IN WITH ME OR--?
HE'S THE HEART SURGEON.
AND I'M NOT WITHOUT MY ABILITIES.
OKAY, LET'S DO IT.
WE'RE NOT THE ONLY ONES HERE.

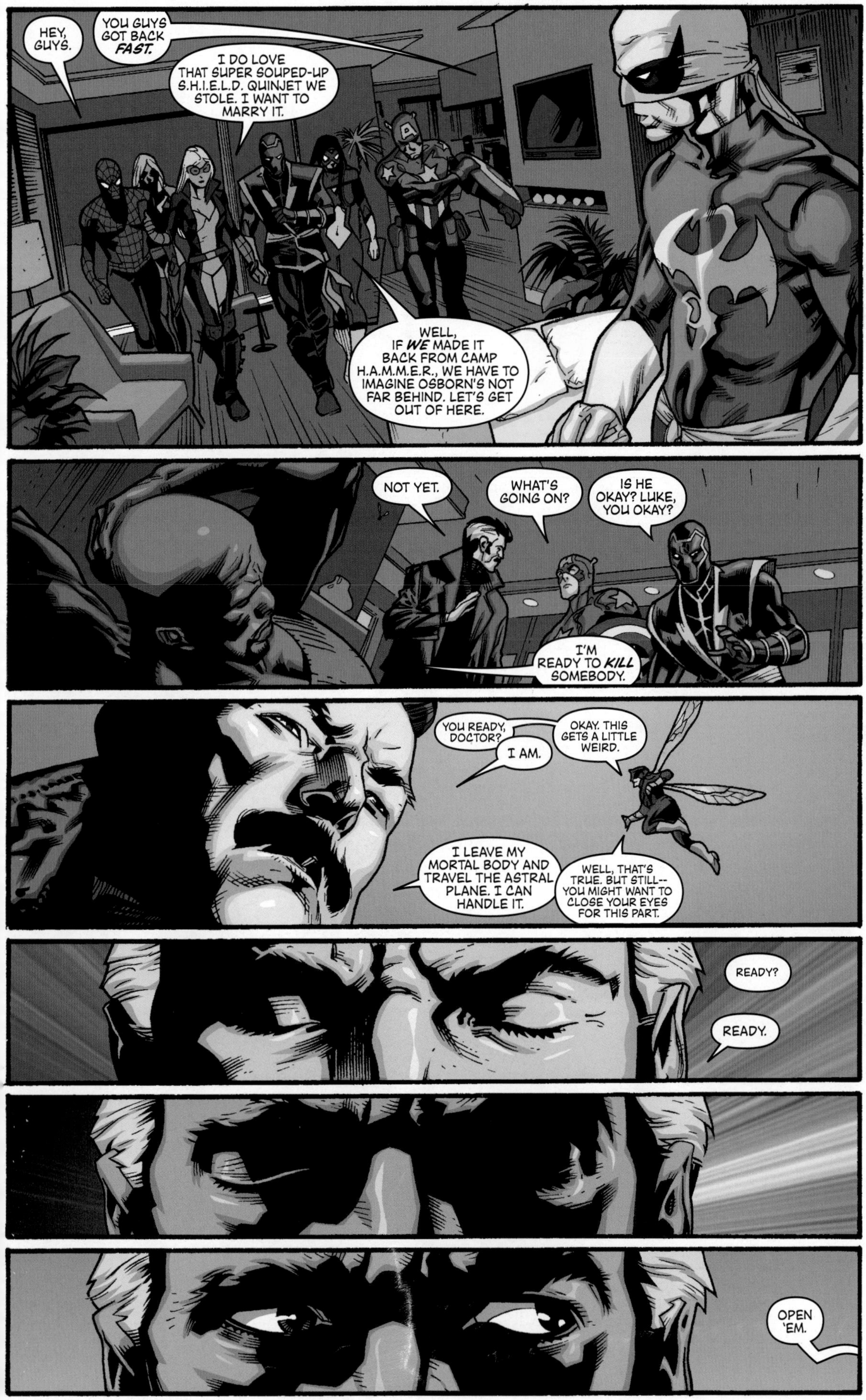
HEY, GUYS.
YOU GUYS GOT BACK FAST.
I DO LOVE THAT SUPER SOUPED-UP S.H.I.E.L.D. QUINJET WE STOLE. I WANT TO MARRY IT.
WELL, IF WE MADE IT BACK FROM CAMP H.A.M.M.E.R., WE HAVE TO IMAGINE OSBORN'S NOT FAR BEHIND. LET'S GET OUT OF HERE.
NOT YET.
WHAT'S GOING ON?
IS HE OKAY? LUKE, YOU OKAY?
I'M READY TO KILL SOMEBODY.
YOU READY, DOCTOR?
I AM.
OKAY. THIS GETS A LITTLE WEIRD.
I LEAVE MY MORTAL BODY AND TRAVEL THE ASTRAL PLANE. I CAN HANDLE IT.
WELL, THAT'S TRUE. BUT STILL-- YOU MIGHT WANT TO CLOSE YOUR EYES FOR THIS PART.
READY?
READY.
OPEN 'EM.

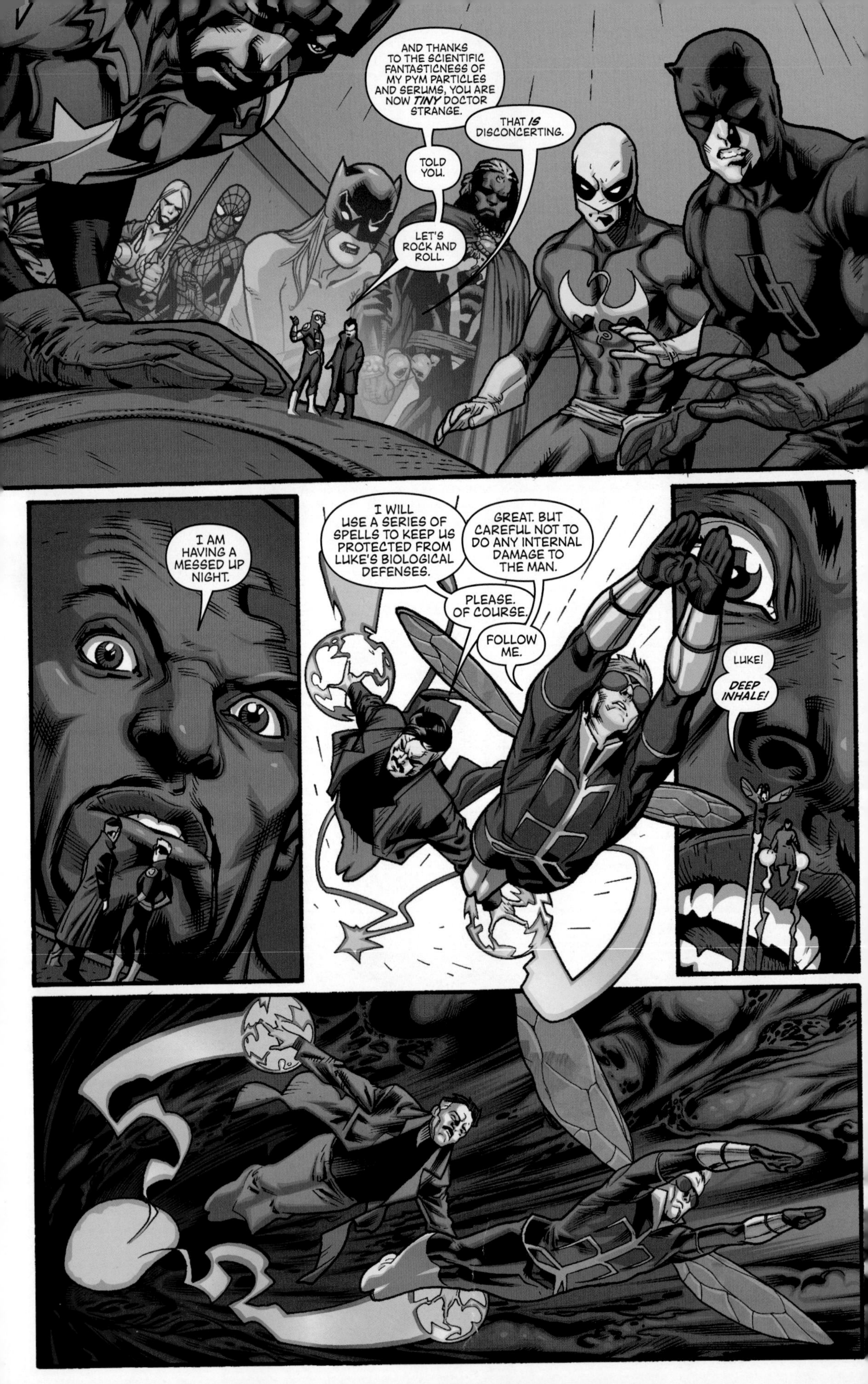
AND THANKS TO THE SCIENTIFIC FANTASTICNESS OF MY PYM PARTICLES AND SERUMS, YOU ARE NOW *TINY* DOCTOR STRANGE.
THAT *IS* DISCONCERTING.
TOLD YOU.
LET'S ROCK AND ROLL.
I AM HAVING A MESSED UP NIGHT.
I WILL USE A SERIES OF SPELLS TO KEEP US PROTECTED FROM LUKE'S BIOLOGICAL DEFENSES.
GREAT. BUT CAREFUL NOT TO DO ANY INTERNAL DAMAGE TO THE MAN.
PLEASE. OF COURSE.
FOLLOW ME.
LUKE!
DEEP INHALE!

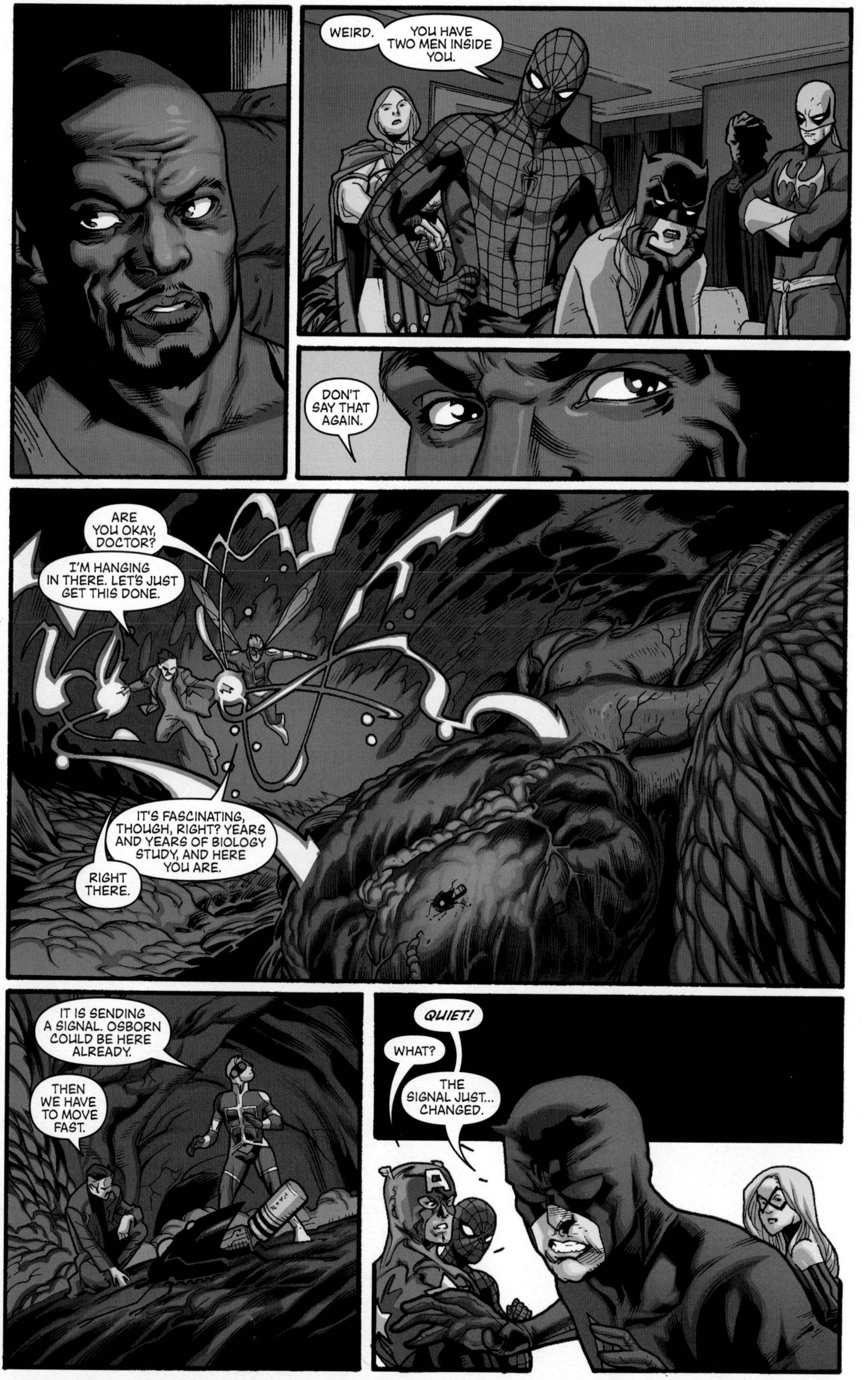
WEIRD.
YOU HAVE TWO MEN INSIDE YOU.
DON'T SAY THAT AGAIN.
ARE YOU OKAY, DOCTOR?
I'M HANGING IN THERE. LET'S JUST GET THIS DONE.
IT'S FASCINATING, THOUGH, RIGHT? YEARS AND YEARS OF BIOLOGY STUDY, AND HERE YOU ARE.
RIGHT THERE.
IT IS SENDING A SIGNAL. OSBORN COULD BE HERE ALREADY.
THEN WE HAVE TO MOVE FAST.
QUIET!
WHAT?
THE SIGNAL JUST... CHANGED.

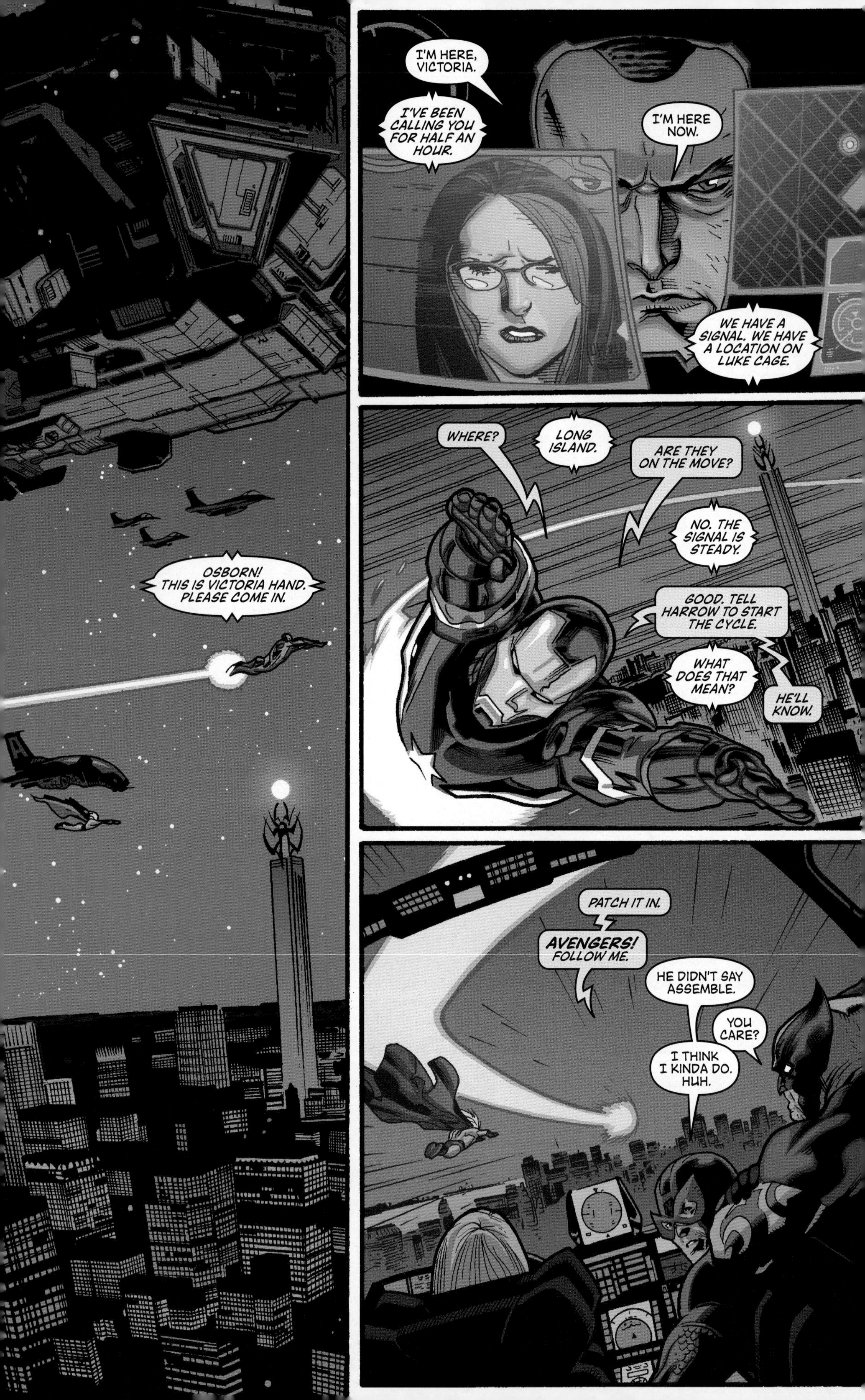
OSBORN! THIS IS VICTORIA HAND. PLEASE COME IN.
I'M HERE, VICTORIA.
I'VE BEEN CALLING YOU FOR HALF AN HOUR.
I'M HERE NOW.
WE HAVE A SIGNAL. WE HAVE A LOCATION ON LUKE CAGE.
WHERE?
LONG ISLAND.
ARE THEY ON THE MOVE?
NO. THE SIGNAL IS STEADY.
GOOD. TELL HARROW TO START THE CYCLE.
WHAT DOES THAT MEAN?
HE'LL KNOW.
PATCH IT IN.
AVENGERS! FOLLOW ME.
HE DIDN'T SAY ASSEMBLE.
YOU CARE?
I THINK I KINDA DO. HUH.

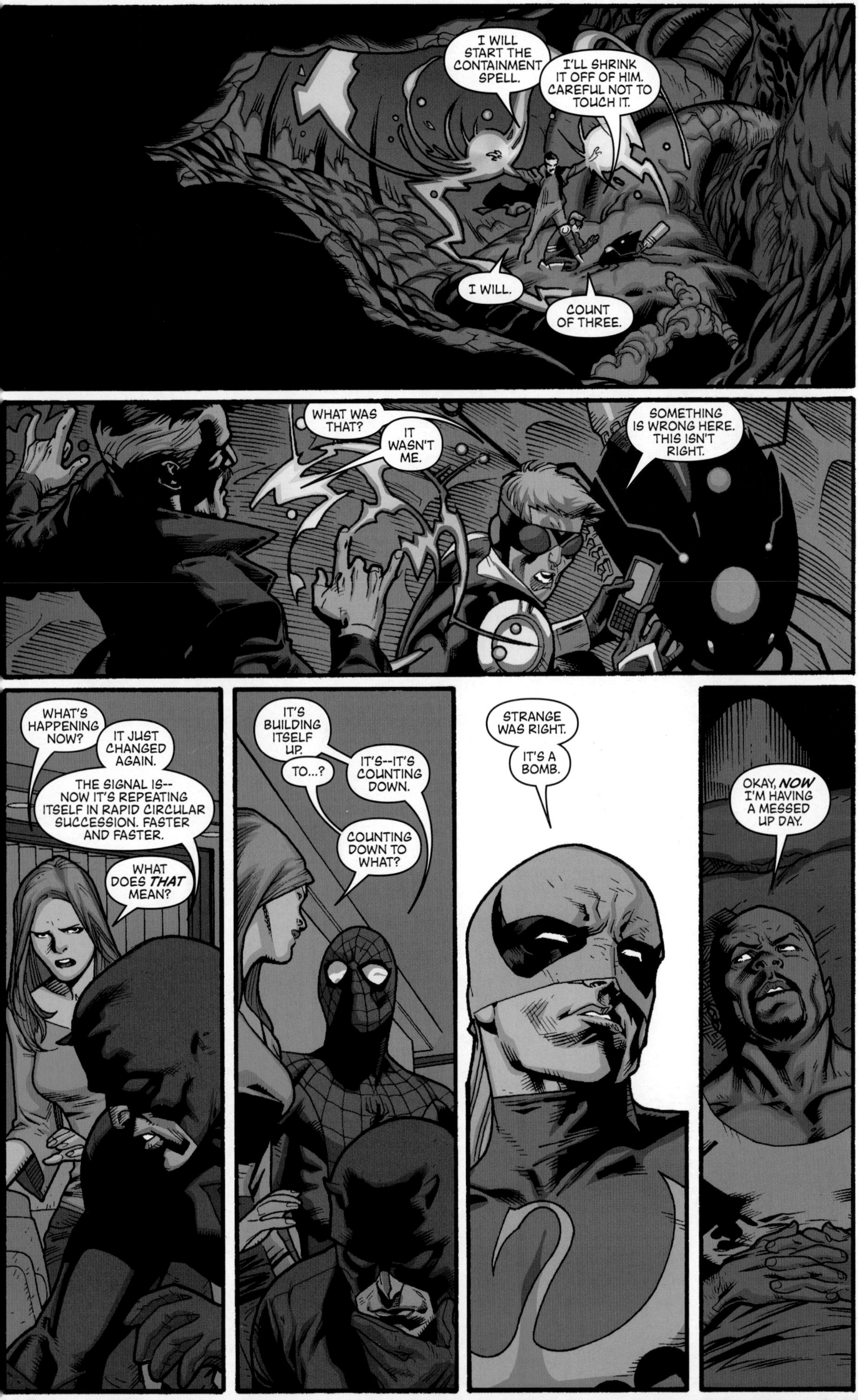
I WILL START THE CONTAINMENT SPELL.
I'LL SHRINK IT OFF OF HIM. CAREFUL NOT TO TOUCH IT.
I WILL.
COUNT OF THREE.
WHAT WAS THAT?
IT WASN'T ME.
SOMETHING IS WRONG HERE. THIS ISN'T RIGHT.
WHAT'S HAPPENING NOW?
IT JUST CHANGED AGAIN.
THE SIGNAL IS-- NOW IT'S REPEATING ITSELF IN RAPID CIRCULAR SUCCESSION. FASTER AND FASTER.
WHAT DOES *THAT* MEAN?
IT'S BUILDING ITSELF UP.
TO...?
IT'S--IT'S COUNTING DOWN.
COUNTING DOWN TO WHAT?
STRANGE WAS RIGHT.
IT'S A BOMB.
OKAY, ***NOW*** I'M HAVING A MESSED UP DAY.

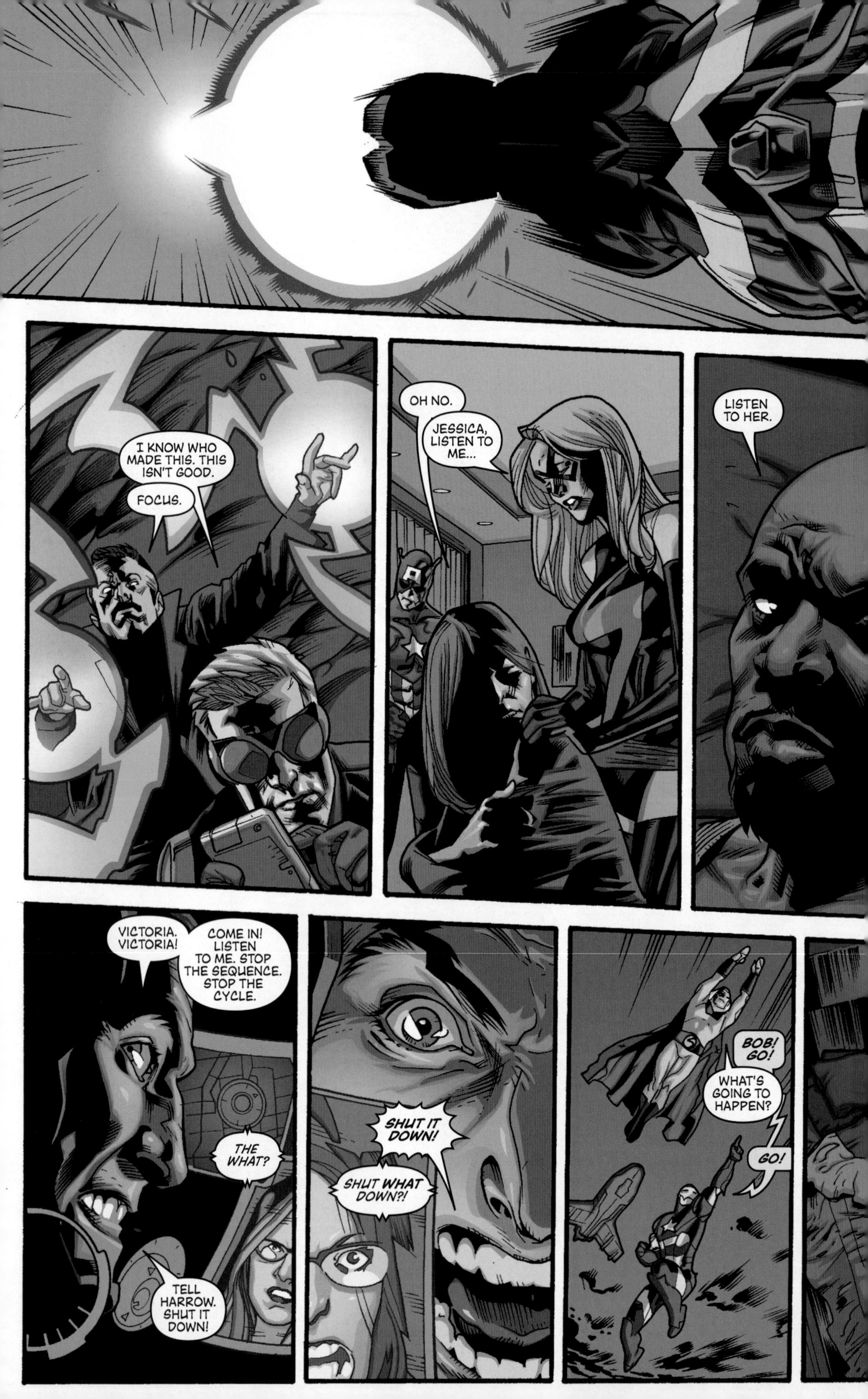
I KNOW WHO MADE THIS. THIS ISN'T GOOD.
FOCUS.
OH NO.
JESSICA, LISTEN TO ME...
LISTEN TO HER.
VICTORIA. VICTORIA!
COME IN! LISTEN TO ME. STOP THE SEQUENCE. STOP THE CYCLE.
THE WHAT?
TELL HARROW. SHUT IT DOWN!
SHUT IT DOWN!
SHUT WHAT DOWN?!
BOB! GO!
WHAT'S GOING TO HAPPEN?
GO!

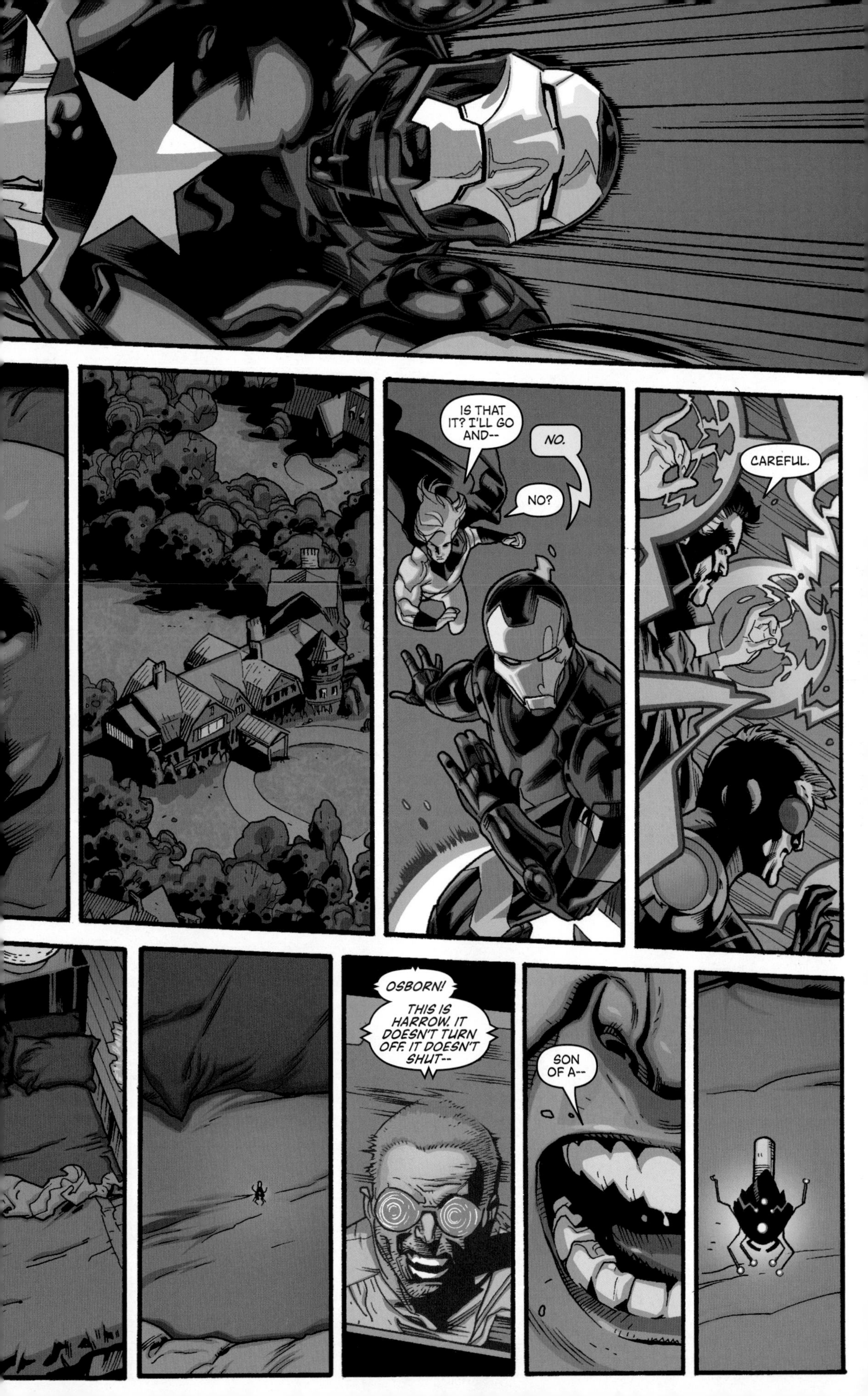

IS THAT IT? I'LL GO AND--
NO.
NO?
CAREFUL.
OSBORN!
THIS IS HARROW. IT DOESN'T TURN OFF. IT DOESN'T SHUT--
SON OF A--

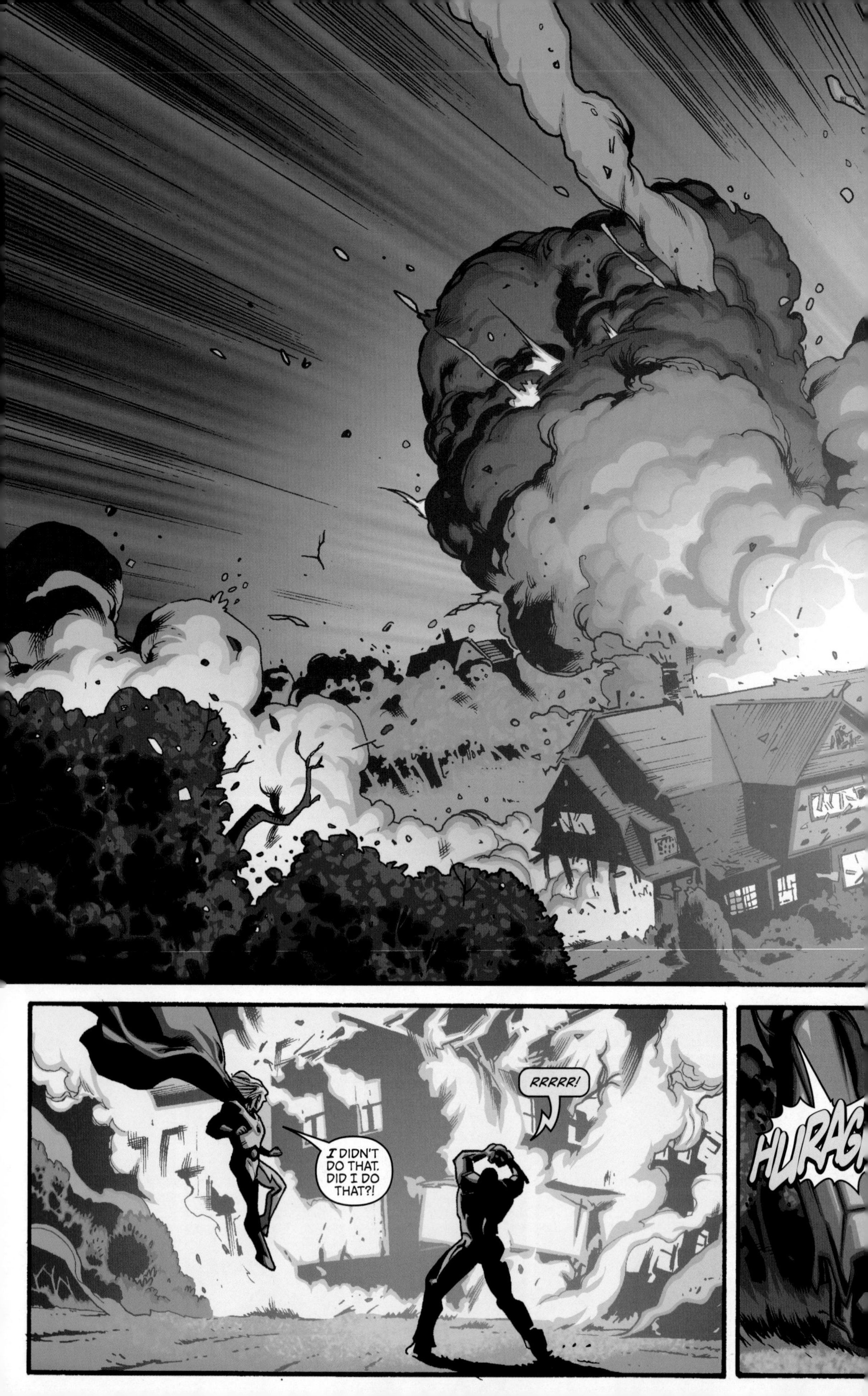
I DIDN'T DO THAT. DID I DO THAT?!
RRRRR!
HURAG

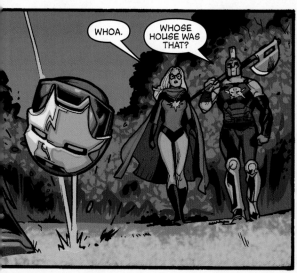

WHOA.

WHOSE HOUSE WAS THAT?

MINE.

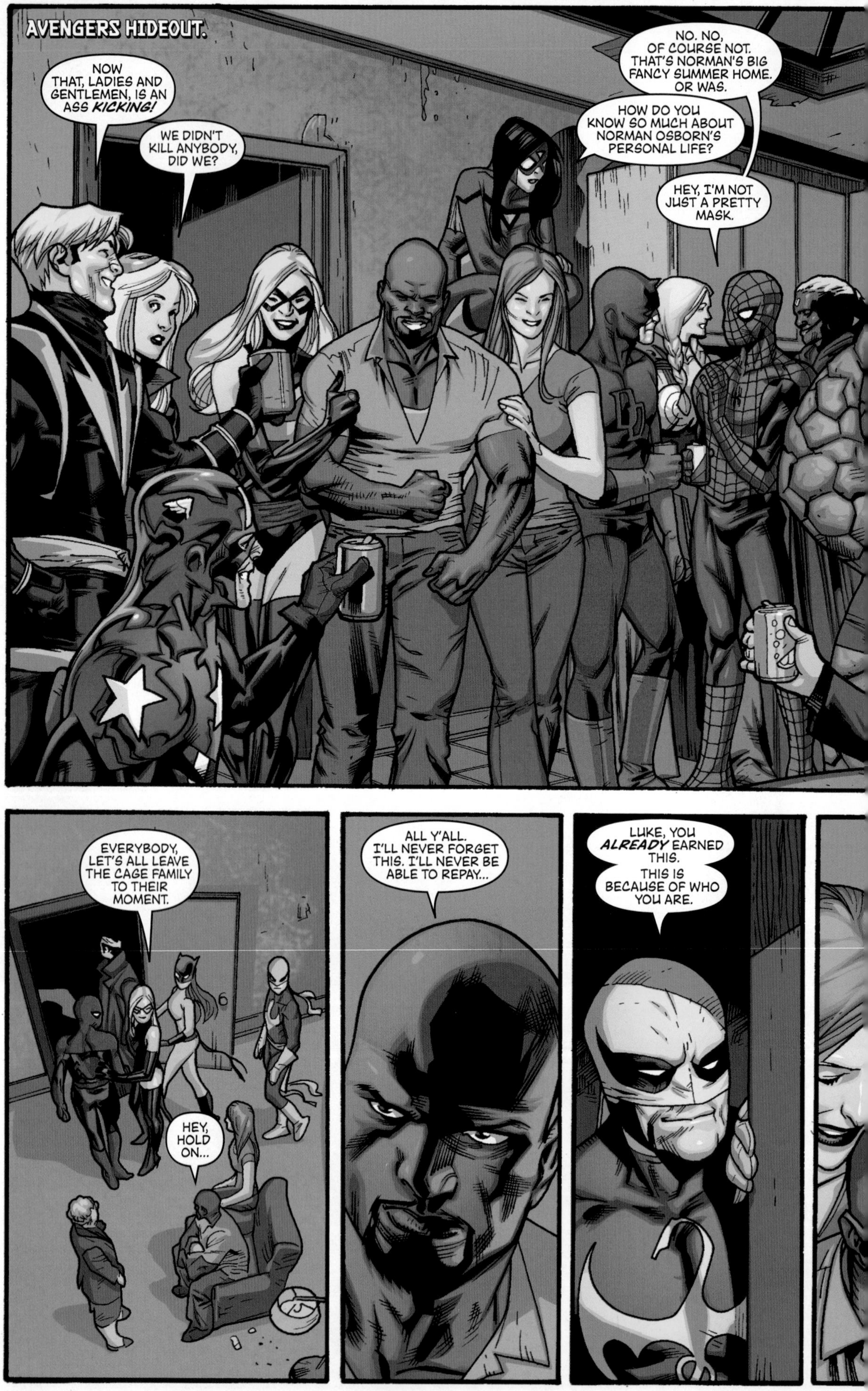
AVENGERS HIDEOUT.
NOW THAT, LADIES AND GENTLEMEN, IS AN ASS KICKING!
WE DIDN'T KILL ANYBODY, DID WE?
NO. NO, OF COURSE NOT. THAT'S NORMAN'S BIG FANCY SUMMER HOME. OR WAS.
HOW DO YOU KNOW SO MUCH ABOUT NORMAN OSBORN'S PERSONAL LIFE?
HEY, I'M NOT JUST A PRETTY MASK.
EVERYBODY, LET'S ALL LEAVE THE CAGE FAMILY TO THEIR MOMENT.
HEY, HOLD ON...
ALL Y'ALL. I'LL NEVER FORGET THIS. I'LL NEVER BE ABLE TO REPAY...
LUKE, YOU ALREADY EARNED THIS.
THIS IS BECAUSE OF WHO YOU ARE.

I'M OKAY, I'M OKAY.

YOU'RE SO NOT.

AGH... I WILL BE.

LUKE, SOMEONE HAS BEEN ASKING FOR YOU.

THANK GOD.

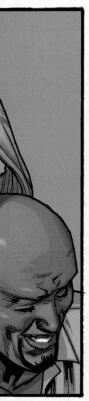

BUT WHAT YOU HAVEN'T EARNED IS HER. THIS BABY. YOU OWE THIS BABY A LIFE. A SAFE, NORMAL LIFE.

THAT IS SO NOT FAIR, MOM.

NO.

NO... HEY...

SHE AIN'T WRONG.

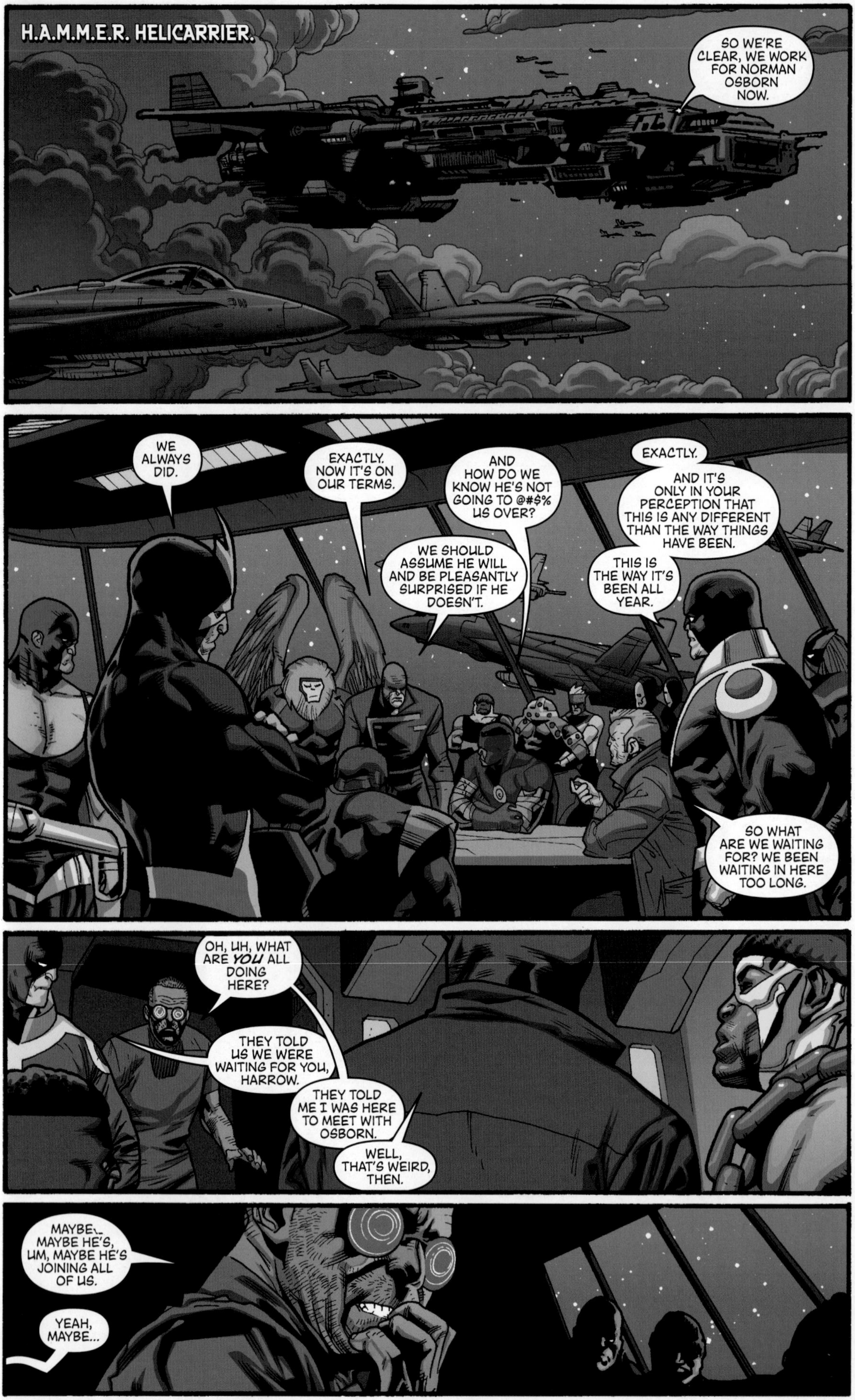
H.A.M.M.E.R. HELICARRIER.
SO WE'RE CLEAR, WE WORK FOR NORMAN OSBORN NOW.
WE ALWAYS DID.
EXACTLY. NOW IT'S ON OUR TERMS.
AND HOW DO WE KNOW HE'S NOT GOING TO @#$% US OVER?
WE SHOULD ASSUME HE WILL AND BE PLEASANTLY SURPRISED IF HE DOESN'T.
EXACTLY.
AND IT'S ONLY IN YOUR PERCEPTION THAT THIS IS ANY DIFFERENT THAN THE WAY THINGS HAVE BEEN.
THIS IS THE WAY IT'S BEEN ALL YEAR.
SO WHAT ARE WE WAITING FOR? WE BEEN WAITING IN HERE TOO LONG.
OH, UH, WHAT ARE YOU ALL DOING HERE?
THEY TOLD US WE WERE WAITING FOR YOU, HARROW.
THEY TOLD ME I WAS HERE TO MEET WITH OSBORN.
WELL, THAT'S WEIRD, THEN.
MAYBE... MAYBE HE'S, UM, MAYBE HE'S JOINING ALL OF US.
YEAH, MAYBE...

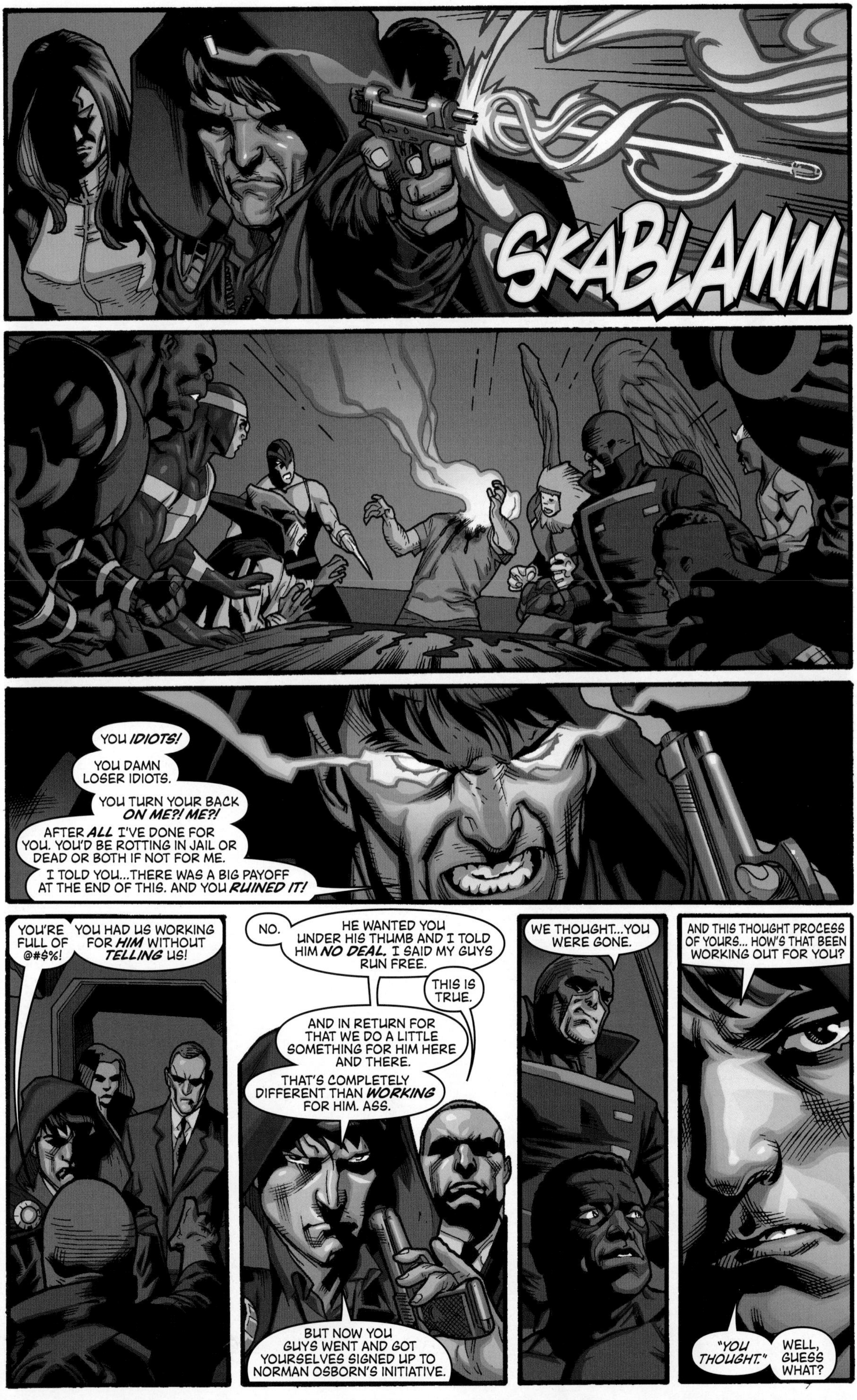

SKABLAMM
YOU IDIOTS!
YOU DAMN LOSER IDIOTS.
YOU TURN YOUR BACK ON ME?! ME?!
AFTER ALL I'VE DONE FOR YOU. YOU'D BE ROTTING IN JAIL OR DEAD OR BOTH IF NOT FOR ME.
I TOLD YOU...THERE WAS A BIG PAYOFF AT THE END OF THIS. AND YOU RUINED IT!
YOU'RE FULL OF @#$%!
YOU HAD US WORKING FOR HIM WITHOUT TELLING US!
NO.
HE WANTED YOU UNDER HIS THUMB AND I TOLD HIM NO DEAL. I SAID MY GUYS RUN FREE.
THIS IS TRUE.
AND IN RETURN FOR THAT WE DO A LITTLE SOMETHING FOR HIM HERE AND THERE.
THAT'S COMPLETELY DIFFERENT THAN WORKING FOR HIM. ASS.
BUT NOW YOU GUYS WENT AND GOT YOURSELVES SIGNED UP TO NORMAN OSBORN'S INITIATIVE.
WE THOUGHT...YOU WERE GONE.
AND THIS THOUGHT PROCESS OF YOURS... HOW'S THAT BEEN WORKING OUT FOR YOU?
"YOU THOUGHT."
WELL, GUESS WHAT?

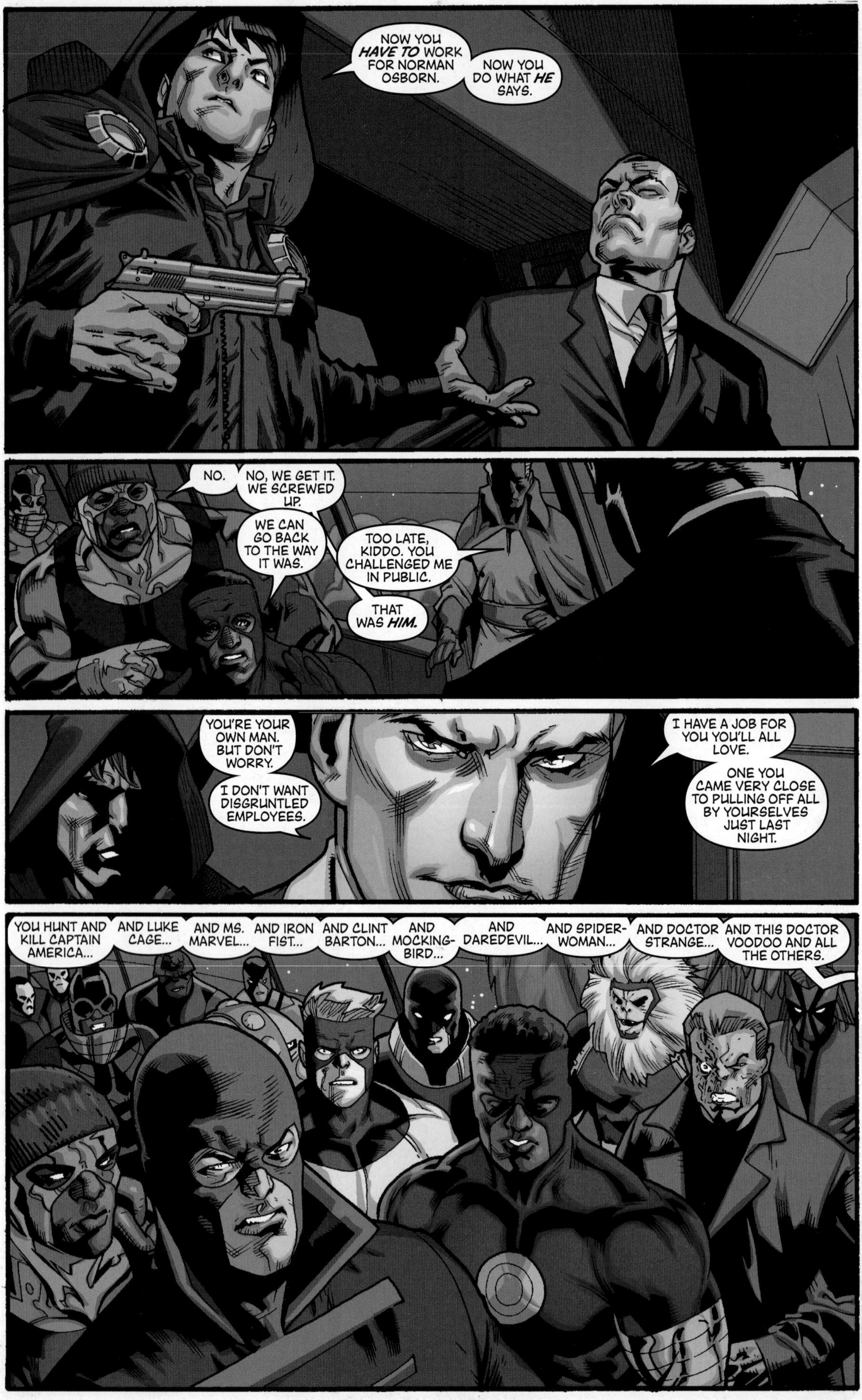
NOW YOU HAVE TO WORK FOR NORMAN OSBORN.
NOW YOU DO WHAT HE SAYS.
NO.
NO, WE GET IT. WE SCREWED UP.
WE CAN GO BACK TO THE WAY IT WAS.
TOO LATE, KIDDO. YOU CHALLENGED ME IN PUBLIC.
THAT WAS HIM.
YOU'RE YOUR OWN MAN. BUT DON'T WORRY.
I DON'T WANT DISGRUNTLED EMPLOYEES.
I HAVE A JOB FOR YOU YOU'LL ALL LOVE.
ONE YOU CAME VERY CLOSE TO PULLING OFF ALL BY YOURSELVES JUST LAST NIGHT.
YOU HUNT AND KILL CAPTAIN AMERICA...
AND LUKE CAGE...
AND MS. MARVEL...
AND IRON FIST...
AND CLINT BARTON...
AND MOCKING-BIRD...
AND DAREDEVIL...
AND SPIDER-WOMAN...
AND DOCTOR STRANGE...
AND THIS DOCTOR VOODOO AND ALL THE OTHERS.

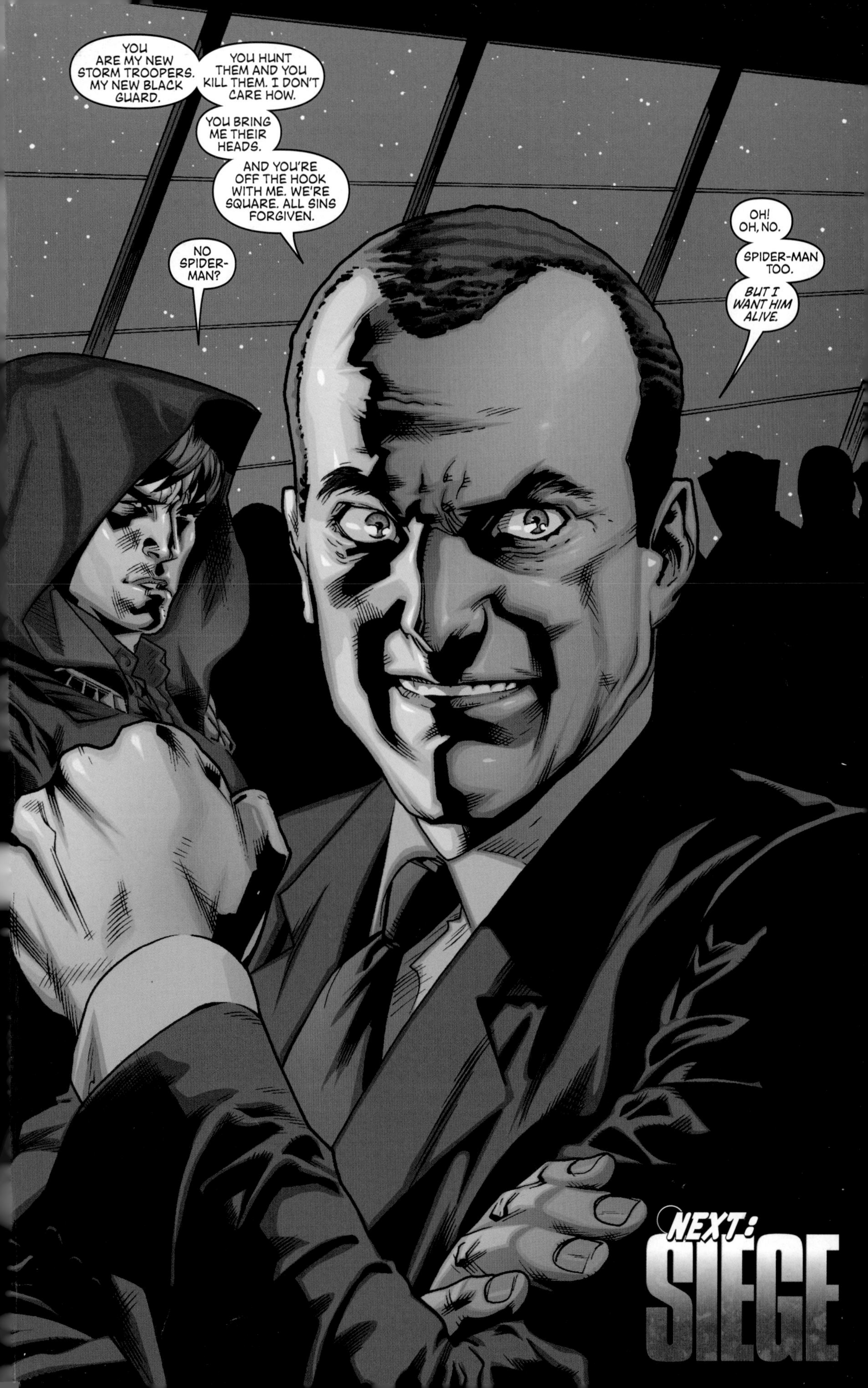
YOU ARE MY NEW STORM TROOPERS. MY NEW BLACK GUARD.
YOU HUNT THEM AND YOU KILL THEM. I DON'T CARE HOW.
YOU BRING ME THEIR HEADS.
AND YOU'RE OFF THE HOOK WITH ME. WE'RE SQUARE. ALL SINS FORGIVEN.
NO SPIDER-MAN?
OH! OH, NO.
SPIDER-MAN TOO.
BUT I WANT HIM ALIVE.
NEXT: SIEGE

#56

70th Anniversary Frame Variant
by Jackson Guice